The
CAMBRIAN
RAILWAYS
by
R.W. Kidner

THE OAKWOOD PRESS

© Oakwood Press 1992

ISBN 0 85361 439 3

First published 1954

Reprinted 1960, 1965 and, with additions, 1978, 1982

Second enlarged edition 1992

Typeset by Gem Publishing Company, Brightwell, Wallingford, Oxfordshire

Printed by Alpha Print (Witney) Oxon Ltd

CAMBRIAN RAILWAYS

TO DRIVERS AND OWNERS OF LOCOMOTIVES OR THE PERSONS HAVING CHARGE OF SAME. NOTICE IS HEREBY GIVEN THAT THIS BRIDGE IS INSUFFICIENT TO CARRY ANY WEIGHT BEYOND THE ORDINARY TRAFFIC OF THE DISTRICT, AND THE OWNER DRIVER OR OTHER PERSON IN CHARGE OF ANY LOCOMOTIVE IS HEREBY WARNED NOT TO ATTEMPT TO DRIVE THE SAME UPON OR OVER THIS BRIDGE WITHOUT HAVING PREVIOUSLY OBTAINED THE CONSENT OF THE CAMBRIAN RAILWAYS COMPANY. DATED THIS 2ND DAY OF JANUARY 1893.

Published by
The OAKWOOD PRESS
P.O.Box 122, Headington, Oxford.

Contents

Abbreviations

A&WC	Aberystwyth & Welsh Coast Railway
B&M	Brecon & Merthyr Railway
CR	Cambrian Railways
CWR	Central Wales Railway
HH&B	Hereford, Hay & Brecon Railway
L&N	Llanidloes & Newtown Railway
M&M	Manchester & Milford Railway
MS&L	Manchester, Sheffield & Lincolnshire Railway
N&M	Newtown & Machynlleth Railway
O&N	Oswestry & Newtown Railway
OE&W	Oswestry, Ellesmere & Whitchurch Railway
PSNWR	Potteries, Shrewsbury & N. Wales Railway
S&M	Shropshire & Montgomeryshire Light Railway
SpR	Shropshire Railway
WHR	Welsh Highland Railway
W&L	Welshpool & Llanfair Railway
WM&CQ	Wrexham, Mold & Connah's Quay Railway

Special thanks are due for assistance in preparing this new edition to C.J.W. Powell, Gwyn Briwnant Jones, Ralph Tutton and W.K. Mackenzie.

An up train with a Great Western bogie coach leading, hauled by 2–4–0 No. 54, seen here coming on to Barmouth viaduct photographed around 1900.

Dr T. E. Rudder

Introduction

The plural title of The Cambrian Railways is sometimes overlooked. It arose from the fact that the forming companies were of much the same size, and since all were at first worked by the same contractors, none had any fierce loyalty or sense of its own importance. Once formed, the Board showed the same tendencies as other railways and proposed expansion in many directions. Fortunately, weak finances precluded these options, ranging from a deepwater port at Porthdynllaen to face-to-face competition for slate at Blaenau Ffestiniog, and the company settled down to working what it had got; later accretions were mostly a reluctant acceptance of something nobody else wanted.

The plural title does conceal also a lack of strategic planning; all the lines had limited objectives, and in a sense Wales's own railway failed to secure its future; one cannot for instance now travel from Aberystwyth to Cardiff by rail except through England. It could be argued that if the Cambrian had joined with the Mid-Wales earlier than it did, or taken over the Manchester & Milford when David Davies had strong influence there, a route from south to north Wales might exist today, having survived the Beeching axe. It would not have been easy; geography was always against it. But there again, the reason the Cambrian suffered so badly from geography was that it could not afford too many tunnels. It could not afford them because the traffic was not there; it ran through land which was either pastoral or totally useless, until the vogue for tourism began later.

The Cambrian was not an isolated line; it had connections with nine other railways, and accepted through coaches from several of them; its own stock was seen in Manchester, London and Cardiff. It did try for mineral traffic, but the North Wales slate traders had been happy with narrow-gauge railways and sailing ships for too long to change, and the lead mines in Mid-Wales proved to have no future. It tried owning ships briefly; it tried a feeder bus service when motor buses were a new idea; it dallied with railmotors and halts. It had good managers and excellent staff; if it failed, it did so still in good heart; and the Great Western treated it well. British Rail was brutal, and would have liked to have been more so. But what is left is an intrinsic part of Wales and should now be safe.

Spelling and Pronouncing

Most names of places in Wales have had differing spelling over the years, notably the recent reversal of Anglicisation, e.g. Dolgelley to Dolgellau, Towyn to Tywyn, Portmadoc to Porthmadog. Some have been completely changed; Newtown now appears in Welsh language railway tables as Y Drenewydd and Welshpool as Trallwng. Where possible, places have been spelt in this text as they were at the time in question.

Readers may wish to understand how names are pronounced. The following is a rough guide, though obviously it is a big subject. LL, DD = th; AI, AU = eye; U = ee; F = V; Ff = F; W = er; Y = u except at ends. C is always hard. A place which will be much on the reader's lips is Machynlleth; the nearest in English would be Merhunthleth.

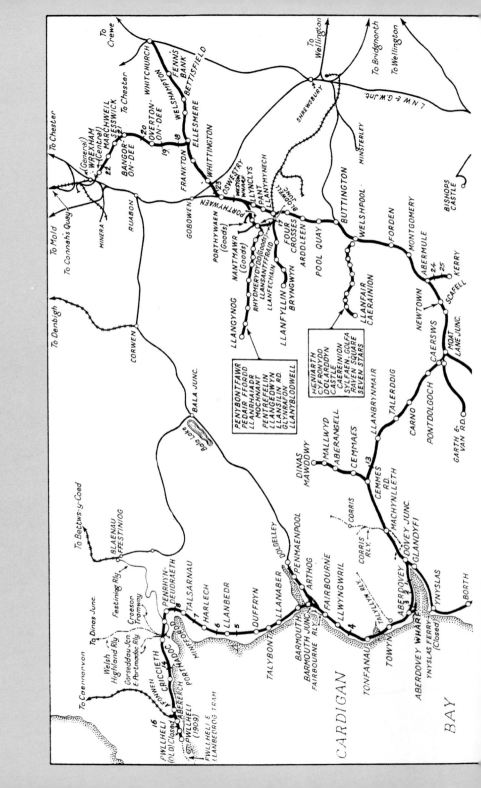

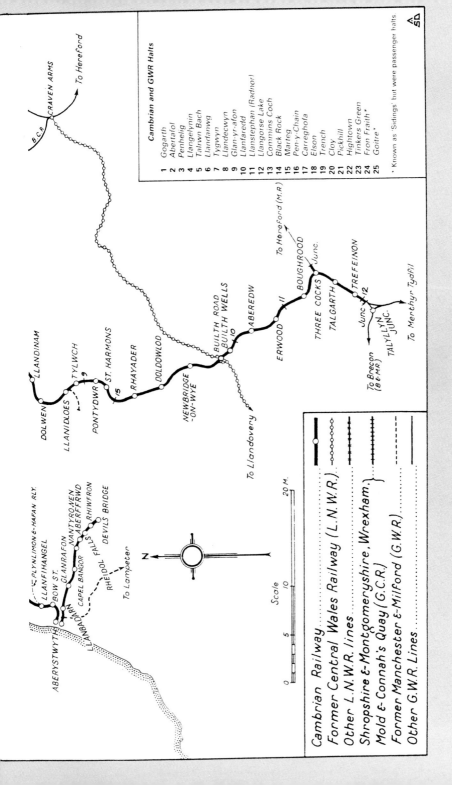

Cambrian and GWR Halts

1 Gogarth
2 Abertafol
3 Penhelig
4 Llangelynin
5 Talvwn Bach
6 Llandanwg
7 Tygwyn
8 Llandecwyn
9 Glan-yr-afon
10 Llanfaredd
11 Llanstephan (Radnor)
12 Llangorse Lake
13 Connins Coch
14 Black Rock
15 Marteg
16 Pen-y-Chain
17 Carreghofa
18 Elson
19 Trench
20 Cloy
21 Pickhill
22 Hightown
23 Tinkers Green
24 Fron Fraith*
25 Goitre*

* Known as 'Sidings' but were passenger halts

Cambrian Railway..........................
Former Central Wales Railway (L.N.W.R.)..........
Other L.N.W.R. lines....................................
Shropshire & Montgomeryshire, Wrexham,}
Mold & Connah's Quay (G.C.R.)
Former Manchester & Milford (G.W.R.)..........
Other G.W.R. Lines.......................................

Scale

0   5   10   20 M.

The Llanidloes & Newtown Railway Sharp, Stewart 0–4–2 locomotive *Wynnstay* of 1859 was passed over by Savin to the Brecon & Merthyr Railway, but the four sister engines remained in the Cambrian stock list. *Locomotive Publishing Co.*

Locomotive *Cambria* a 'Queen' class 0–6–0 built by Sharp, Stewart in 1860 for the Oswestry & Newtown Railway, seen here about 1870 at Machynlleth.
Locomotive Publishing Co.

Cambrian No. 24 was former Mid-Wales Railway No. 4. It is doubtful whether it gave much service after being absorbed into Cambrian stock in 1888, although not officially withdrawn until 10 years later. *Locomotive Publishing Co.*

Chapter One
Five Railways Become One

A casual glance at a railway map of Wales at first suggests a bewildering lack of purpose; lines straggle, twist and come to abrupt ends. However if laid against a map which shows the mountains and the estuaries, it makes better sense. There is of course the grand sweep from Chester along the north coast to Holyhead, but all that area was falling into the hands of the London & North Western Railway when the founding fathers of the Cambrian came together. It was in the 1850s that railway fever hit Wales with full force. There had been abortive schemes from the 1830s for lines across the Principality. These were of two kinds; one from east to west, a quick dash across to imagined West Coast ports for the trade with America; and the other from north to south, seeking to exchange coal and iron for Lancashire manufacturers. The first kind foundered when it became clear that there were no natural ports on the west coast, and the second gave up when the costs of tunnelling through the Cambrian Mountains became plain. The field was therefore left open for promoters of local lines whose ambitions were more easily satisfied.

At the time the first of the lines which would form part of the Cambrian was opened, its area was not entirely devoid of transport. The Chester & Holyhead Railway had driven as far south as Mold, and the Vale of Clwyd to Denbigh. The Shrewsbury & Chester was at Oswestry, not actually in Wales but important to the Cambrian's future. Various parts of the Shropshire Union Canal ran from Whitchurch across to Ellesmere and Llangollen and down through Welshpool to Newtown, and in many places tramways fed the canal with local minerals. The seaport of Portmadoc was already active, with tramways coming in from the slate mines; on the Dovey estuary a horse-tramway from Corris reached Machynlleth and the lower wharves before the Newtown & Machynlleth Railway. The surprising thing is that within five years there was hardly a place in North Wales out of reach of a railway station. How did this come about?

In part, it was due to the enlightened attitude of a number of large land-owners. Lord Sudeley, Lord of the Manor of Newtown, had petitioned against the Oswestry & Newtown Railway (O&N) Bill, but later supported it. Earl Vane, at Machynlleth, later Lord Londonderry, was an active railway supporter, and the Earl of Powis, who was also Lord of Duparts, was equally co-operative. The Earl of Bradford, who owned a lot of land in the Llanymynech area, a generation later caused some trouble when he appeared to want to control both the route and the timetable of the Tanat Valley line.

There was also of course the need, apparent to thinking people, to bring modern transport to a grievously neglected area. A good idea of the situation at the time can be gained from an advertisement in a London newspaper of 1846; '*Blanche*, master John Evans, now loading at Pickled Herring Upper Wharf, Southwark, for Aberystwyth, Aberdovey, Machynlleth and Carmarthen. Last day of loading 22nd September, 1846'.

Of the planned north-to-south railways, most used the town of Llanidloes as the gateway from north to mid-Wales, because the Cambrian Mountains made any route further west too difficult. A Manchester & Milford Railway

Locomotive *Llanerchydol* on an up train at Aberdovey about 1900, still in original condition apart from some slight additional protection for the footplatemen.
Locomotive Publishing Co.

The original form of the 'Seaham' class tanks, built by Sharp, Stewart in 1866; this example is believed to be at Llanfyllin in about 1890. *Locomotive Publishing Co.*

(M&M) of 1845 and a North & South Wales Railway of 1850 used it, the latter also aiming at Milford Haven. G.H. Whalley MP, busy trying to garner support for a line from Newtown to Llanidloes, also had his sights set further. When soon afterwards he became involved in the Oswestry & Newtown Railway, he claimed that the two lines, with an extension southwards to Carmarthen, would provide a route from the Mersey to the Bristol Channel.

There were several schemes for railways south from Llanidloes; since Carmarthen had had a railway since 1852, this town was one to aim for; but the Llanidloes & South Wales railway intended to run south to Newbridge and there join a projected line from Shrewsbury to Llanelli. The first part of this route became what was termed the 'Mid-Wales Section' of Mr Whalley's Manchester, Liverpool, Swansea & Milford Haven Junction Railway, later shortened to the Mid-Wales Railway.

For some time the two big English companies, the Great Western and the London & North Western, had been keen to enter mid-Wales, but each had frustrated the other. In 1853 three schemes came to Parliament; the GW-backed Shrewsbury & Chester Railway's Newtown Extension, the LNW-backed Montgomeryshire Railway from Shrewsbury to Aberystwyth, and the local Llanidloes & Newtown (L&N) Railway. Parliament threw out the first two but granted the third, which received its Bill in August 1853. The first sod was cut at Llanidloes on 3rd October, 1855, but after that progress became slow, although the line was almost ready by 1859, when the Mid-Wales Railway finally got its Act.

A year later the refurbished Manchester & Milford Railway obtained an Act for a line from Llanidloes through the mountains to Pencader, and Parliament failed to note that for 1½ miles from Llanidloes to Penpontbren it and the Mid-Wales were on the same course. The resulting stalemate was only broken by the L&N in 1862 agreeing to build that 1½ miles, and own it but not itself use it. However, this is leaping ahead; neither the Mid-Wales nor the Manchester & Milford were part of the Cambrian, though the former was taken in later, and it is of more interest to see what was happening north of Llanidloes.

The 13-mile route of the L&N was opened for goods traffic on 30th April, 1859, and for passenger traffic on 31st August the same year. The opening train of 48 carriages(!) was drawn by the engines *Llewellyn* and *Milford*, which had arrived by road as neither terminus was connected to another railway. There were intermediate stations at Moat Lane (Caersws), Llandinam and Dolwen; the terminus at Llanidloes was north of the later one built to accommodate the Mid-Wales and Manchester & Milford Railway as well as its own traffic (though the M&M never used it, as will be explained later).

The isolation did not last long; the Oswestry & Newtown had obtained its Act in 1855, though nothing happened at first. In 1856 a Committee of Investigation was appointed to see why no progress was being made; it made no observations of note, except to recommend that the formation (but not the bridges) be made for one line of metals only. This was not unusual in Wales;

This view of the sand siding and start of the wharf branch at Aberdovey shows how the main line (*far right*) had to rise sharply to go round the back of the village.

H.W. Burman

The rocky shelf of Friog which gave the Cambrian and its successors so much trouble; the train is running down towards Fairbourne station and comprises a 2–4–0 (No. 1 or 10) with a close-coupled set of four 4-wheeled coaches and a corridor bogie.

Author's Collection

for instance the road overbridges between Borth and Aberystwyth are of double-track width with single-track girders, on one side only.

In August 1857 the cutting of the first sod of the O&N was effected without arousing too much local disorder. It is tempting to laugh at Welsh railway ceremonies, but rather should one stand back in awe. At the birth of the O&N the great guns at Powys Castle, captured by the famous Lord Clive in India, boomed forth; there was a solemn invocation of the Almighty by Archdeacon Clive, and a place was found in the procession, behind the cavalry and between the Mayor and the Board of Directors, for the wheel-barrow to be used by Lady Williams-Wynn: no common barrow, but of solid mahogany emblazoned with the company's arms.

The promotion of the O&N was a joint affair between the local land-owners, the better-off tradesmen, and the contractors. In the case of all the early Cambrian lines the party of the third part was Thomas Savin, at this time in partnership with David Davies, later MP for Cardigan Boroughs, chief proprietor of the Ocean Collieries in the Rhondda Valley, and the moving spirit in the Barry Dock & Railway. Not only did they actively promote the railways, but they became involved with the financing of them, and for a time operated them on lease.

While the rails were moving ahead, there was a rather rude hiccup in local railway politics. At the sod-cutting for the Mid-Wales Railway in 1859, George Whalley openly and publicly criticised the business methods of the appointed contractors, Davies & Savin. By taking shares in lieu of payment, and arranging to lease the lines when open, contractors were becoming the masters and the shareholders the servants. There were ugly scenes amongst the crowd, most of whom favoured Davies; later Whalley lost his seat on the Mid-Wales Board, and for other reasons Davies & Savin gave up the contract. However, the pair remained primarily responsible for all local railway-building; the Mid-Wales was the only line between Oswestry and Merthyr that one or other did not build.

However, much power still rested with the land-owners, Earl Vane, Lord Sudeley, Sir Watkin Williams-Wynn of Wynnstay, and others, partly because they had the ear of the Lords Committees, which could pronounce life or death for new schemes. One must also mention Benjamin Piercy, a local man born at Trefeglwys, who became a noted engineer; though he spent some of his time abroad, he was an important figure in Welsh railway politics.

There can be no doubt that Savin was the saviour of the O&N, for when that company was temporarily out of funds in 1859, and likely to have to suspend construction, the LNWR became very active in promoting its line from Shrewsbury to Newtown via Welshpool. This would have meant the end of the O&N as a separate entity, and if construction had ceased the LNWR would undoubtedly have gone ahead. So Savin on his own account raised the sum of £45,000 to pull the company out the morass, and work on the line went ahead. It was opened from Oswestry (Cambrian station) to Pool Quay on 1st May, 1860. Later the same month an unofficial – but well patronised – special was run over unballasted track as far as the intended junction at Buttington (then called Cefn Junction) with the Shrewbury &

Locomotive No. 15 was one of the last class of goods engines, built in 1918, and is seen here about the time of Grouping, shunting at Criccieth.   *J. Whittaker*

Army Volunteer Camps provided much revenue in the Aberystwyth area before World War I; in this picture, taken about 1912, a huge tented camp can be seen on the fields west of Bow Street station, now occupied by the Plant Breeding Station.
Lens of Sutton

Welshpool line (later GW and LNW Joint, opened 27th January, 1862), and on to Welshpool. On 14th August this section was formally opened, and the isolated piece between Newtown and Abermule; the intervening section followed on 10th June, 1861. On that date trains began to work through from Oswestry to Llanidloes, over the metals of the L&N beyond Newtown.

The year 1860 was a busy one, and several things happened which would later affect the Cambrian lines. The West Midland Railway announced that it would build a line from Shrewsbury to Portmadoc via Llanfyllin and Llanginog. There were valuable mineral deposits near those places, and Piercy and Savin decided they would counter this ploy by announcing a branch to Llanfyllin from their O&N line; this had the desired effect. Then the LNWR was eager to convert its Shropshire Union Canal to a railway, but was headed off by being given running powers into Welshpool by the O&N. A bit further away, George Whalley had turned his attention to planning a line from the LNWR at Craven Arms to Montgomery, via Bishops Castle. This would have connected with the O&N, but the Bishops Castle Railway's section from Lydhamheath to Montgomery was never built. Down south, the Mid-Wales Railway had been denied its route to Llandovery (the LNWR won this one for its Central Wales protégé; fortunately the ancient Hay Tramroad running from Hay-on-Wye to Brecon came up for sale at this time, and after complex manoeuvres the Mid-Wales obtained a route from Newbridge via part of the old tramroad to Brecon, joining the Brecon & Merthyr Railway at a remote spot later called Talyllyn Junction. Thus it came about that the northern railways' trains to the south would run via Dowlais, and not via Carmarthen.

Importance also attached to the fact that the partnership of Davies & Savin was dissolved at the end of October 1860. The former had been becoming increasingly worried at the extravagant plans of the other; it seems probable that the last straw was a plan by Savin to build a railway up the coast and to develop holiday resorts with hotels at various places, which later became in modified form the Aberystwyth & Welsh Coast Railway (A&WC). The upshot was that Davies went on constructing the Newtown & Machynlleth (N&M) and the Manchester & Milford Railway, while Savin took as his partner his brother-in-law Ward and completed the Brecon & Merthyr and Hereford, Hay & Brecon Railways before turning to the Coast Line, which he constructed in partnership with his brother John. Savin was also working all the lines so far opened, having with Davies signed contracts providing shareholders with a guaranteed return of 5 per cent on their capital out of receipts.

The L&N had been an easy line to build, with no complications; the O&N however was otherwise. A few miles south of Oswestry it met and crossed the Shropshire Union Canal near Llanymynech. Here and to the north there were valuable mineral deposits, which had tempted the canal builders 60 years earlier; the canal followed the intended line of railway all the way to Newtown, and some promoters had expressed fears of what might result from having to share traffic with the canal. To counter this, the O&N promoted and built a short branch from just north of Llynclys station to quarries at Whitehaven and Porthywaen. The former was already served by the 3 ft gauge Crickheath Tramway, running east to the canal where a solid

The original stone building at Machynlleth still stands, though not at present used by the railway. This view was taken in the 1950s.
Oakwood Collection

The station building at Machynlleth, which was constructed from the stone from Talerddig cutting; 2–4–0 No. 43 is in the platform, photographed 1910. *Lens of Sutton*

A postcard view of the grand joint station built at Llanidloes by the L&N for the use of itself, the Mid-Wales Railway and the Manchester & Milford Railway. *Lens of Sutton*

wharf with passing width was built. There were several other ancient tram-roads; one from coal pits at Coed-y-Go on Sweeney Mountain crossed under the Cambrian north of Llynclys Junction; another passed underneath the new Pant station. Savin personally built a branch of about 2 miles from Porthywaen to coal-pits he set up at Coed-y-Go (Gronwen) called the New British Coal Pits, but the coal was of poor quality and it lasted only a few years.

The Cambrian toyed with the idea of a branch line in Newtown to the canal, but decided against it; plans were also made for a branch with curves of 5 and 6 chains radius across the canal at Llanymynech to some gravity-worked inclines coming down from the vast limestone cliffs of Llan-ymynech Rocks, but again it did not proceed. The competition was certainly real for some years; the canal had a branch from Burgedin No. 2 lock to Tyddyn, which was close to the intended station at Pool Quay. There were canal depots at Buttington, Welshpool, Berriew, Pennant and other points in the Severn Valley; and though canal transport might be slow, there was no denying that by its junctions with other canals in the Midlands and North, there was no town of importance that could not be reached.

With Newtown now in rail connection via Oswestry with the ouside world, the rails were moving towards Machynlleth under the guidance of Davies and Piercy. The N&M was the most difficult line yet attempted. It was a rule of thumb for Welsh railways to 'follow the river' so far as was possible. Now, after leaving the valley at Pontdolgoch, the new line had to get through a mass of mountains to drop down to a minor valley at Llanbrynmair and thus to the Dovey at Cemmes Road. Piercy planned the route, which rose to a summit of 693 feet at Talerddig, and he or Davies decided that in view of the stability of the rock, a cutting rather than a tunnel could be made. It would be the deepest rock cutting in the United Kingdom, and in parts the walls were originally almost sheer. The rise was at 1 in 71 from the west, and 1 in 52 from the east; the nine mile rise from Cemmes Road was what taxed engines the most.

Countess Vane had cut the first sod in 1858, and by 1861 Davies was near to completing the Talerddig cutting. The new line diverged from the Llanidloes & Newtown near Moat Lane station; it was decided to build a large interchange station at the junction, abandon the old Moat Lane station, and build a new one at Caersws, the only large village in the vicinity. At Machynlleth a large area of rock was quarried out on the north of the town for a new depot, incidentally at the point where the horse-worked Corris Railway came across the Dovey and passed beside the new station on its way to the wharves at Derwenlas.

'Bradshaw' for February 1860 shows a short section of the line between Caersws and Pontdolgoch as open with one train per day, but this did not appear in later issues, and the N&M announced a year later that the section between Moat Lane and Pontdolgoch was 'nearly complete'. In October 1862 David Davies, whose house was at Llandinam, organised a trip for local people to Machynlleth, though the earliest public (but unapproved) ride seems to have been on 25th September, 1862, when a Temperance Excursion ran from Newtown to view Talerddig cutting and the embankment at Commins Coch.

While the Newtown & Machynlleth was nearing completion, the Corris, Machynlleth & River Dovey Tramroad put forward plans in the 1862/3 session to convert its line to standard gauge and to make a connection with the N&M line just east of the station. There was to be a new bridge of three spans across the Dovey, shortly after which the route joined the old horse-tramway route, which would need widening and in some places easing of curves. It would proceed northwards from the terminus to join the line from Bala to Dolgelley. The Upper Corris branch was also to be extended some six miles to Tir-Stint (or Stent). With gradients up to 1 in 35 and a tunnel of 1958 yards, it is not surprising that the Dolgelley line was not built, although an Act was obtained in 1864. The line remained a horse-worked tramway, and the Upper Corris branch was not extended. Although the A&WC had to insert an arch in its bridge over the main road at the west end of Machynlleth station for the tramway, and to arrange for a level crossing near Derwenlas (Glandyfi), little use was made of the tramway west of Machynlleth once the Coast Line deviation was open and slate could go by rail to Aberdovey.

The official opening of the Newtown & Machynlleth took place on 3rd January, 1863, though public trains had probably been running a few days earlier. Two 0–6–0 engines, at that time named *Countess Vane* and *Talerddig*, hauled the train, which on return from Newtown comprised 36 carriages. It is reported that the young Marquis of Blandford, Earl Vane's nephew and a Spencer-Churchill, rode on the leading engine playing on a 'cornet-a-piston', but presumably only on arrival at Newtown and probably at Machynlleth on return.

The two engines were of the 'Queen' class, delivered only a few days after *Queen* itself, and were ordered by Davies & Savin on behalf of both the O&N and N&M, since their stock was pooled at the time. Neither kept its name, *Countess Vane* became *Castell Deudraeth* and *Talerddig* became *Cader Idris*; both names were used again, the first on 2–4–0 No. 41 and the latter on 0–6–0T No. 13.

On 4th May, 1863 the Oswestry, Ellesmere & Whitchurch Railway (OE&W) opened between the last-named points, and throughout on 27th July, 1864. The company had had to promise Sir John Hanmer, whose quarries had been made use of, a station in the parish of Hanmer, a siding at Penn's Lane, and a new approach to the bridge over the canal at Cornhill. The junction with the GWR was to have been where the line crossed over it at Whittington, but in the event it was at Oswestry. The GWR had desired to build this line. A note on a copy of the Act of 1861 in the National Library appears to have been written by a GWR official. In pencil, it reads: 'The GWR have not running powers. The line from Ellesmere to Whitchurch which was a very objectionable one, was put forward separately if not independently, and it was not exposed with all its faults to the Great Western till some time in March'. The LNWR Whitchurch station became a junction.

During this time it became obvious that the continuence of a number of small contiguous lines all under separate management could not be justified. An Amalgamation Bill was prepared, by which in July 1864 the

Barmouth Bridge.

An early postcard view of Barmouth Bridge in original condition with sliding opening span.   *Author's Collection*

A 'Barnum' 2–4–0 taking an up train out of Barmouth about 1930; note the 'excursion' platform behind added by the GWR, which was on the up side of the crossing gates.   *D.J. Powell*

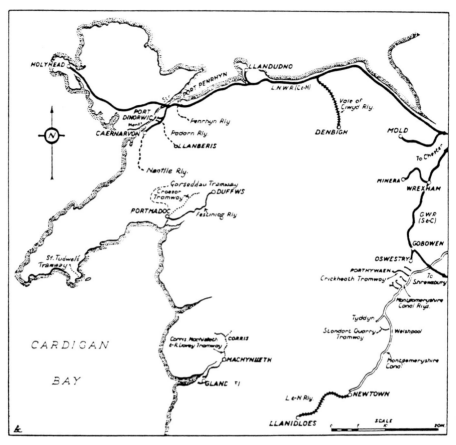

North and Mid Wales Railways in 1860.

Llandre station, showing the unusual bow-fronted building, with clock. The wooden down platform was added about 1912 and the sidings are behind it. After the station closed, a ground frame by the level crossing (behind the camera) replaced the box on the up platform.   *Oakwood Collection*

O&N, L&N, N&M and OE&W became the Cambrian Railways. The A&WC was brought in in 1865, but the Mid-Wales remained outside. Meanwhile, on 12th December, 1863 the companies had severally taken over the working of their lines on Savin relinquishing his leases, and Savin's firm became simply the manager. The rolling stock was purchased by the companies: they had in fact advanced up to two-thirds of its cost to Savin for its original purchase by him.

The most useful engines in the 'pool' now formed were a number of light 0–6–0 and 2–4–0 types bought from Sharp, Stewart. There were also six light 0–6–0ST engines which had been bought from Manning, Wardle mainly for construction work; the ownership and whereabouts of these was at all times perplexing, and they were sold before very long.

It is not certain how many engines were in the new 'pool'. Savin did not at that time use numbers, and some engines changed their names, leading to confusion. The L&N in theory had four engines, the O&N three by 1861, later 17 more were added making a total of 24. However, four engines at least were loaned for the opening of the Brecon & Merthyr Railway in 1863 and to work the Hereford, Hay & Brecon in 1864. One of the small 0–4–0ST engines ordered for the Kerry and Porthywaen branches of the O&N was reported as loaned by Savin to the Dowlais Ironworks Railway down south. The Committee administering the locomotive pool cannot have been very diligent, since when Savin went bankrupt in 1866 the whereabouts and ownership of many engines was still in doubt.

The O&N opened a short 3¾ miles-long branch line on 2nd March, 1863 from Abermule on its main line to Kerry. There was some hope of mineral traffic, but little developed, and apart from two periods when narrow gauge tramways ran from Kerry station to timber-felling areas, it remained the least used of all Cambrian lines, with a one-coach sized train calling at three intermediate 'sidings' which were not even recognised as halts.

A more important O&N branch was that to Llanfyllin, from a junction just north of Llanymynech station, facing Oswestry. The peculiar siting of the junction was no doubt due to the desire to tap the stone traffic from Llanymynech Hill which was running down to a canal wharf north of the town. There had been a plan to run a branch from the main line across the canal to reach the stone, but instead the Llanfyllin branch was arranged to pass over the mineral tramways near their foot and an interchange siding put in, Rock Siding.

The branch had enjoyed a remarkably elaborate 'first sod' ceremony on 20th September, 1861 at Llanfyllin. The official participants had come by special train from Oswestry to Llanymynech, and then embarked for Llanfyllin in a collection of road vehicles, some of which according to the *Oswestry Advertizer* 'beggared description'! At Llanfyllin they marched to various notables' houses picking up local support for the ceremony, carried out by a Mrs Dugdale at Llyn, with the usual ceremonial spade and barrow. The interminable speeches at the Wynnstay Arms which followed said little about the project, except that so far land had only been purchased for 5½ miles of the line. Benjamin Piercy made much of the hostility of the Great Western Railway to the project, while Savin confined himself to a bantering

A fine view as the driver of a train from Dolgellau exchanges tokens at Barmouth Junction East box; the locomotive is 0–4–4T No. 3 and the stock is Great Western.

H. W. Burman

speech, saying he had sometimes been called 'a small haberdasher' – which indeed he had been. G.H. Whalley, the Chairman of the O&N was in his element, and the whole thing ended in a fireworks display, including 'Roman candles, Serpents and Saxon Lights'. At the intermediate village of Llansantffraid a battery of five guns fired all day, and a large painting of an engine and tender was titled 'Llansantffraid to Manchester via Ellesmere'.

The branch opened on 17th July, 1863, and led an unexciting life except during the building by Liverpool Corporation of the Lake Vyrnwy dams (1880–90) for which stone imported via Aberdovey was off-loaded at Llanfyllin. The line crossed over the Nantmawr branch of the Potteries, Shrewsbury & North Wales Railway at Wern, and the process by which a connection here in 1896 led to trains from Llanfyllin arriving from the south, instead of at Rock Siding, is described later.

By 1863 Savin was no doubt less cheerful, and may even have wished he were still a draper, as problems piled up with his most ambitious project, the Coast Line. There had been two schemes: the Machynlleth, Aberystwyth & Towyn, and the Aberystwyth & Welsh Coast. Savin backed the latter, which included a crossing of the Dovey estuary and later an extension from Pwllheli to the west Lleyn coast, neither of which was achieved. There were to be hotels and holiday developments at several places and a port at the mouth of the Leri Cut at Ynyslas. There were daunting water crossings beyond the Dovey, at Barmouth and the Traeth Mawr; and as it turned out, terrible difficulties where the Cader Idris foothills came down to the sea at Friog.

An easy section between Machynlleth and Borth was opened on 23rd June, 1863; the line had to cross the Corris tramroad twice, on the level at Cei Ward, Derwenlas, and by the road bridge on the west side of Machynlleth station. Borth station was a converted farmhouse; the well known Grand Hotel and Cambrian Terrace came later. Another easy section, from Aber-dovey to Llwyngwril, followed on 24th October, 1863.

Meanwhile, Savin had the problem of the crossing of the Dovey estuary. Two plans were drawn up, one embodying a road; the line would leave the Machynlleth line east of Ynyslas station, the junction facing west, and take a curving route, with a straight opening span at the north end, coming off the viaduct at Penhelig and running round the back of Aberdovey. This would involve tunnelling, but a route along the front was not possible from the viaduct, though it would have been from the later deviation line. It was not an option, however, for the strand provided the only occupation for the village, fishing and boat building, and that could not be stopped. Finding footings for the viaduct was not easy, and when found, the sheer cost of the long viaduct frightened even Savin. So both bridge plans were laid aside and it was decided to build a deviation line from Glandyfi to Penhelig. Meanwhile a ferry would maintain communication across the estuary; this was useful mainly for the contractors, but also provided for passengers wishing to use the isolated open section of line from Aberdovey to Llwyngwril, being worked by the O&N, as was the Machynlleth–Borth section.

0–6–0 No. 31 was a post-War engine and one of the last to be withdrawn (in 1954).
This is a local train near Harlech, but the class was often used for heavy excursions.
H.W. Burman

The Neilson 0–6–0s were different in having sand-boxes on the front splashers. This
example, No. 88, was rebuilt by the GWR in 1926 and lasted until 1944 and is seen
here at Llanbedr. *H.W. Burman*

The exact situation at the Leri bridge at Ynyslas in 1863 is a matter of conjecture. By the time of the first Ordnance Survey (1887) there was a wharf on the east side of the 1829 Cut with a steeply curving branch siding to Ynyslas station, joining where the later up platform was. There had also been a branch from a junction 300 yards west of the station, cut back to a short siding, which may have been a temporary track to Penrhyn Point ferry (for Aberdovey). This place had to be used at low tide, which here seems to be for most of the day, and is 1½ m across the beach from Ynyslas station. There was a path through the mud and sand but it seems unlikely that passengers for Aberdovey and beyond would have been expected to walk it. Later the saw-mill which was by the east wharf was moved across the river, and the west branch reinstated that far, and a wharf built on the west side of the cut. The ferry itself was mostly rowed, thought steam tugs and ferries were available some of the time. The deep water channel to Ynyslas was narrow and marked by posts to guide stranger boats. It seems that at times the Spring tides (that is non-neap tides) made it impossible to get the ferry up the cut, and it went up the Clettwr river to Trer-Ddol. Altogether, getting workmen, stores, and passengers across the estuary can never have been easy.

The train service from Aberdovey to Llwyngwril was worked by two engines, both Manning, Wardle 0–6–0STs, *Cardigan* and *Merion*. There are conflicting accounts of how they reached Aberdovey. One states that *Merion* went on a cart from Machynlleth, possibly before the line to Borth was available, and that the other was barged across, using a pier which was built at Penrhyn Point, where the present ruined refuge can be seen. The latter, built in 1933, replaced one built in 1880, and it seems there was no structure here at the time the pier was built. This collapsed at least once, and would have been taken down after 1867. Gwyn Briwnant-Jones, who has studied the matter in detail, states that the pier was finally stabilised by using 40 tons of rail, and that thereafter locomotives and stock were sent across on barges towed by steam tugs, and that the steam ferry *Elizabeth* provided a passenger link.

The A&WC Board was an unduly contentious one; in 1864 opposition between Whalley and Piercy on the one side, and Savin on the other, could only be resolved by the former members' resignations. This left the company without an Engineer, and Henry Conybeare, of London, who had been occupying a similar post with the Brecon & Merthyr Railway, was appointed. On 23rd June, 1864 the difficult piece of line between Borth and Aberystwyth was opened; this had required two heavy cuttings; no doubt if it had had the money, the company would have built tunnels and saved a century of double-heading on this section. On 27th July the Oswestry to Whitchurch railway opened for traffic, and passengers from the north could now reach Aberystwyth via the LNWR or via Gobowen. By a coincidence this was the same week that the O&N, L&N, N&M and OE&W decided to come together as The Cambrian Railways. As stated earlier, the A&WC had to be left out at that time, though since Savin was working this at the request of the Cambrian companies, it was an academic distinction.

The east end of Aberdovey railway wharf seen here about 1905, reproduced from a Wrench Series postcard. While not exactly bustling, a coal wagon is being unloaded to the right of the horse 'growler' which has been parked there.   *Author's Collection*

A rebuilt 'Queen' class 0−6−0 No. 1 standing on the Aberdovey quays about 1910. New boiler, addition of a cab and a six-wheeled tender makes No. 1 look very different from its original form.   *H.W. Burman*

The Act for the deviation line from Glandyfi was passed in July 1865; the same Act covered the Aberdovey Harbour Branch, given as one third of a mile. However, much of this must have already been built to connect with the ferry. The deviation was a blow to the prospects of the Coast Line; there was extra mileage from Aberystwyth, for it was 1½ miles from Ynyslas to Aberdovey direct and 12 miles via Dovey Junction. Then the junction, known at first as Glandyfi Junction, produced no revenue since it had no road to it; it was purely an interchange point. Nor was there any reward from the deviation itself, built on the water's edge and having no stations. It opened on 14th August, 1867.

Another short section of the A&WC opened on 3rd July, 1865, from Llwyngwril to Barmouth Ferry, a temporary station where Fairbourne station was built later. The reason for the delay in this section was the engineers' difficulties with the foothills of Cader Idris where they reached the sea at Friog Rocks. The cliffs were penetrated, but they were not subdued, as time would show. On the same date the line beyond Barmouth Ferry to Penmaenpool, on what was to be the Dolgelley branch, was opened, running along the south bank of the Mawddach. At Penmaenpool there was a wooden toll bridge across the narrowing estuary, which the Cambrian purchased in 1900.

The ferry to Barmouth lay well over a mile from the station, at Penrhyn Point, where carriages and horses were kept to transport users. Since Penrhyn is the Welsh for headland, it is not surprising that this ferry station had the same name as that for Aberdovey further south.

The extension of service from Penmaenpool to Dolgelley is generally supposed to have occurred in 1869; however it should be noted that Earl Vane in his half-yearly Report on 6th March, 1866 stated that the railway was open from Aberdovey to Dolgelley; possibly he felt that Penmaenpool counted as Dolgelley.

However, the terrors of the Mawddach crossing, which often involved changing boats on a sandbank in the middle (see Chapter 5), would soon belong to the past, as the contractors began putting vast quantities of timber into the 113-span Barmouth Bridge; at the north end a span which could be tilted and rolled back over the adjoining one gave access for shipping. The whole thing gave good service until 1899, when it began to be rebuilt in its present form.

Next came the Traeth Bach and Traeth Mawr, where the rivers Glaslyn and Dwryd emptied themselves into a wide expanse of tidal sand and marsh. The most direct route would have been to cut across from north of Harlech to Morfa Bichan, the later Black Rock Halt, but the Cambrian decided on a long route via Penrhyndeudraeth, Minffordd and Portmadoc. There were good reasons; for one thing, 60 years earlier Mr Madocks had built the embankment across the Traeth Mawr which now carried the Festiniog Railway, making firm the ground behind where the Cambrian chose to go, And there was much slate traffic to be had; it came down the Festiniog Railway from half a dozen important quarries in the Blaenau area, and two other narrow gauge railways, the Croesor and the Gorseddau, were preparing to do the same for other quarry areas.

In the event, the railway did not cut heavily into the seaborne slate trade from Portmadoc; later an exchange siding with the Festiniog was put in at Minffordd and one with the Croesor at Portmadoc, but much of the slate went for export, and the harbour wharves remained busier than the station sidings. A plan was drawn up in 1865 for a railway branch to the harbour, but not implemented.

The railway regained the coast before Criccieth and followed it to the first terminus at Pwllheli, some way east of the later and better known one. Rails had been laid all the way by early 1867, but passenger working did not begin until 10th October of that year.

One person who had been watching the progress of the Coast Line closely was the owner of the Bryneglwys Quarries some six miles inland from Towyn. Aware that he was probably the only slate-quarry owner without access to river, canal or railway, he had gambled on the line reaching Towyn and begun to build a narrow gauge railway to meet it; this was opened in 1866, the Talyllyn Railway, with a 'wharf' beside the Coast Line for the transfer of his weighty product.

John Savin's own copies of the book of plans for 'Railway No. 4' and 'Railway No. 5' are preserved in the Welsh National Library; they cover respectively the section from Barmouth to Portmadoc and from Portmadoc to Llanystumdwy. It is of interest that No. 4 shows only a level crossing with the Gorseddau tramway at Portmadoc, though that with the Croesor was also necessary before the line was completed. No. 5 shows a branch line turning east at 8 m. 73 ch. from the datum point; this was the start of a line to Caernarvon, and the Cambrian did own a few chains of it, but it was an LNWR line; the Cambrian had given that company running powers to Pwllheli and Portmadoc in return for the dropping of an 1852 proposal for an LNWR railway from Caernarvon to Portmadoc. This line was opened to Caernarvon (Pant) station on 2nd September, 1867, and worked by Cambrian engines for a while. The junction station became known as Afon Wen, literally a place on the beach with no habitations.

One of the least sensible of the A&WC proposals was that in 1865 for a branch from Portmadoc to Blaenau Ffestiniog; it would have passed slightly north of the present Festiniog Railway Dduallt station, and any traveller on that railway could easily judge its impracticability.

In 1866, while the line was being carried triumphantly across the Mawddach, Savin went bankrupt. He was over-extended, as Davies had judged he would be when they split up in 1860. Many of his assets were shares in unsuccessful railways, and it is surprising that he carried on his balancing act for so long. Suddenly a number of railways in Wales were faced with operating their own concerns, which had previously been left to him, and sorting out who owned what engines and stock, with few accountancy records to help. Several years later (1870) the Chairman of the Brecon & Merthyr Railway (B&M), where some supposedly Cambrian engines had been found, was still complaining bitterly that Savin's liquidators refused to meet his officials. The Cambrian Directors had been at pains to try to extract from the B&M quite a large sum outstanding for the hire to them of engines which had been on their own capital account.

The B&M was a 'Savin' line, as was the Hereford, Hay & Brecon (HH&B), with which it carried out a legally-unsound amalgamation in 1865, later annulled. The B&M did not feel equal to working the Hereford line when Savin gave up doing so after his financial crash, and requested the Mid-Wales to take this on from 1st October, 1868. Fortunately, at the end of a year the Midland Railway, which planned to use the HH&B line as part of a route to Swansea, took over.

The company's offices were moved in 1866 from Welshpool to Oswestry, at the same time as the workshops there, set up by Savin to designs by Sharp, Stewart, became its responsibility, together with the maintaining of engines and stock which Savin had been looking after. There was probably a great deal that required attention; it would seem that some lines had been completed in a hurry; 'new stations' reported in the local newspapers for the years 1872/3 included Criccieth, Portmadoc, Llwyngwril, Barmouth Junction, Glandovey, and Montgomery. In one case the phrase 'replacing the present shed' was used.

The half-yearly report in March 1866 was extremely optimistic. After reporting the conclusion of the amalgamation of the various original railways, Earl Vane stated that a Bill was being prepared to amalgamate with five more lines. He mentioned four: the Nantlle (a horse tramway partly taken over by the Caernarvonshire), the Corris, the Caernarvonshire, and the Beddgelert (from Portmadoc to Nanthywynant). He said that progress on the unopened portions of the Cambrian was being made: 'the engine now runs along a considerable extent of it' (surely Savin was using more than one engine for construction) and it would all be open for summer. The new works intended included harbours at Ynyslas and Porthdynllaen (at the end of the Lleyn peninsular), the St Tudwal's Extension, and other items; powers would be taken to run steamboats to Ireland.

George Owen reported the completion of Oswestry Works, and that the engines recently added to work the Ellesmere branch were 'of first class construction'. H. Conybeare told of a suspension of work on the Barmouth viaduct due to violent storms; however by 1st June 'we shall have all works done to complete the line from Machynlleth to Caernarvon'. The only service at present on the Coast Line was from Aberdovey to Dolgelley, but soon 'communication to the south would be opened up by the completion of the Manchester & Milford Railway'. It would certainly not have been apparent to any shareholders present that the Cambrian did not, and would not ever, have a railway to Caernarvon, or that there was bitter enmity with the M&M due to non-payment of its dues at Llanidloes; or for that matter that none of the projects mentioned would be carried out.

The Schedule of Deviations for the same year is also interesting; at Ynyslas the branch to the wharf was to be continued as a mile-long loop, one track each side of the Twyni Bach, coming together at Penrhyn Point where there would be a pier. As stated earlier, the arrangements for passengers to be ferried to Aberdovey from 1863 until the opening of the 'deviation' line from Glandyfi suggests that such a line may have been already running on a temporary basis, and this may have been an attempt to regularise this; in fact no permanent part of it was ever built. Another wharf on the other side of the

Inside Oswestry Works: the second engine from the foreground is 0−4−4T No. 9 and, next to it, 2−4−0 No. 11.   *Oakwood Collection*

When the Cambrian took over the running of the Mid-Wales Railway, its plates were fixed on the cab sides of the engines; this is Mid-Wales Railway 0−4−2 No. 2, the only one which kept its original number.   *Locomotive Publishing Co.*

Leri cut would be served by a two-furlong branch with a junction facing west; when this was built, the junction faced east. There was also further mention of the 'St Tudwal's Extension'; this was eight miles of fairly tortuous track from near Pwllheli, crossing the ancient St Tudwal's tramway and terminating at Porthbach Point, south of Abersoch. In fact, no part of the western Lleyn peninsular saw the Cambrian until it began running buses there in 1906. The tramway was a 1¾ m line opened in 1846 serving various lead mines, and running to a pier in St Tudwal's Roads south of Abersoch.

As stated earlier, the Coast Line itself was opened in October 1867, delayed by Savin's financial problems, and also by the failure of the Gurney Overend Bank, which had repercussions on Cambrian finances. The final step for the erstwhile A&WC was a short one, from Penmaenpool to Dolgelley. There is some conflict on the actual date here, but it seems probable that the line opened on 21st June, 1869 to a temporary Dolgelley station at the end of Cambrian-owned metals, and that trains ran into the GW-owned station a few months later.

Returning to the two tracks built southwards by the L&N to Penpontbren Junction, mentioned earlier: the easternmost one from 19th September, 1864 carried Mid-Wales Railway trains from Llanidloes to Brecon, running over the Brecon & Merthyr Railway from Talyllyn Junction. This was a triangular junction, and the Mid-Wales had its station at the north corner, with a platform for Brecon and one on the east loop for trains to Dowlais and later to Merthyr and Newport. Soon after opening, the Mid-Wales Railway set up a locomotive shed at Llanidloes, next door to the L&N one. The Mid-Wales was not a 'Savin' railway, but had good relations with the Cambrian through Benjamin Piercy. Nevertheless there was some resentment that the Cambrian made no attempt to synchronise its services to Llanidloes with that of the other company. A few years later, when the Brecon & Merthyr had secured its connections south of Dowlais, the Cambrian was to benefit from heavy summer-time traffic in excursion trains by this route from South Wales to Aberystwyth. At Llechryd station, later called Builth Road, the Mid-Wales connected with the Central Wales line sponsored by the LNWR, from Shrewsbury to Swansea. Here a passenger from the south could join a through coach via the LNWR to Liverpool, Manchester and many other places; therefore the passenger traffic which might have come up to Llanidloes and on to Oswestry, or to Shrewsbury via Buttington Junction, was diverted, as was much goods traffic.

What then of the westernmost of the two lines to Penpontbren Junction? This had been laid for the exclusive use of the Manchester & Milford Railway's line to Llangurig, intended to pass through the Cambrian Mountains in a long tunnel to Yspytty Ystwyth. In fact construction ceased about a ¼ mile west of Llangurig, and the line never opened, though track was laid. The M&M decided as it approached Ystrad Meurig from the south, that it would turn north-west and make a dash for Aberystwyth, with David Davies driving his contracting team fast. There was a complex series of agreements between the M&M and the Mid-Wales; the latter would build a branch from Marteg to Llangurig to join up with the constructed portion from Penpontbren, and the M&M would link to this branch, at the same time allowing the Mid-Wales a further link which would enable it to run into Aberystwyth over the M&M tracks.

The Cambrian company noted that the M&M was not paying its one-third share of the running costs of the magnificent joint station at Llanidloes, nor of the line from there to Penpontbren. The M&M repeatedly stalled, and finally resorted to semantics by claiming that the agreement called upon them to make payment when the junction at Penpontbren was open, and it was not yet open. The fact is that Capt. Huish when he 'passed' the junction for the Board of Trade had commented on the fact that the two lines were not connected to each other at the 'junction'; but this had never been intended, the junction effectively being at Llanidloes station. There was a signal box and signals at Penpontbren, so the claim that the junction was not open was feeble. In 1872 a rumour was started, possibly by the Cambrian, that the train service to Llangurig was to begin operating shortly; but the gambit failed and the M&M never paid in full. A similar situation arose in regard to the payment for the M&M use of Aberystwyth station; the Cambrian sued, but the M&M went bankrupt.

Semantics were again employed, this time for the Mid-Wales, when in 1876 it applied to the House to abandon its branch from Marteg to Llangurig. This was the route by which the M&M hoped to reach north Wales, and it was a bitter blow. The M&M applied to Parliament for a Bill to force the Mid-Wales to pay compensation for loss of traffic, but the Law Lords handed down an opinion that the Mid-Wales had only agreed to apply for powers for the branch; they had not agreed to build it. The M&M Bill was thrown out as vexacious. Relations between the two companies at Aberystwyth remained strained.

Auto-trains were tried out on the Ellesmere and Wrexham lines in 1913, when two six-wheeled coaches were rebuilt into one bogie saloon trailer, No. 211, here being worked by 2–4–0T No. 56.   H.W. Burman

Chapter Two
Consolidation

The Board had been re-organised in 1868 with ten Directors, four elected by the 'Coast Line' Section, four by the Inland Section, and two nominees of Earl Vane and the Earl of Powis. There was a great deal of squabbling and a further restructuring was needed in 1878. Nevertheless, in the following year David Davies, who was now a Director, his contracting days behind him, saw fit to issue a broadsheet criticising the company, and resigned. A speech with which he followed up, stating that the Railway was not safe and would shortly be sprinkled with human blood, was angrily condemned by the former Earl Vane, now Lord Londonderry, as 'a stab in the dark'.

No words could conceal the fact that the company was in dire straits financially; in a country-wide recession receipts continued to fall, and by 1884 could not cover the debentures interest. At the insistence of the banks, on 12th July, 1884 the company was placed in Chancery, and John Conacher appointed Receiver. He was an able man, who had joined the railway in 1865 and become Secretary in 1882. By first consolidating some 70 blocks of shares into 10 he was able to get a grip on the finances, and from 1890 he was Manager of the railway. He left within two years to take a post on the North British Railway, but by that time fortunes were on the turn, an important factor being a rapid increase in tourism. When Lord Londonderry died in 1884 a link with the past was broken, and the work began of steering the Cambrian towards late Victorian prosperity.

The Cambrian's neighbour south of Llanidloes, the Mid-Wales Railway, had not been having a good time either. It had dissipated much of its capital obtaining Acts for branches it never built, and possessed neither of its termini, paying the Cambrian for the use of Llanidloes and the line from Penpontbren Junction, and paying the Brecon & Merthyr for the use of Brecon Free Street station and the line from Talyllyn. True, it got paid by the Midland for the use of the line from Three Cocks to Talyllyn Junction, but when in 1880 overtures were made to the Cambrian, the Board was not tempted. Towards the end of the decade however, there was a change of heart; the holiday traffic from the South Wales coalfields at least was worth having; had the Mid-Wales died, this would have passed to the Great Western's route via Carmarthen, and the Manchester & Milford. So in 1888 a working agreement was reached, by which in effect the Cambrian took over the line, although legal amalgamation did not take place until 1904.

The Mid-Wales and the Cambrian had made an agreement as early as 1864 that either company could use the other's carriages; indeed Cambrian stock was often seen at Newport and Cardiff. When David Davies gave a party for the 21st birthday of his son at Llandinam (where his house lay close to the station), hundreds of workpeople from his Ocean Collieries in South Wales were brought to it in Cambrian carriages. Therefore the 1888 Agreement produced no startling effects, though it did result in Moat Lane becoming in effect the junction for the Mid-Wales line. The station there was improved and later an engine shed built, which was useful for Cambrian locomotives hauling the Aberystwyth excursions, sometimes all the way from Merthyr Tydfil, as they could be turned at Moat Lane shed when the train had necessarily to reverse its direction there.

Buses lined up outside Pwllheli station about 1912; the two on the left are those built for the Cambrian Railway in 1911 on ex-LGOC 'E' type chassis; the others are various competitors on the Nevin and Edeyrn route. *J. Nickels*

The second station at Pwllheli was built in 1909; in this postcard view it is not yet open. A horse tramway ran down Embankment Road to the seafront; the car-shed is behind the railway refreshment room.
Author's Collection

Before rationalisation set in, a picture of Pwllheli looking towards the buffer stops on 9th June, 1965.
Oakwood Collection

The 1888 Agreement is an interesting document; somewhat amusing is the clause that 'the Mid-Wales Company will not disturb the exercise of quiet enjoyment by the Cambrian Co. of any of its rights and powers'. The revenues were to be kept separate; the Mid-Wales revenue would pay the tolls to the Brecon & Merthyr Railway, while the Cambrian would take all revenue from the Aberdovey wharf branch. One old chestnut popped up again; the Mid-Wales would deduct £750 from its revenue for the use of Llanidloes station; the Cambrian would keep any revenue arising from the use of the joint line by the Manchester & Milford Railway – that hope was apparently not quite dead.

The Mid-Wales was ordered to surrender to the Cambrian by 1st April 'all rolling stock and plant except three locomotive engines, old rail stores, and the furniture of the London Office'. Since all the Mid-Wales engines then in use received Cambrian Railway numbers, the three mentioned here would appear to be ones which the Mid-Wales had hired out or sold, but which were found on the books by the solicitors' accountants!

The Cambrian did not take over the spur line joining the two stations at Builth Road, as this had been transferred to the LNWR in 1866. Nor did it yield to persuasion to take over the derelict line from Penpontbren Junction to Llangurig. When the Manchester & Milford Railway went bankrupt in 1875 it is believed some rails from this line were lifted and sold to pay debts, though officially they were lifted in 1883. When 20 years later the M&M merged with the Great Western, Parliament ordered that the Llangurig branch should be handed to the Cambrian 'at no cost'; however the gift was refused; the line had never been fenced, and since there had already been one lawsuit due to a horse falling into a cutting, the CR no doubt regarded this thin 3-mile strip of real-estate across barren land as more trouble than it was worth.

Until 1916 passengers to Fairbourne station continued to the Barmouth Ferry by horse tram, which had begun in 1890; here two bogie cars on the 2 ft gauge line are seen at the Ferry terminus about 1904. In its later steam days the terminus was moved several times. *Author's Collection*

The Earl (seen here) and *The Countess*, named after the occupants of Powys Castle remained the only motive power on the Welshpool–Llanfaircaereinion branch from 1903 to closure in 1956. *F. Moore*

The W&LR made its way through Welshpool town by ancient tramway wayleave, and here a train squeezed between the houses prepares to cross the ungated Church Street; the church clock shows that this is the 3.45 from Welshpool. *Oakwood Collection*

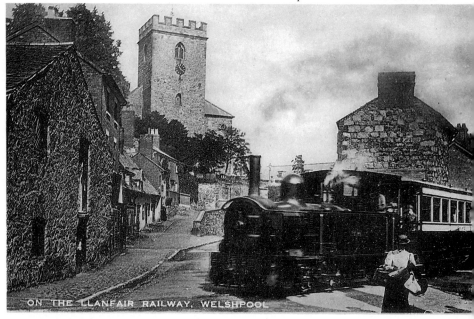

Chapter Three
The Last Branches

The northern end of the Cambrian system has received less attention than the more scenic coastal lines, but at one time it seemed about to achieve more importance. It was the key to the Welsh Union Railway, a loose confederation of Welsh railways intent on providing a rail route to the industrial north which did not depend upon either the GWR or the LNWR. When first mooted in the mid-1860s it had involved the Buckley, Chester & Mold, Mold & Denbigh, Vale of Clwyd, and Hoylake Railways, and looked to the Cambrian like a non-starter which it did not wish to join. In the south there was less doubt; the Brecon & Merthyr and Mid-Wales had always had such ambitions. Interest died for some time, but in 1881 when Piercy rejoined the Wrexham, Mold & Connah's Quay Railway (WM&CQ) after a spell abroad, he put his mind to it and a viable plan began to form. This involved a reconstructed WM&CQ main line (not via Buckley), connection at Wrexham with a Cambrian branch from Ellesmere, and a spur to the LNWR at Hope.

There was however another faction which had a different idea; J.W. McClure was a new Cambrian Director, and was also on the Board of the Manchester, Sheffield & Lincolnshire Railway (MS&LR), a fiefdom of the great Sir Edward Watkin. He and others wished to join the WM&CQ not to the LNW but to the MS&L, by means of a bridge at Shotton, then jointly with the Wirral Railway to build a line from there to Bidston, the North Wales & Liverpool Railway. From Bidston an existing Wirral Railway line would take traffic into Birkenhead. Perhaps to secure the southern end, Watkin became Chairman of the Neath & Brecon Railway and brought Connacher in to manage it as well as the Cambrian.

In 1889 the Welsh Railways Through Traffic Act was pushed through the Houses of Parliament by Watkin's friend Gladstone; the bridge over the Dee was named after Gladstone's home station of Hawarden. It was all set; an independent route to the north; never mind that it was mostly single line and peppered with severe gradients. The first step was made on 1st November, 1887 when a short connecting line was opened from Wrexham Exchange station to Wrexham Central, where the Cambrian line from Ellesmere was to be met. The Ellesmere & Wrexham Railway, a nominally independent company, was approved in 1885 but took a long time to build, not arriving at Wrexham Central until 2nd November, 1895. The final link, from Shotton to Bidston, opened on 18th May, 1896.

Unfortunately, the mountain had brought forth a mouse; little through traffic followed. Piercy had died in 1888 and Sir Edward Watkin had retired due to ill health. The Ellesmere & Wrexham Railway settled down to life as a rail-motor-served branch line; the MS&L became the Great Central and started frying much bigger fish. A through service from the Cheshire Lines Railway via the new route ran to Aberystwyth, but was withdrawn in 1915. Only once did the Welsh Union route come into its own; in 1918 due to congestion on all routes to the north, Welsh coal for the Grand Fleet at Scapa Flow went that way; the trains were known as 'Jellicoe Specials'. What epic journeys they must have been; down the 'Seven Mile Bank' on the B&M,

banked up to Rhayader and then to Pantydwr summit, 1½ miles of 1 in 80 up to Frankton; and from the WM&CQ summit at Buckley Junction there was a nasty drop at 1 in 5̊3 with severe curves into Hawarden. Only desperation would send coal trains by such a route.

In the 1890s the Cambrian received an unexpected traffic boost from the decision by Birmingham Corporation to build a series of giant reservoirs in the Elan Valley, west of Rhayader. A substantial railway was built by the Corporation from Elan Junction, south of the short tunnel at Rhayader, to the workings. Because the junction was on a gradient of 1 in 60, the Board of Trade required the actual exchange sidings to be some hundreds of yards up the branch, at Noyadd. To this point the Cambrian Railway brought materials and equipment in three to four short train loads per day, hauled by one of the old 'Seaham' class 2–4–0T engines. The Corporation's 0–6–0ST locomotives were more powerful and appear from the working instructions to have been able to take up the Valley in one go all the wagons brought by three trips of the 'Seaham'. The Cambrian handled all negotiations with the Corporation, though they did not yet legally own the Mid-Wales line; there was an attempt to insist that all materials came over the Cambrian main line, but this failed, and much of it came via the LNWR and the spur line at Builth Road.

As early as 1893 the Cambrian was organising excursions to view the workings. From 1894 the Elan Valley Railway had its own carriages, about 17; five ex-Cambrian and the remainder early GWR. However they did not run into Rhayader station, but worked from Noyadd sidings upwards. The Cambrian ran a workmen's train early on Monday mornings, returning on Saturdays, but negotiations to run this to Noyadd failed and the passengers had to walk from Rhayader station. Most workmen lived in the Cor-poration's Elan Village, and the workmen's train on the CR is thought to have been only two old carriages, for the few whose families lived in or near Llanidloes.

The dams took 12 years to complete; finally on 21st July, 1904 all was ready for the opening by King Edward VII. The Cambrian had to put together a Royal Train of four-wheelers, as nothing else was allowed on the branch; they chose 1st/2nd class Compo. No. 34, 1st saloons Nos. 9 and 11, and full brake No. 31. For the occasion many rules must have been 'bent', for as the LNW and GWR trains of notables from Birmingham and elsewhere poured into Rhayader station, they were hauled in open trucks up the valley by Corporation engines (not fitted with continuous brakes), while the incoming stock was sent away to wait in any available siding. The King's LNWR Royal Train arrived late at Rhayader station; the Cambrian engine (No. 83) had stalled near Elan Junction and had to be assisted by a waterworks engine. However, all went more or less according to plan; the Cambrian's 'Royal Train' was hauled up the valley by a Corporation engine from Rhayader station; there is no evidence that the engine was brake-fitted, and consider-ing the gradient up to Craig Goch, where the main ceremony took place, this was a remarkable risk to take. The Cambrian was probably requested to supply a brake-fitted 'Seaham', but would have declined; they were always careful not to take responsibility for anything that happened beyond Noyadd Siding.

On the 1 in 50 gradient, two miles before the top of the climb, is Rheidol Falls Halt;
here a down-valley train comprises three coaches, both passenger brake vans and five
open wagons, about 1925.   *Author's Collection*

A set-piece photograph on the Rheidol Railway before opening; in addition to the
gentleman lolling too near the rails, another is on the front of the engine; the place is
Nant-yr-Fynwg curve, Rhiwfron.   *Author's Collection*

However, from 1906 the Corporation having sold its engines, the Cambrian did agree to work any traffic required, for a fairly heavy fee, and kept a 'Seaham' at Builth Road shed for the purpose. The large signal box at Elan Junction was closed in 1908 and the double-line loop there singled. By 1916 the branch track needed some replacements, and the Corporation was advised that scrap prices were so high that they could lift the track, sell it, and relay later if necessary from the proceeds. This was done, from Noyadd up the valley; it was never relaid. The short section from Elan Junction to Noyadd was lifted a few years later.

In the meantime, two events of no great importance had occurred. In June 1880 the Potteries, Shrewsbury & North Wales Railway (PSNWR), which made connection with the Cambrian at Llanymynech, closed entirely. Shorn of its intended sections between Stoke-on-Trent and Shrewsbury, and Llanymynech and Portmadoc, it had no chance; it had been opened on 13th August, 1866, and apart from mineral branches from Kinnerley to Breidden and Llanymynech to Nantmawr it generated little revenue. The Cambrian (CR) was prepared to take over the latter branch, which it did six months after closure; the Breidden (or Criggion) branch was not resuscitated until 30 years later, and not by the Cambrian. The CR continued to work the Nantmawr traffic even after the Shropshire Railway (SpR) bought the old PSNWR in 1888; this company proved to have insufficient funds to re-open its lines, though it remained the nominal owner. On 27th January, 1896 the Cambrian arranged with the SpR to use the Nantmawr connection, which was south of Llanymynech station, for its branch to Llanfyllin, then connecting at Rock Siding north of the station. To effect this, a spur was put in at Wern where the former PSNW crossed the Llanfyllin branch; the track between that point and Rock Siding was lifted.

The second event was also a closure. The Van Railway had been opened on 14th August, 1871 from its own station at Caersws to a lead mine in which Earl Vane and David Davies had interests; a passenger service was run until 1879 to a terminus at Garth & Van Road, about ½ mile short of the mine. In 1887 the Manager, the poet Ceiriog Hughes, died and not long after David Davies also; the railway and mine deteriorated and closed in 1892. By 1896 the Cambrian considered that future prospects had sufficient substance to justify re-opening. It had another interest; it had by agreement been taking large quantities of mine spoil for ballast. This had the advantage of being toxic to weeds, but it was found later that the dust from it did not improve engine bearings. The line re-opened for mineral traffic only on 29th July, 1896; the two small Manning, Wardle tank engines were taken over as CR Nos. 22 and 25, but the two carriages were left to rot at Caersws and Pwll-glas stations.

The mine machinery was improved; the water-wheel and long leat up the hill went; in 1909 Lord Herbert Vane-Tempest and David Davies's grandson showed off the mine to Prince Francis of Teck, travelling in the saloon No. 9 used at the opening of Elan dams. However, after the Great War the demand for lead dropped and the mine closed again in 1920. The railway maintained a shadowy existence until 1940; the Van station and sheds at Caersws were passed over to the Bridge Engineers and used to stable service vehicles until the 1970s.

Rheidol Railway No. 1, a 2–6–2T by Davies & Metcalfe, in Cambrian Railways livery with No. 3 behind, at Devil's Bridge about 1920.   *W.L. Good*

This Bagnall's 2–4–0T which had belonged to the Hafan & Talybont Tramway (which connected with the CR at Llanfihangel) is shown here after purchase by the Vale of Rheidol Railway, and before the removal of the spark-arresting chimney in 1904. It lost its name in 1915, becoming No. 3 and ultimately GWR No. 1197.   *F. Moore*

A considerable expense fell upon the company in the rebuilding at
Barmouth Bridge from 1899; the sliding span was replaced by a swinging
one, based on four steel spans in place of the old eight. Barmouth Harbour
was outside the town, lying ¼ mile east of the bridge, at Aber-amffra. There
were continual calls for more and more dredging of the channel, but these
ceased in the late 1890s and the cost of the new swinging span was not really
justified.

The passing of the Light Railways Act in 1896 stimulated many
marginally viable railway schemes all over the country, North Wales
included. One of the first was the Tanat Railway, a fresh attempt at an
Oswestry & Llanginog Railway which had failed in the early 1880s. As
revived, the scheme was for a line coming off the Porthywaen branch not far
from Llynclys Junction, joining the Nantmawr branch at Llanyblodwell, and
going on up to Llanginog, where there were quarries. Llanyblodwell was
renamed Blodwell Junction, the station there having at one end a junction
between the Tanat Valley and the Llanymynech spur, and at the other a
junction between the Tanat Valley and the remainder of the Nantmawr
branch. The line was opened on 5th January, 1904, worked by the Cambrian
Railway; all trains worked through to Oswestry, and a through carriage from
Llanginog was detached at Blodwell Junction for working to Llanymynech,
to connect with trains to Welshpool and beyond. This was at the request of
the Earl of Bradford, and ceased about 1916.

Another early light railway was the Vale of Rheidol, from Aberystwyth to
Devil's Bridge. The latter place had been the objective of an earlier proposed
branch line of the Manchester & Milford Railway. There was some lead
mining in the Rheidol valley, but tourism was now a greater hope. The line
was built to the 2 ft gauge, on an almost continuous rising gradient above
Capel Bangor; there was also a short branch from the engine sheds in
Aberystwyth to the Rotfawr Wharf on the south side of the Harbour. The line
opened on 22nd December, 1902. It was purchased by the Cambrian on 1st
July, 1913.

Another narrow gauge light railway, this time of 2 ft 6 in. gauge, was
opened on 9th March, 1903 (to passengers 4th April) from the station yard at
Welshpool to Llanfaircaereinion, its purpose being mainly passengers and
agricultural. Its route out of Welshpool was difficult; the only choice was the
wayleave of an old Montgomeryshire Canal tramway of 1818 to the Stondart
Quarry, which was still available though unused for 50 years. This ran
narrowly between houses and streets, and was the reason why the line,
when 'privatised' 50 years later, had to terminate rather inconveniently near
Raven Square. The line was worked by the Cambrian Railway with two
engines and three carriages, a modest stock, and various wagons.

Colonel H.F. Stephens was a great enthusiast for Light Railways, and
collected several under his management; ever optimistic over lines of
marginal viability, he was persuaded to re-open the railway between
Shrewsbury (Abbey) station and Llanymynech, the old 'Potts'. In 1888 the
Shropshire Railways had done some renewal of track and bridges, but much
of that had in its turn decayed. However, the 1865 rails and chairs were
mostly useable. At Llanymynech the sad little wooden station on the east

side of the Cambrian one was patched up, though the engine shed there was knocked down. The new railway, called the Shropshire & Montgomeryshire Light Railway (S&M), opened on 13th April, 1911; the special train for notables from Shrewsbury included the two Cambrian saloons used by King Edward to open the Elan dams in 1904. A large notice was put up at Llanymynech opposite the CR platform announcing 'The Shortest Route to Shrewsbury', and it certainly was that, but not necessarily the quickest, and later the service and the stock which ran it became quite unacceptable. The S&M did not claim back the Nantmawr branch, therefore this development hardly affected the Cambrian at all.

The Mawddwy Railway, which connected with the Cambrian at Cemmes Road, was not a light railway legally, having been built before the Act was passed. However, in 1910 an application was made for a Light Railway Order, mainly due to pressure from David Davies. What had happened was that this railway, which was almost entirely owned by the Buckley family, had been allowed to reach such a wretched state that by April 1901 passenger services had had to be suspended, and by 1908 all carrying ceased. The reason for this is not clear; from 1892 when slate quarries were opened at Maes-y-Gamfa, connected by tramway to Aberangell station, there was a regular income. No money had been spent on running the line, except for the adding to stock of two decrepit ex-North London Railway carriages, and fitting the regular engine *Mawddwy* with its vacuum brake. The negotiations to buy out Sir Edmund Buckley and to obtain an Order took some time, and it was not until 29th July, 1911 that the line was re-opened, for passengers and goods, worked by the Cambrian Railway. The whole line was relaid; the weeds were neatly disposed of by using toxic ballast from the Van Mines. One engine, *Mawddwy*, was taken into CR stock, and one coach survived as a service vehicle, one other having a further life grounded at Nesscliff S&M station.

A railway whose life was so brief as to be hardly worth mentioning was the Hafan & Talybont, a 2 ft 3 in. gauge line which ran from the sidings at Llanfihangel (Llandre) to Talybont, Hafan, and some granite quarries in the foothills of Plynlimon. This was opened in May 1897, carried passengers as far as Talybont from 28th March, 1898, and closed entirely the next year, for reasons of finance and disappointment at the output of a mine, and the quality of granite setts from the quarry. Some of the wagons were sold to the Rheidol Railway and remained in use long enough to carry GWR livery; a 2–4–0T engine was also sold to the Rheidol Railway, and remained in service as No. 3 until 1923, being the only engine allowed on the harbour branch.

The Cambrian was uneasily aware that it covered only part of the developing tourist areas of Wales, and joined with the GWR and LNWR in issuing circular tickets for tours which involved all three lines. However, it also issued its own 1000-mile ticket for the reasonable price of £2 17s. 6d. (in 1912), and in summer a fortnightly ticket for unlimited travel between Machynlleth, Aberystwyth, Pwllheli and Dolgelley, 32s. 6d. first class, 22s. 6d. second class, or 17s. 6d. third class. Guide books were at that time rail-oriented, and the Cambrian arranged for publicity inserts in guides such as the famous Baddeley & Ward. This included a feature on Welsh golf courses, and sure enough the insert offered special cheap tickets for golfers. Nowadays they call it 'marketing'; to the Cambrian it was just good management.

By 1909 the construction at Pwllheli of a north embankment along reclaimed harbour land had enabled the Cambrian to extend its line 45 chains westwards to a new terminus. This lay adjacent to the new Embankment Road on the west side of the harbour, down which a horse-tram now ran to the South Beach, ¾-mile away. The station was of a new type, with a centre island platform, and lines each side having engine release roads. Wooden station buildings extended across the end, with a refreshment room on the harbour side. The goods sidings and engine shed remained at the old station, the canopy of which was moved to Aberdovey. In front of the new station was a large standing area of motor buses; the Cambrian had themselves put on two buses in the summer of 1906 running from the original station to Nevin and Edeyrn on the Lleyn Peninsular. There was at that time no satisfactory British type of bus and the choice fell on the Swiss-built Orion; with a horizontal engine somewhat underpowered it was not a successful type. The body had an open front saloon for smokers and a closed part to the rear; they were single-deck. It is known that in 1911 the railway purchased from the London General Omnibus Co. two chassis of their E-type (E60/110), German Milnes-Daimlers which had given good service in the capital; new all-enclosed bodies were mounted. However, a stock list of Cambrian passenger and goods stock dated 1908 included 'four motor buses', and it is possible that others were purchased between the two pairs of which photographs exist. The 'charabangs' were now becoming very popular and the forecourt of Pwllheli station was soon crowded with competitors, including Tocia Motors, who built up a large fleet. Possibly for this reason, the railway buses ceased to run after 1913.

This was a period of prosperity for the Cambrian, which could afford to double the line from Newtown to Moat Lane. A good part of the revenue was coming from summer camps for the 'Volunteers' (later the Territorial Army) held in the Aberystwyth area. There was a large one in the grounds of Lovesgrove House, Capel Bangor, in 1910 for which a halt was opened on the Devil's Bridge line, and another west of Bow Street; to cope with the extra traffic, wooden second platforms were erected at Borth and at Llandre, then still Llanfihangel. This traffic ceased after July 1914, for now the Volunteers were being readied for the War in regular barracks.

There was one satisfactory event for the Cambrian; the dues on the joint line and station at Llanidloes owed by the M&M were partly paid.

In 1911 the Great Western finally took over the Manchester & Milford Railway. In 1904 the Cambrian had made an offer for this bankrupt concern, but was turned down in favour of a working agreement with the GWR. It was admitted that the Cambrian terms were better, but the M&M felt the hot breath of Chancery might reach it there. It was no great loss to the Welsh company; it would have inherited some very strange engines and run-down coaches. The M&M did have a branch to Aberystwyth Harbour (St David's Wharf) but there was little trade there and the branch seems to have been inactive before the take-over, which incidentally was objected to by the LNWR and the Midland Railway. In the latter case the reason no doubt was that it gave the GWR a route alternative to its own from Swansea via Brecon and Three Cocks; the former did not wish to see its great rival countering its own approach to Aberystwyth via the joint Welshpool line. In the event, the GWR did not develop the line and posed no problem, though it did run motor buses in Aberystwyth, including a service to Aberaeron in connection with a new GWR-sponsored light railway to Lampeter.

The Cambrian participated in various tours; one example (1911) was a circular trip from Aberystwyth via Machynlleth and the Corris Railway (steam-worked since 1883), and road to Dolgelley, with return via Barmouth, all for 5s.

The first years of World War I were not total, except for those at the front; the Midlands in particular had many thousands profitably engaged in munitions production, and they needed holidays. So it was that heavy trains of LNWR stock were still running on to the Cambrian lines. It would be untrue to say that the lines played a major part in the War, except for one brief time in 1918 already mentioned, when the English lines were unable to cope with the insatiable demand from the Grand Fleet at Scapa for Welsh steam coal, and the Welsh route to the north, hardly won 20 years earlier, was used to the full at last. Coal trains from the Valleys ran on to the Cambrian at Talyllyn Junction, having passed over several South Wales railways. They were short, because the Brecon & Merthyr line to Talyllyn had fierce gradients, as had the Mid-Wales section of the Cambrian; having struggled up to Oswestry, it was not over; the line of the Wrexham, Mold & Connah's Quay Railway, which would be met at Wrexham, was also steeply

'Beaconsfield' class 4–4–0 No. 60, after its 1914 rebuild, on a local train about to leave Aberdovey for Machynlleth.
H.W. Burman

No. 10 was an ex-GWR 2−4−0 built at Wolverhampton in 1883 and taken on by the Cambrian in 1921; note that the railway's name was carried high on the coal rail.
H.W. Burman

graded. Furthermore, only a small part of the route could accept powerful engines; the Mid-Wales in particular was confined to its less powerful 0−6−0s in theory, though no doubt the latest Aston engines were used in fact.

After it was all over, railways in general were taking a rueful look at run-down equipment and a changed world. It was clear that the Cambrian had to join some big brother, and for a time this seemed likely to be the LNWR, so much the strongest in North Wales. But in the event it was the GWR. Was this the right choice? The Cambrian connected with the LNWR at Welshpool, Builth Road, Whitchurch and Afon Wen; with the GWR at Welshpool, Brecon, Dolgelley, Aberystwyth; there was not much in it. Perhaps the GWR had a little more patience with small branch lines than the LNWR; in any case the GWR set to work modernising the engine and carriage stock, opening new halts, and improving the through London services. Perhaps 'modernising' the locomotive stock is not the right word, for the new engines were almost all of the Dean '2301' class of 0−6−0, which was 40 years old. But this large class performed wonders everywhere on the GWR and not least on the Cambrian, where it formed the backbone of goods and passenger services right up to BR times.

The actual date of amalgamation was 25th March, 1922; on the new GWR Board the Cambrian had one Director, David Davies. The Cambrian came in with five railways which it did not own but only worked. These were the Mawddwy; Van; Wrexham & Ellesmere; the Shropshire, which was a paper railway apart from the short line from Llanymynech to Nantmawr quarries; and the narrow gauge Welshpool & Llanfair. Two other connecting lines, the Festiniog and the Talyllyn, were left out and remained independent; the five quoted officially joined the GWR on 1st January, 1923.

Chapter Four

Locomotives and Coaches

Apart from some contractors' locomotives ordered in their own names, David Davies and Thomas Savin normally placed orders for engines to work 'their' lines in the name of one of the companies, which paid up to two-thirds of the cost, though they had little say in the use to which they were put. Up to 1864 engines were only distinguished by names; thereafter numbers were allotted, but the first available list shows engines supposedly owned by the B&M and HH&B numbered in with ones which certainly were Cambrian, and also with some of the contracting engines. Savin switched machines from one line to another depending upon need, and the precise history of each cannot always be determined. For example the 0−6−0 purchased in 1862 for the opening of the Brecon & Merthyr was named *De Winton* after a Brecon banker, and certainly worked there for a time, but some authorities include it as Cambrian Railway No. 16, while others give it as Brecon & Merthyr No. 6. After Savin set up the Oswestry Works, engines of various railways attended there for repairs, and may have seemed to some to be Cambrian engines. The Joint Committee set up to operate the engines of the L&N, O&N and N&M in a pool, purchased in 1863 eight Savin engines no longer needed for contracting work, most of which were sold within five years.

Engines whose history is doubtful included *Llywelin*, an engine which helped to open the L&N, *Dove*, a Sharp, Roberts 2−2−2 of 1839, which worked on the L&N from 1857 to 1859, but may not have remained long enough to work passenger trains. *Llandinam* was a Manning, Wardle which was probably Davies's property; *Hero* which was present at the opening of the OE&WR was probably borrowed from the LNWR; *Tiny*, which is known to have worked Savin's New British Coalpits branch at Porthywaen, is said to have been ordered for the HH&B, but appeared briefly on Cambrian lists from 1867. Another HH&B engine *Hereford* was at Oswestry Works in 1869 (where it was renamed *Lady Cornelia* in honour of the Guests of Dowlais) but remained a B&M engine, as it was reported later supplying steam for pumping at Brecon shed. At 31st December, 1866, before Savin's stock had been properly sorted out, the Cambrian claimed ownership of 14 passenger and 13 goods engines, 6 tank engines and 6 'ballast' engines. The list published here of engines built up to 1866 suggests: Passenger engines 3, 7, 28−31, 41−44, 53−56 (total 14); goods engines 11, 12, 19, 26, 27, 34, 35, 39, 40, 45, 46, 51, 52 (total 13); tank engines 36, 38, 57−59 (total 5); ballast engines 1, 2, 14, 17, 21, 24 (total 6). Of the tank engines, No. 37 was probably counted, though thought to be on loan in the south.

Because the Cambrian Railways had running rights over the Mid-Wales Railway, Savin could move engines anywhere within an area stretching from Hereford, Dowlais and Brecon in the south to Whitchurch in the north. The period of uncertainty in records is up to 1863, when the O&N Joint Committee was formed; at that time there were 17 engines working the Brecon & Merthyr and the same number the constituents of the Cambrian. At the sorting-out following Savin's bankruptcy, most of the engines which appeared still to be his property went to the Cambrian; however, it is

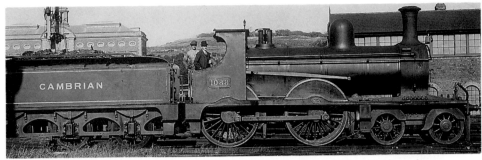

No. 61 was one of the small 4−4−0s built in 1893; here it is still in Cambrian livery but has its new GWR brass number, 1088. *F. Moore*

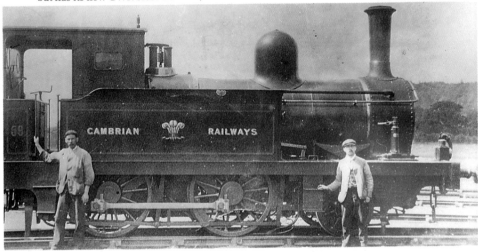

'Seaham' tank No. 59 here has its new boiler and square cab fitted in 1894 but has lost its name; it was to last another 50 years in service. *R.E. Thomas*

No. 7 was one of the small class of 0−4−4Ts, which were often used for railmotor work; here although in CR livery, it is working with GWR trailer No. 25. *F. Moore*

somewhat puzzling that No. 4 *Wynnstay*, an L&N veteran and named after the estate of the great Sir Watkin Williams-Wynn, should have been allowed to stay in the south. Only five engines on the Savin list were retained by the B&M; this list did not include B&M engines working south of Dowlais, the 'Old Rumney' line. Six which had been on the B&M went back to the CR, and one (No. 7) seems to have been recovered from the Denbigh, Ruthin & Corwen Railway, as the Vale of Clwyd had become. One of the small 0–4–0ST engines is said to have been found on the Dowlais Ironworks private railway.

Davies and Savin seem to have been amongst the first to recognise the usefulness of the Manning, Wardle 'K' class 0–6–0ST for railway contracting, and purchased eight in the period 1861–3. With 12 in. × 17 in. cylinders, 3 ft 1½ in. wheels, and with a weight of 16½ tons evenly distributed, they were indeed good work engines, but their small wheels ruled them out for serious traffic and all were sold by 1878. There have been conflicting accounts of their history, but it seems probable that the O&N Locomotive Committee took them over in 1863, together with Savin's Nos. 1 and 2 which were of a different type, and hired them back to Savin. However only Nos. 13, 14, 17, 18 and 24 ended up in Cambrian ownership, Nos. 10, 15 and 22 becoming Brecon & Merthyr stock.

Manning, Wardle Locomotives

MW	List No.	Date	Name	CR No.	B&M No.	Remarks
35	10	1861	Pioneer	–	17	For B&MR
36	13	1861	Whixall	13	–	For OE&WR
45	14	1862	Nantclwyd	14	–	For Vale of Clwyd Rly
49	15	1862	Hereford	–	16	For HH&B Rly
52	17	1862	Merion	17	–	On Coast Line
55	18	1862	Cardigan	18	–	For B&MR. On Coast Line
58	22	1862	Usk	–	15	For B&MR
66	24	1863	Borth	24	–	On Coast Line

The Cambrian also inherited three more engines of the same type: Manning, Wardle No. 140 *Mawddwy* of 1864 from the Mawddwy Railway, which became Cambrian No. 30; also Manning, Wardle Nos. 374 of 1872 and 668 of 1877 from the Van Railway, which became CR Nos. 25 and 22. This last was withdrawn in 1896 and in 1901 replaced by another Manning, Wardle engine, which however was a 0–4–0ST and therefore easily distinguishable. The second Mawddwy Railway engine, Manning, Wardle No. 268, was not taken over.

The Manning, Wardle saddle-tanks saw much service after leaving the Savin or CR stock; *Borth* for example was later *Vixen* for T. Docwra & Son and *Mendip* for H. Jackson & Co.

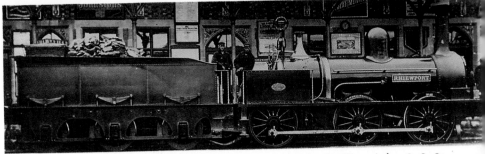

Locomotive *Rhiewport* was one of several repeat orders for the 'Queen' class 0–6–0s from Sharp, Stewart, supplied in 1864. Seen here at Aberystwyth about 1880, its number (45) is only just visible on the front splasher.   *Locomotive Publishing Co.*

Three of these 0–4–0ST engines were supplied by Sharp, Stewart to the O&NR in 1863; later their jobs included working the Kerry branch and the Porthywaen sidings – the Porthywaen branch brake van is behind the shed.   *Locomotive Publishing Co.*

The six Metropolitan Railway tanks made surplus by electrification were not a good buy in 1905; formerly MR No. 15, this one was 40 years old when purchased.

F. Moore

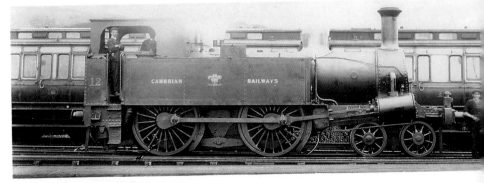

List of Savin and CR Locomotives built up to 1866

No.	Name	Type	Works	Maker's No.	Built	Built for	Remarks
1	Enterprise	0–6–0T	E.B. Wilson	601	1858	Davies & Savin	
2	–	0–4–0	MW	19	1860	,,	Originally Ruthin
3	Milford	0–4–2ST	SS	1123	1859	,,	
4	Wynnstay	0–4–2	,,	1146	1859	L&NRy	B&M No. 12
* 5	Montgomery	,,	,,	1147	1859	,,	
6	Glansevern	,,	,,	1148	1859	,,	B&M No. 11
7	Llanerchydol	,,	,,	1224	1860	,,	
* 8	Leighton	,,	,,	1225	1860	,,	
9	Volunteer	,,	,,	1226	1860	,,	
10	Pioneer	0–6–0ST	MW	35	1861	T. Savin	B&M No. 17, Blanche
11	Queen	0–6–0	SS	1301	1861	O&N Ry	
12	Prince of Wales	,,	,,	1302	1861	,,	
*13	Green Dragon	0–6–0ST	MW	36	1862	T. Savin	Originally Whixall
14	Nantclwyd	,,	,,	45	1862	,,	
15	Hereford	,,	,,	49	1862	,,	B&M No. 16, Lady Cornelia
16	De Winton	0–6–0	,,	41	1862	,,	B&M No. 6
17	Merion	0–6–0ST	MW	52	1862	,,	
*18	Cardigan	,,	,,	55	1862	,,	
19	Hercules	0–6–0	SS	1341	1862	O&N Ry	
20	Vulcan	,,	,,	1342	1862	,,	B&M No. 3
21	Lilleshall	0–4–0ST	Lilleshall		1862	T. Savin	Sold 1868
22	Usk	0–6–0ST	MW	58	1862	,,	B&M No. 15
*23	Tiny	0–4–0ST	,,	63	1862	,,	
24	Borth	0–6–0ST	,,	66	1863	,,	
25	Dwarf	0–4–0ST	Worsdell & Evans		1860	,,	Used on O&N, not CR
26	Tubal Cain	0–6–0	SS	1343	1863	O&N Ry	
27	Cambria	,,	,,	1344	1863	,,	
28	Mazeppa	2–4–0	,,	1400	1863	,,	
29	Pegasus	,,	,,	1401	1863	,,	
30	Albion	,,	,,	1412	1863	,,	
31	Minerva	,,	,,	1413	1863	,,	
32	Antelope		Slaughter, Gruning		1853		B&M No. 7
33	Elephant				1854		B&M No. 8
34	Cader Idris	0–6–0	SS	1310	1861	N&M Ry	Originally Talerddig
35	Castell Deudraeth	,,	,,	1311	1861	N&M Ry	Originally Countess Vane
36	Plasfynnon	0–4–0ST	,,	1431	1863	O&N Jt	
*37	Mountaineer	,,	,,	1432	1863	,,	On B&M, later CR
38	Prometheus	,,	,,	1433	1863	,,	
39	Sir Watkin	0–6–0	,,	1445	1863	N&M Ry	
40	Cyfronydd	,,	,,	1446	1863	,,	GWR 899
41	Countess Vane	2–4–0	,,	1485	1864	O&N Jt	GWR 1330
42	Glandovey	,,	,,	1486	1864	,,	
43	Plynlimmon	,,	,,	1487	1864	,,	GWR 1331
44	Rheidol	,,	,,	1488	1864	,,	Reb. 2–4–0T, 1907; GWR 1190

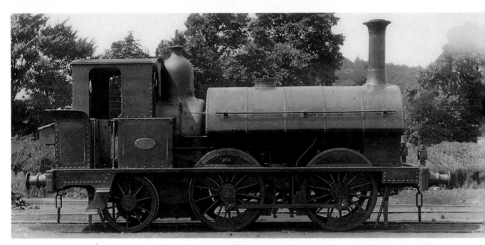

Locomotive *Milford*, an 0–4–2ST supplied by Sharps to Davies in 1859, and the first engine to work for the L&NR; seen here about 1900 as CR No. 3.   *Locomotive Publishing Co.*

The 'Prince of Wales Feathers' armorial device, applied to locomotives for a time from 1898.

No. 13, originally named *Talerddig*, was ordered in 1875 specifically for banking trains to the summit of the same name. *Locomotive Publishing Co.*

No. Name	Type	Works	Maker's No.	Built	Built for	Remarks
45 Rhiewport	0−6−0	,,	1530	1864	Cambrian	GWR 900
46 Towyn	,,	,,	1531	1864	,,	GWR 901
47 Wye	2−4−0	,,	1579	1865	,,	B&M Ry No. 10
48 Usk	,,	,,	1580	1865	,,	B&M Ry No. 9
51 Snowdon	0−6−0	SS	1590	1865	,,	GWR 910
52 Harlech	,,	,,	1597	1865	,,	GWR 911
53 Gladstone	2−4−0	,,	1633	1865	,,	GWR 1332
54 Palmerston	,,	,,	1632	1865	,,	
55 Treflach	,,	,,	1655	1865	,,	GWR 1333
56 Whittington	,,	,,	1656	1865	,,	Reb. 2−4−0T, 1907; GWR 1191
57 Maglona	2−4−0T	,,	1681	1866	,,	GWR 1192
58 Gladys	,,	,,	1682	1866	,,	GWR 1196
59 Seaham	,,	,,	1683	1866	,,	GWR 1197

* These engines were not in Cambrian Stock at 31st December, 1866, but taken over in 1867.

The railways which made up the Cambrian had little choice in the type of engine they would use for their passenger services; since 'singles' were ruled out by the gradients, it had to be 2−4−0, 0−4−2 or 0−6−0, though the last was at that time regarded as a goods type. Savin seems to have had good relations with the firm of Sharp, Stewart & Co. and it was fortunate for his railways that he and Davies elected to order from them; they certainly gave better service than the engines their neighbour the Mid-Wales ordered from Kitsons. Following a rather dubious purchase by Davies of a 0−4−2ST with only 4 ft 6 in. wheels for the O&N in 1859, a class of six tender 0−4−2s with 5 ft driving wheels was obtained in 1859−60. From the same company came

A fine view of No. 3214 and 3217 on an eight-coach train, climbing the steep bank at Talerddig in the summer of 1938.   *N.E. Stead Collection*

The '3 class' comprised of six locomotives only. 0–4–4T engines for passenger work on services mainly north of Oswestry; No. 5 was built by Nasmyth Wilson in 1895.

F. Moore

The '94' class was too heavy for use on some parts of the system, with an axle weight of 15¼ tons. This engine was built by Robert Stephenson in 1904.

H.W. Burman

The '61' class of 4–4–0 numbered 21 engines, beginning in 1895 and the last one 1904. No. 84 was withdrawn by the GWR in 1926 without being rebuilt.

Locomotive Publishing Co.

Six engines comprised the *Beaconsfield* class; they were built between 1878 and 1886 by Sharp, Stewart, and worked on the Mid-Wales line after that was purchased, being light and small-wheeled.   *Locomotive Publishing Co.*

Deep front sandboxes distinguished the three goods engines built by Vulcan Foundry in 1894; this example, No. 80, became GWR No. 883 but was withdrawn in 1925.
                                                                                    H.W. Burman

'Queen' class 0−6−0 No. 48 after its 1889 rebuild; this was formerly Mid-Wales No. 9, and had a long life, being rebuilt again by the GWR in 1926.
                                                                          Locomotive Publishing Co.

the first 'Queen' class 0–6–0s, eight in 1861–4, also two of the same ordered for the N&M; four 2–4–0s also built in 1863 had 5 ft 6 in. driving wheels. In the same year three 0–4–0STs with only 4 ft wheels were purchased for working into the light and tortuous sidings of the Porthywaen branch.

By the time the Cambrian had to take over working from Savin in 1866, there were 49 engines in all; they included 14 2–4–0s of the 'Albion' class, and the same number of 'Queen' class 0–6–0s; also three 2–4–0T engines built by Sharp, Stewart in 1866, the 'Seaham' class. However, in the great sort-out of Savin's locomotive list, the Cambrian had to allow the Brecon & Merthyr to keep five of 'their' engines working on that line – Savin had taken eleven in all, but they got six of them back.

Following Savin's bankruptcy, no new engines were purchased until 1872; numbers made blank by sales or transfers were filled, as follows:

Cambrian Replacements, 1872–1878

No	Name	Type	Makers	Maker's No.	Built	GWR No.
1	Victoria	0–6–0	SS	2231	1872	
4	Alexandra	,,	,,	2232	1872	897
6	Marquis	,,	,,	2306	1873	
10	Marchioness	,,	,,	2307	1873	
13	Talerddig	0–6–0T	,,	2452	1875	
14	Bronerion	0–6–0	,,	2511	1875	898
15	Glansevern	,,	,,	2513	1875	
16	Beaconsfield	4–4–0	,,	2789	1878	1115
17	Hartington	,,	,,	2790	1878	1116
18	Orleton	0–6–0	,,	2510	1875	

Nos. 14 and 15 lay unsold with Messrs Sharp, Stewart for three years and were not bought by the Cambrian until 1878. No. 18 was purchased from the LNWR; it had been Denbigh, Ruthin & Corwen Railway No. 1, built in the same batch as Cambrian Nos. 14 and 15.

The two 4–4–0 engines represented a notable advance at a time when this arrangement was still rare; they had 5 ft 6½ in. driving wheels and were the first two of the 'Beaconsfield' class, which became closely associated with the through trains from South Wales via the Mid-Wales Railway after it was taken over. They were Nos. 16 and 17 and were followed in 1886 by Nos. 20 and 21, filling numbers left vacant; more numbers were vacant by 1888, 2, 22, 23, 24, 25, 32, 33, 47–50; all these except for 50 were taken by Mid-Wales engines brought into the Cambrian stud in that year.

The Mid-Wales Railway had ordered from Kitson's twelve engines, six 0–6–0s with 4 ft 6 in. wheels and six 0–4–2s with 5 ft driving wheels. The 0–6–0s Nos. 7–12 were built in 1864/5 and the 0–4–2s, Nos. 1–6 in 1864. Owing to its failure to build various branch lines, the company found its stock exceeding requirements, and in 1866 leased, and later sold, Nos. 2, 6, and 10 to the Manchester, Sheffield & Lincolnshire Railway, and No. 11 was

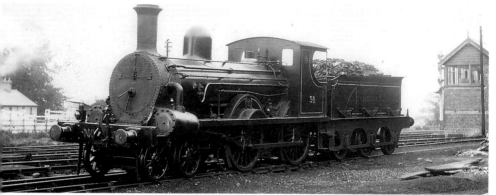

Because the ex-Metropolitan engines were too heavy for some lines, two were rebuilt as tender engines, but were not successful; No. 34 (*above*) ex-MR No. 13, was withdrawn in 1922.

Locomotive Publishing Co.

The Cambrian had several Manning, Wardle saddle-tanks at various times; this one, M&W 140 of 1864, was originally *Alyn* of the PSNWR, then *Mawddwy* of the Mawddwy Railway, then CR 30 and GWR No. 824, as seen here in 1934 at Moat Lane shed. *Author*

he third design used by the railway after 891. Note the word 'RAILWAYS' not ailway and the better dimensions of the ragon within the shield.

The style of the first and second designs with the initials CRC within the circle. These two first designs had colour changes but were the same size and the reason for change cannot be ascertained.

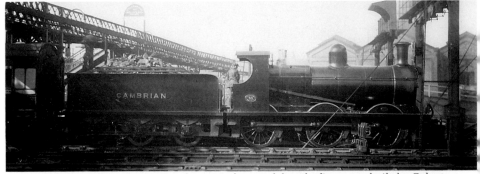

The class '93' 0–6–0s were heavy and powerful; only five were built by Robert Stephenson in 1903; that above, No. 93 itself, seen at Oswestry about 1920, lasted until 1954.   *Real Photographs*

No. 96 was one of the 1903 batch of large 4–4–0s; here seen as GWR No. 1029, it did not last long, being withdrawn in 1928.   *Real Photographs*

Three Chapman & Furneaux 0–6–0Ts were purchased from the Lambourn Valley Railway; that seen here rebuilt as GWR No. 821 was originally *Aelfred* on the LVR.
W.H. Whitworth

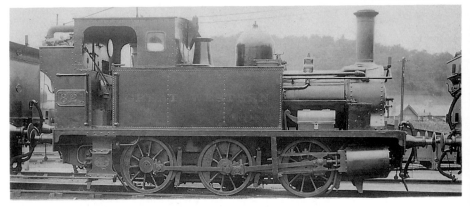

sold to the Denbigh, Ruthin & Corwen Railway, becoming LNWR property later. In 1872 the remaining engines were renumbered 1–4 for the passenger engines and 5–8 for goods engines, while a year later two more 0–6–0s were purchased, this time from Sharp, Stewart, the same as the CR 'Queen' class, which became Nos. 9/10. The Kitson engines were not all serviceable when taken over by the Cambrian in 1888.

The list of Mid-Wales' engines taken over by the Cambrian was as follows:

MW No.	Type	Maker	Maker's No.	Built	Cam. No.	GWR No.
2	0–4–2	Kitson	1235	1864	2	
1	,,	,,	1237	1864	22	
3	,,	,,	1239	1864	23	
4	,,	,,	1238	1864	24	
5	0–6–0	,,	1249	1864	25	
6	,,	,,	1252	1865	32	
7	,,	,,	1247	1864	33	
8	,,	,,	1248	1864	47	
9	,,	SS	2339	1873	48	908
10	,,	,,	2347	1873	49	909

No. 47 was withdrawn from service almost immediately, and the other engines except for Nos. 2, 33, 48, 49 were all withdrawn by 1898. No. 33 lasted until 1904, followed by No. 2 in 1905; Nos. 48 and 49 were still in service in 1922; the latter never carried its GWR number.

The company was now enjoying better times, and during the 20 years from 1890 to 1910 a great improvement took place in the locomotive stock, 4–4–0 and 0–6–0 engines of increasing power replacing many of the old Sharp, Stewart machines as shown below. A few 0–4–4T engines were also purchased (to work the newly opened Wrexham–Ellesmere branch), together with some others of dubious value second-hand from smaller lines. In the same list are given some post-1918 accretions which are explained later.

It might here be observed that throughout its history the CR locomotives bore a strong resemblance to those of the Furness. Both lines largely purchased Sharp, Stewart standard types. Alexander Walker, who had been Savin's locomotive superintendent, remained in charge at Oswestry until 1882, when William Aston took over. He was succeeded in 1899 by Herbert Jones, who retired in 1918, being succeeded in turn by G.C. McDonald.

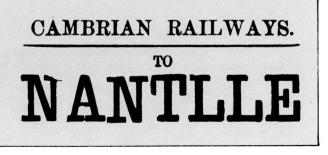

CAMBRIAN RAILWAYS.

TO

NANTLLE

Cambrian Locomotives

Cam. Diag.	Cam. No.	GWR No.	Type	Maker	Maker's No.	Date	Remarks
17	1	1329	2−4−0	Beyer, Peacock		1883	Ex-GWR No. 212 (1921)
5A	2	1129	4−4−0T	„	421	1864	Ex-Met. No. 10 (1905)
5	3	10	0−4−4T	Nasmyth, Wilson	460	1895	
5	5	11	0−4−4T	„	461	1895	
5	7	15	0−4−4T	„	462	1895	
5	8	19	0−4−4T	„	558	1899	
5	9	20	0−4−4T	„	559	1899	
18	10	1328	2−4−0	Beyer, Peacock		1883	Ex-GWR No. 213 (1921)
2	11	1068	4−4−0T	Oswestry Works		1904	
5A	12	1130	4−4−0T	Beyer, Peacock	422	1864	Ex-Met. No. 11 (1905)
9	15	844	0−6−0	„	5944	1918	
2	19	1082	4−4−0	Oswestry Works		1901	
	22		0−6−0ST	Manning, Wardle	668	1877	Ex-Van Rly (1896)
	22		0−4−0ST	„	1523	1901	
5	23	21	0−4−4T	Nasmyth, Wilson	560	1899	
7	24	819	0−6−0T	Hunslet	8011	1903	Ex-LVLR Eadweade (1904)
	25		0−6−0ST	Manning, Wardle	374	1877	Ex-Van Rly
7A	26	820	0−6−0T	Chapman & Furneaux	1161	1898	Ex-LVLR (1896) Eahlswyth (1904)
9	29	849	0−6−0	Beyer, Peacock	5945	1918	
12	30	824	0−6−0ST	Manning, Wardle	140	1864	Ex-Mawddwy Rly (1910)
9	31	855	0−6−0	Beyer, Peacock	5946	1919	
2	32	1085	4−4−0	R. Stephenson	2871	1897	
5A	33	1131	4−4−0T	Beyer, Peacock	423	1864	Ex-Met. No. 12 (1905)
5A	34	1113	4−4−0T	„	424	1864	Ex-Met. No. 13 (1905)
7A	35	821	0−6−0T	Chapman & Furneaux	1162	1898	Ex-LVLR Aelfred (1904)
5A	36	1114	4−4−0T	Beyer, Peacock	426	1864	Ex-Met. No. 15 (1905)
5A	37	1132	4−4−0T	„	2675	1885	Ex-Met. No. 66 (1905)
9	38	864	0−6−0	„	5031	1908	
9	42	873	0−6−0	„	5947	1919	
2	47	1086	4−4−0	R. Stephenson	2872	1897	
3	50	1110	4−4−0	Sharp, Stewart	3696	1891	
9	54	874	0−6−0	Beyer, Peacock	5948	1919	
3	60	1112	4−4−0	Sharp, Stewart	3697	1891	
2	61	1088	4−4−0	„	3001	1893	
2	62	1090	4−4−0	„	3902	1893	

Cam. Diag.	Cam. No.	GWR No.	Type	Maker	Maker's No.	Date	Remarks
2	63	1091	4–4–0	,,	3903	1893	
2	64	1093	4–4–0	,,	3904	1893	
2	65	1096	4–4–0	,,	3905	1893	
2	66	1097	4–4–0	,,	3906	1893	
2	67	1100	4–4–0	,,	3907	1893	
2	68	1101	4–4–0	,,	3909	1893	
2	69	1102	4–4–0	,,	3976	1894	
2	70	1103	4–4–0	,,	3977	1894	
2	71	1104	4–4–0	,,	3978	1894	
2	72	1105	4–4–0	,,	3979	1894	
10	73	875	0–6–0	Neilson	4691	1894	
10	74	876	0–6–0	,,	4692	1894	
10	75	878	0–6–0	,,	4693	1894	
10	76	879	0–6–0	,,	4694	1894	
10	77	880	0–6–0	,,	4695	1894	
10	78	881	0–6–0	Vulcan Foundry	1445	1895	
10	79	882	0–6–0	,,	1446	1895	
10	80	883	0–6–0	,,	1447	1895	
2	81	1084	4–4–0	Sharp, Stewart	4070	1895	
2	82		4–4–0	,,	4071	1895	(Dest. Abermule)
16	82	3521	4–4–0	Swindon	1095	1887	Ex-GWR No. 3521
2	83	1110	4–4–0	Sharp, Stewart	4072	1895	No. 1106 until 2/26
2	84	1107	4–4–0	,,	4073	1895	
2	85	1108	4–4–0	R. Stephenson	2873	1898	
2	86	1109	4–4–0	,,	2874	1898	
10	87	884	0–6–0	Neilson	5401	1899	
10	88	885	0–6–0	,,	5402	1899	
9	89	887	0–6–0	R. Stephenson	3089	1903	
9	90	888	0–6–0	,,	3090	1903	
9	91	859	0–6–0	,,	3091	1903	
9	92	891	0–6–0	,,	3092	1903	
9	93	892	0–6–0	,,	3093	1903	
1	94	1014	4–4–0	,,	3131	1904	
1	95		4–4–0	,,	3132	1904	(Dest. Abermule)
16	95	3546	4–4–0	Swindon	1122	1888	Ex-GWR No. 3546
1	96	1029	4–4–0	R. Stephenson	3133	1904	
1	97	1035	4–4–0	,,	3134	1904	
1	98	1043	4–4–0	,,	3135	1904	
9	99	893	0–6–0	Beyer, Peacock	5029	1908	(Former No. 15)
9	100	894	0–6–0	,,	5030	1908	(Former No. 31)
9	101	895	0–6–0	,,	5032	1908	(Former No. 42)
9	102	896	0–6–0	,,	5033	1908	(Former No. 54)

No. 34, rebuilt BP&Co., 1915 as 4–4–0; No. 36 ditto Oswestry 1916. (Diagram 5B.)

Following the liquidation of Savin's contracting engines, the Cambrian's stock presented a fairly tidy appearance. But this was not to continue. In 1896, along with the defunct Van Railway, two 1870s-built Manning,

Wardle saddle tanks were acquired; and in 1911, playing fairy godmother to the equally moribund Mawddwy Railway, two more Manning, Wardle machines (this time built in the 1860s) were added. One of these started life in 1864 as *Alyn* and was used to build the Potteries, Shrewsbury & North Wales Railway; it became *Mawddwy*, and was rebuilt in 1893; as CR No. 30 it was rebuilt at Oswestry in 1911, and after becoming GWR No. 824 received a Great Western chimney and other fittings. This gallant old-timer went to the wall in 1940, after 76 years working quietly on two little-visited branch lines. The other Mawddwy engine, *Disraeli* (MW No. 268, 1868), was broken up at Oswestry. Meanwhile, the Cambrian had been shopping in the second-hand market; it had bought the three engines of the Lambourn Valley Light Railway in 1904 on its adopting GWR steamcars; these were Chapman & Furneaux 0–6–0Ts and were needed to replace the 'Mountaineer' class 0–4–0STs on the Kerry branch and elsewhere; and six Beyer, Peacock bogie tanks from the Metropolitan Railway in the next year, MR Nos. 10, 11, 12, 13, 15 (1864), 66 (1885). Five of these were already 40 years old, and seemed a curious choice, for they were too heavy to be used on the lightly-laid sections of the line, while carrying insufficient water for main-line use. In an attempt to remedy this, Jones rebuilt two in 1915/16 as tender engines, reducing the weight from 33½ tons to 27½ tons, and increasing the water capacity (by drawing old tenders from stock) from 900 to 1,700 gallons. The attempt was not a success. All six engines went to the scrap heap almost immediately after the Grouping.

From 1903 Jones fitted both passenger and goods engines with Belpaire fireboxes; these engines were not permitted on the Mid-Wales line, nor of course on the branches which were lightly laid with flat-bottom track, and have required the ministrations of ancient and light machines to the bitter end. Two of the large bogie class of 4–4–0 (Nos. 19, 11) were actually built at the Oswestry Works in 1901 and 1904, respectively, although possibly the boilers were supplied by R. Stephenson who had built the previous four engines of the same class.

In 1907 two of the Sharp 2–4–0s were rebuilt as tank engines to work push-pull trains; these were Nos. 44 and 56.

The last new locomotive arrived from Beyer, Peacock in 1919 (0–6–0, No. 54). In 1921, however, four engines were purchased that had seen service on the Great Western. Two (Nos. 1 and 10) were 2–4–0 machines built in 1861 as 2–2–2s for the West Midland Railway, renewed as 2–4–0s at Wolverhampton in 1883, sold to A.R. Angus for signalling experiments on the derelict West Somerset Mineral Railway in 1911, and purchased by the Cambrian via the Bute Docks Supply Company. Their tenders were rather shallow and the name 'Cambrian' had to be painted on the coal-rails. The other two engines were bought from the GW to replace the engines smashed in the Abermule collision; they were Swindon-built outside-frame 4–4–0 engines, Nos. 3521 and 3546. Although allotted Cambrian numbers 82 and 95, they never carried them.

At the Grouping there were 99 Cambrian engines; the standard livery was black lined in gamboge and edged with vermilion; express engines carried the coat-of-arms on the leading splasher.

Locomotives running on the Cambrian had always been a matter of 'horses for courses'. The Mid-Wales branch, because of some shaky high iron viaducts, was restricted as between Llanidloes and Three Cocks to the earlier types of 0−6−0 and 4−4−0; the through trains to South Wales were mainly in the hands of the small-wheeled 'Beaconsfield' 4−4−0s. The Kerry branch was only worked by one of the 0−4−0ST engines until they were scrapped in 1905/6, while the 'Seaham' class 2−4−0Ts worked the Llanfyllin and Llanginog branches. There were places on the Porthywaen branch where a light saddle tank was preferable, as also on the Van branch. The Mawddwy, though originally a lightly-laid line, had been improved and the Sharp 2−4−0s worked most trains. The northern branches, to Whitchurch and Wrexham, were where one could see the two larger 2−4−0Ts and the few 0−4−4Ts. On the Coast Line the latest and heaviest 4−4−0 and the new 0−6−0 types could show their strength. The 'Queen' class 0−6−0s could be seen anywhere, but from the turn of the century one or two began to be scrapped, and they were placed on the sort of duties they would perform in diminishing numbers for another 30-odd years; ballast trains, short runs to mineral sidings, and so on.

Although Cambrian engines worked over the South Wales lines from the first when required, the reverse did not happen. At times a Taff Vale engine would take a train to Talyllyn in place of a B&M one, but they handed over there, in the east loop. Midland Railway engines did of course work over the portion of the Mid-Wales branch between Talyllyn and Three Cocks, latterly Johnson 0−4−4Ts on the passenger trains and Johnson 0−6−0s on goods.

The study of Cambrian locomotives requires particular care because of the haphazard numbering system, and the fact that so many numbers were used twice or more. There were cases of a number being used thrice; No. 22 was a 0−4−2 until it was replaced by an ex-Van Railway engine in 1896, which was replaced by a new 0−4−0ST in 1901. The other cases, Nos. 15, 31, 42 and 54, arose from the moving of four of the 1908 0−6−0s to the end (Nos. 99−102) soon after they were built, although the numbers they had carried remained blank until filled by the large 0−6−0s in 1918/9.

Of the original 'Queen' class 0−6−0s, four survived after 1922; the Mid-Wales Railway one, No. 908, was reboiled in 1927 with a '2021' boiler and Belpaire firebox, and served until December 1938, from 1932 on the Lambourn Valley branch in Berkshire, which was a Light Railway. The 0−4−4Ts had all gone by 1932; all the 'Beaconsfields' were withdrawn between 1922 and 1930; '61' class No. 1110 (1106 until 1926) was used until 1931 to run the Engineers' saloon. Of the large 'Belpaire' 4−4−0s, apart from the one lost at Abermule, three went in 1928 and No. 1043, the last to go, in 1933.

Of the '73' class of 0−6−0, No. 884 lasted to 1947; the 'Belpaire' class all survived to be nationalised except 90−2 and 54, which was damaged at Friog.

The two narrow gauge 0−6−0Ts on the Welshpool & Llanfair (GWR No. 823/4) survived to be nationalised and later to run for the private line; of the two original Davies & Metcalfe 2−6−2Ts on the Rheidol, renumbered 1212 and 1213, the former went to Swindon in 1932, and was scrapped in

Observation car No. 4072 was one of a pair rebuilt from 6-wheeled stock in 1915 and attached to certain trains between Machynlleth and Pwllheli up to the 1930s. This was Cambrian No. 178; the lower photo shows the interior.   *Oakwood Collection*

1935. The 2−4−0T *Rheidol* was given No. 1198 but scrapped in 1924. The original names of the 2−6−2Ts, *Edward VII* and *Prince of Wales* were removed, not by the GWR but by the Cambrian in 1915. No. 1213 was officially rebuilt in 1924, but in fact became a new engine, later numbered 9.

The Cambrian locomotive sheds were: Oswestry, Welshpool, Moat Lane, Llanidloes, Kerry, Llanfyllin, Wrexham, Builth Wells, Machynlleth, Penmaenpool, Brecon, Aberystwyth, Portmadoc, Pwllheli.

Main Dimensions

Cam. Diag.	Engine	No.	Date	Cylinders in.	Driving wls ft	in.	Wt wkg order tons	cwt.
	0−4−2	4	1859	15½ × 22	5	10		
11	0−6−0	11	1863	16 × 24	4	6	26	16
4	2−4−0	28	1863	16 × 20	5	6	27	0
	0−4−0ST	36	1863	14 × 20	4	0	22	6
	0−4−2	2	1864	16 × 22	5	0		
12	0−6−0T	30	1864	12 × 17	3	1	17	7
18	2−4−0	10		17 × 24	6	2	33	16
6A	2−4−0T	57	1866	14 × 20	4	6	28	19¾
6	0−6−0T	13	1875	17 × 24	4	6	35	18
3	4−4−0	16	1878	17 × 24	5	6½	33	3
5A	4−4−0T	2		17¼ × 24	5	10	44	9*
10	0−6−0	73	1894	18 × 26	5	1½	39	15
2	4−4−0	61	1893	18 × 24	6	0	40	5
5	0−4−4T	3	1895	17 × 24	5	3	45	9¾
7A	0−6−0T	26	1898	12 × 20	3	7	23	10
1	4−4−0	94	1904	18½ × 26	6	0	45	4½
7	0−6−0T	24	1903	13 × 18	3	7	24	
9	0−6−0	99	1908	18 × 26	5	1½	41	13
17	2−4−0	1		17 × 24	6	0	35	5
16	4−4−0	82		17 × 24	5	2	41	16
5B	4−4−0	34	1915	17½ × 24	5	10	39	0½
8	2−4−0T	44	1907	16 × 20	5	6	35	6
13	0−6−0T	The Earl	1902	11½ × 16	2	9	19	18
14	2−6−2T	1212	1902	11 × 17	2	6	25	0
15	2−4−0T	3	1896	8 × 11½	2	3	13	0

* Tender conversions 60t. 15cwt.

Carriages

The early carriages purchased for the various lines were all similar; three-compartment firsts, four-compartment compos and seconds, five-compartment thirds, and third brakes, the last two having outside framing and extremely cramped seating. There were several builders, but Ashbury of Manchester and Joseph Wright of Birmingham (later Metropolitan Carriage & Wagon Co.) were the main suppliers. By 1867 the Cambrian had 94 carriages; 3 first, 16 second, 29 compos, 38 thirds, 8 third brakes, and one

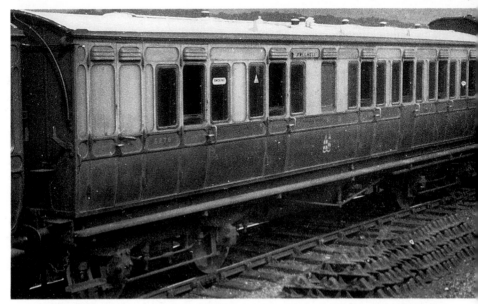

Carriage No. 237 was built by MCW in 1895, with four third and two first-class compartments, lavatory and luggage compartment. It was 45 ft long and became GWR No. 6276, lasting to 1940. *Oakwood Collection*

Carriage No. 264 was a 33 ft composite saloon brake, here seen demoted to third class only, after withdrawal in 1925. *Oakwood Collection*

The carriages on this typical train are (*right to left*) a six-compartment 6-wheeled 3rd, a six-wheeled lavatory 1st brake, a six-wheeled five-compartment third and a full brake. *G.H.W. Clifford*

Saloon No. 9 had a small and a large 1st class section divided by a luggage space; it was built at Oswestry in 1889. It was allocated GWR No. 9218 as a saloon, but soon after down-graded to brake 3rd 418, lasting until 1936.   *GWR Official*

Composite No. 48 (originally 1/2nd) was built at Oswestry in 1885 and though given No. 6321 it never carried it, being withdrawn in 1923.   *GWR Official*

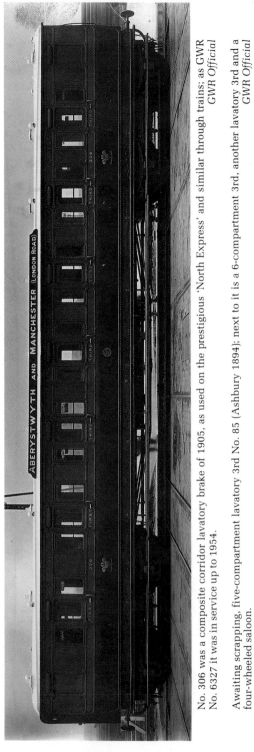

No. 306 was a composite corridor lavatory brake of 1905, as used on the prestigious 'North Express' and similar through trains: as GWR No. 6327 it was in service up to 1954.

GWR Official

Awaiting scrapping, five-compartment lavatory 3rd No. 85 (Ashbury 1894); next to it is a 6-compartment 3rd, another lavatory 3rd and a four-wheeled saloon.

GWR Official

saloon. They were about 21½ ft long (first class) and up to 25½ ft for the others, weighing some 8 tons. Soon Oswestry was building its own coaches, one of the first being a splendid saloon for Earl Vane, running on six wheels and painted yellow and lilac. This left Oswestry in 1870 to carry the Earl from Machynlleth to his Northumberland property, and was in use mainly for this purpose until 1892, when it was taken into company stock as No. 228. Oddly enough in 1899 the Cambrian purchased another ducal saloon from the Highland Railway; it had been used by the Duke of Suther-land with his private engine at Golspie. It became CR No. 1; it was not scrapped until 1931, having latterly been a compo./luggage saloon.

From 1882 most coaches built were 28½ ft six-wheelers. Though a large number were six-compartment thirds, and somewhat uncomfortable, there were also some centre-brakes, and lavatory compos used on the through trains from South Wales to Aberystwyth. Oil-gas lighting arrived in 1894, and the first corridor carriages the next year; starting at 45 ft long (only eight feet more than the later six-wheelers), they increased over the years to 54 ft. Although there were a few 7- and 8-compartments thirds, almost all were composites of some sort, many tri-compos with a small luggage compart-ment, suitable for use singly to add on to LNWR trains to Manchester or Euston. Even after second class was abolished for the second time in 1912, there were nine different arrangements of bogie carriage, seven of which had a luggage compartment. Corridors were internal until 1905. These bogie coaches were somewhat inefficient in terms of weight per passenger, the number of compartments varying from two first and two third (with large luggage space) to four thirds, two seconds, one first and no luggage compartment.

There were a number of carriages of special note; for example four-wheeled saloons 9 and 10 of 1889, which took part in Royal and non-Royal local occasions, and were loaned to the LNWR for a Royal opening of Port Sunlight. Then there was the postal carriage 200 of 1888, followed by a full sorting carriage (bogie) No. 293 in 1902. An oddity was No. 116, an early (1873) six-wheeled third which was converted into a parcels van by simply cutting a sliding door into the middle. In 1915 two six-wheeled thirds were rebuilt as observation cars (Nos. 176 and 178) which worked for 20 years on the Coast Line, being attached at Machynlleth to the rear of certain trains and shunted to the end of the train before it left Pwllheli.

As regards stock taken over from other railways, the Mawddwy had seven, of which only ex-North London Railway 1022 survived, to become a Cambrian service vehicle. The Mid-Wales probably had about two dozen serviceable carriages, but as they would have been of the same types as the early Cambrian ones, they cannot be identified.

In 1922 the Cambrian carriage numbers were up to 334; as there had always been a policy of numbering new stock in gaps left by old ones, there were only two numbers not then in use. However, the same series numbers included 47 horse-boxes, 7 carriage trucks, a meat van, a hound van and four poultry vans, so the passenger stock amounted to 272 vehicles, of which a good number were full brakes.

Guard's van No. 10, one of the common single-ended type; later a few were built with
platforms at each end.   *Cambrian Railway Official*

A 10-ton boiler wagon, No. 2510, built at Oswestry in 1907.
                                                                          Cambrian Railway Official

Carriage van No. 290 was 21 ft long; later numbered in the record as GWR No. 35, it
did not last long enough to carry this number.   *Cambrian Railway Official*

In 1913 the bodies of two old six-wheelers were used to make up a new push-pull trailer, No. 211, seating ten first and 56 third class passengers, weighing 26 tons; mated with one of the two larger 2−4−0Ts, it worked the Wrexham branch. At this time incandescent gas-mantles were introduced instead of the bats-wing flames for lighting, and some stock was steam-heated. The livery since 1909 had been altered to all-over bronze green; the upper parts had previously been white.

A good deal of alteration to stock went on at Oswestry; several thirds were altered to full brakes, and one to a hound van; a few became service vehicles. It appears from the register that there were 320 revenue-earning vehicles passed over to the GWR, though this included a few items which the larger company regarded as goods department stock. The figure does not include narrow gauge vehicles. These comprised 17 on the Rheidol line: three 32 ft bogie compos, six similar thirds, three thirds converted to open-side 'summer cars', three four-wheeled brake vans and two open cars converted from timber wagons. The Welshpool & Llanfair stock comprised three 35 ft bogie coaches, two compo. brakes and a third; as the Cambrian was only the working company, these were excluded from the stock list.

After gas-lighting was introduced in 1897, ten mobile gas-holder wagons were acquired, but not numbered in the carriage series. The gas-oil plant was at the north end of the Oswestry Works.

Goods Stock

The Cambrian goods stock differed somewhat from most lines in its preponderance of small two-plank 8-ton open wagons, needed for stone, slate and sand. There was also a large number of timber bolster wagons, of which 88 had come from the Mid-Wales Railway stock. A register of 1908 shows 1578 open wagons and 92 covered; also 191 cattle trucks, 400 timber bolsters, 38 lime wagons, 2 gunpowder vans, 39 goods brakes and 68 ballast trucks. Some more modern stock was acquired after this time, including more gunpowder vans and 50 more eight-plank open wagons. Goods brakes, which had been somewhat basic, were from 1912 given verandahs at each end, although the wheelbase was only 11 ft.

Photographs indicate that the Cambrian was very late in abolishing 'dumb' buffers; although new stock had sprung buffers from the 1880s the old stock was not converted until a programme was begun in 1900 which took several years to complete. In later days wagons had 'Cambrian' in large lettering on the side; previously they had 'Cam. Rys' with the Prince of Wales feathers between; it was necessary to show that these vehicles were not Caledonian Railway property.

The narrow gauge goods stock on the Rheidol line included 15 open wagons originally built for the Hafon & Talybont Railway (though possibly not delivered); three were converted to timber bolsters. Later six more wagons and two long-wheelbase timber trucks were purchased; the GWR added two cattle wagons but they were little used, and moved to the Llanfair line, and later still to the Festiniog. The Welshpool & Llanfair had 40 open wagons, four box vans, eight sheep trucks, six timber bolsters and two goods brake vans. The Vale of Rheidol Railway did not use goods brake vans; as far as is known all trains were 'mixed' and for ballast workings passenger brakes were used.

The Cambrian was host to a wide variety of private owners' wagons, mostly three plank for stone or five plank for coal; they belonged to small firms and carried single figure numbers. Even the small chemical factory at Pontithel near Three Cocks on the Mid-Wales line had its name on wagons.

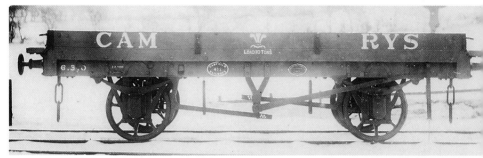

Low-sided wagon No. 471 was able to carry stone or machinery weighing up to 10 tons.   *Cambrian Railway Official*

The Cambrian numbered its horse-boxes in with the carriages; No. 321 was built in 1907 and is shown above on withdrawal in 1925.   *GWR Official*

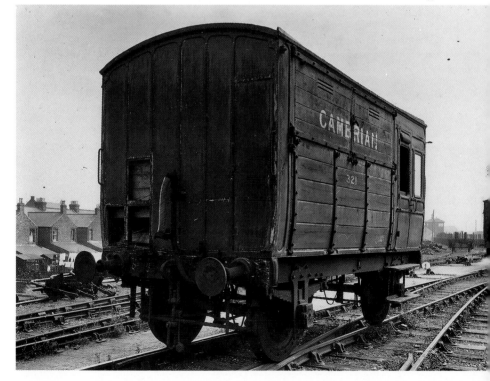

Chapter Five
Train Services

When first opened, none of the Cambrian lines could boast a very frequent service. The Llanidloes & Newtown ran three trains each way only (except on market days), taking 25–35 minutes. When the end-on connection of the L&N with the O&N was made one fast train was instituted (in one direction only) running from Oswestry to Newtown with a stop at Welshpool only. But it ran on as a 'slow' to Llanidloes, and most trains took up to 2 hours 25 minutes for the whole 41 miles, including a 15 minute wait at Newtown to change engines. By 1863 the journey time from Oswestry to Llanidloes had been cut to 2 hours, and for the newly-instituted service to Machynlleth the time was 2 hours 45 minutes. The opening of the isolated section of the A&WC from Aberdovey to Llwyngwril made the timetables more complex, as the ferry journey across the Dovey had to be shown. Only one set of through connections was indicated from Oswestry to Llwyngwril, allowing 40 minutes from Ynyslas to Aberdovey over the ferry. In 1864 the Cambrian was advertising through carriages from Euston as far as Borth, with a coach connection to Aberystwyth. As soon as the Coast Line was complete, through carriages between Euston and Manchester and Aberystwyth and Pwllheli were instituted. The journey from Whitchurch through to Pwllheli took 6¾ hours.

During the period when the line was only open from Aberdovey to Penmaenpool there was also the Mawddach Estuary ferry to consider. The present Fairbourne station is the site of the Barmouth Ferry station, which flourished before the viaduct had been built across the Mawddach, and passengers for Barmouth were officially invited to alight there. But Charles and Adam Black in their *Guide to North Wales* in 1867 drew attention to the hazards of so doing. First there was a drive in an open car (6d.), followed by a walk of 50 to 400 yards depending on the tide, to reach a small boat 'which has only one man to manage it' (3d.) – and 'the sail is often very rough'. Horrors! But wait, there is more. If the tide was low, there was a sand-bar in mid-estuary, over which one had to walk, to embark in another small boat (3d. again presumably) – 'a mode of proceeding not altogether convenient for ladies'. Altogether, said Black, it was a good idea to stay in the train and drive 10 miles back to Barmouth. There was a steam ferry across the river from Penmaenpool to the main road, where a stage might be taken.

By 1869 there were two good trains down the line; one left Whitchurch at 9.45 am and reached Aberystwyth at 2.25 pm and Pwllheli at 4.35 pm, Caernarvon at 5.21. Connections arrived at Llanidloes at 12.40 pm, and Dolgelley at 3.30 pm. The other train was 1st and 2nd class only, and left Whitchurch at 1.12 pm, arriving at Aberystwyth at 5.55 pm and Pwllheli at 7.38 pm. The timetable was completed by one slow train from Whitchurch to Aberystwyth, and trains from Welshpool to Machynlleth, Whitchurch to Oswestry, and Machynlleth to Aberystwyth; also two more trains only up the Coast Line. The Llanfyllin branch had four trains each way, and Kerry five. A cheap excursion was run on summer Mondays from Oswestry (5.25 am) and all stations to Borth and Aberystwyth. The return train left Aberystwyth at 6.15 pm; passengers were allowed to break their journey at

Machynlleth or Ynyslas. The advertisement specified 'cov. cars'; some railways used open unroofed carriages for excursions.

The Mid-Wales Railway when it came under Cambrian direction was working three trains per day down the whole line, with some short workings, especially from Builth Wells to Builth Road. These were from Llanidloes, but before long Moat Lane was the terminal station. No through trains from Manchester or London were laid on down this line, though there were many through trains up from the south via Talyllyn Junction, to Aberystwyth, reversing at Moat Lane. Three or four extra short workings from Moat Lane to Llanidloes over the years gave reasonable connections to that town from most up or down trains. The Cambrian advertised a service from Oswestry to Shrewsbury via Whitchurch. It did not advertise the trains to Shrewsbury over the GW/LNW joint line from Buttington.

At the end of the century there was a boom in travel to 'Hydro' resorts. The Cambrian ran regular trains from Cardiff to Builth Wells, Llandrindod Wells, Llangamarch Wells and Llanyrtyd Wells, the last three being on the LNWR Central Wales line. It is probable that a change of trains was needed at Builth Road, as the connecting spur was not in regular use then. On the other hand, the tables suggest that the Midland Railway train from Swansea to Builth Wells was a through train. Through coaches ran from both the Taff Vale and Rhymney Railway stations at Cardiff, and from the B&M station at Merthyr.

There were three through trains per day from Aberystwyth to Newport taking six hours. There were also through coaches to the GWR via Shrewsbury which were worked non-stop from Welshpool to Wellington; passengers for Shrewsbury were required to change at Wellington.

In 1907 some fresh competition was provided by the GWR putting on a slip coach for Aberystwyth on the Fishguard Express; it was detached at Carmarthen and was the first slip carriage working in Wales. In 1909 Cambrian coaches worked to Paddington, to balance the use of GWR coaches on the Ruabon–Barmouth service.

The Cambrian had its share of Royal occasions; one such was on 25th June, 1896; on this occasion it was a London & North Western train, and the CR provided a pilot to travel on the GWR engine from Buttington Junction to Welshpool, where a Cambrian engine took over.

Another Royal occasion was in July 1911; in connection with the investiture of the Prince of Wales at Caernarvon the LNWR Royal Train was hauled from Afon Wen to Machynlleth double-headed by class '61' 4–4–0s Nos. 81 and 83 on the 14th, and from the latter place to Whitchurch on the 17th. The rule then existing against double-heading on the Coast Line, due to weak bridges, was waived. Banking assistance was given over Talerddig notwithstanding the power 'up front'.

At this time both the GWR and LNWR ran a 9.30 am from London, ending up as the same train at Aberystwyth at 4.20 pm. The train from Euston arrived at Wolverhampton (Queen St) 20 minutes ahead of the GWR train at Low Level; the combined train ran non-stop from Wellington to Welshpool via the Abbey Foregate loop at Shrewsbury.

A more important train perhaps was the 'North Express' from Aberystwyth to Manchester; this called only at Borth, Dovey Junction, Machynlleth,

Cemmes Road, Moat Lane and Newtown; then Welshpool, Oswestry, Ellesmere and Whitchurch. At Oswestry another express could be picked up which ran behind and diverged at Ellesmere to run via Wrexham and Chester with through carriages for Manchester, Nottingham and Leicester. At the height of the summer season through coaches from Barmouth were joined to those which had started from Pwllheli. This era was probably the finest ever for through carriages, which were advertised from 21 cities. The Cinderella was the Mid-Wales line, which had none, and no connection at Moat Lane to the London train. The Mid-Wales Railway had from the start advertised most of its through traffic via a change to the LNWR at Builth Road, and this continued. Passengers for Builth Wells were advised to travel on the LNW to Llandrindod Wells and take the bus.

It may seem surprising that so little use was made of the 'Ellesmere Loop' allowing direct running from the northern lines via Wrexham to Oswestry and beyond. A through train in the summer months comprising composite coaches of the Cheshire Lines, MS&LR and Cambrian, which had from the opening of the Wrexham Branch reversed at Ellesmere, ran non-stop from Wrexham to Oswestry via the loop from 1897, but between 1900 and 1905 there was no train using the loop; in the summer of the latter year a Manchester–Aberystwyth express used it, the train having also a through coach to Barmouth. After 1st October, 1905 no passenger train used the loop, and it must have been taken out of service not long after, as by 1911 the Cambrian was considering other uses for the trackwork of the 'disused' loop. Even before the opening of the branch the MS&L had reported 'considerable difficulty in providing connecting trains with Chester and Manchester' and it would seem that not much effort was made.

None of the branch lines ever developed generous services. By the turn of the century, Dolgelley had nine trains, Ellesmere–Wrexham seven, Llanfyllin five, Kerry six, Welshpool & Llanfair four, and Mid-Wales four. All trains were 'all stations' apart from missing a few ill-favoured places; Trefeinon, Aberedw and Pantydwr on the Mid-Wales, for example. On the main line, the timetables presented the reader with some very complex problems; some trains could only set down at certain stations first and second class passengers, and not third class. Other trains could only pick up or set down passengers from Hereford, Birmingham and beyond. However, there were at least some fast trains; the North Express from Aberystwyth reached Whitchurch in 3 hours 18 minutes, stopping at only 10 stations; the following afternoon train stopped only at 11. The London Express at 1 pm from Aberystwyth got into Paddington at 8.45 pm; however, Coast Line passengers got little benefit from this as their connecting train left almost two hours earlier and called at all stations to Machynlleth. There were eight trains from Machynlleth northwards, one terminating at Towyn and one at Barmouth. The fortunes of the Cambrian did not depend on their local services, but to a large extent on the holiday traffic. The range of services and through coaches on offer show great ingenuity, and considerable faith in the staff's ability to cope on single lines with sudden flushes of trains. Aberystwyth had the largest number of through carriages: from Birmingham, Cardiff, Hereford, Leeds, Leicester, Liverpool, London, Manchester, New-

On this and the next three pages is the summer 1904 CR Timetable.

TANAT VALLEY LIGHT RAILWAY. (No Sunday Trains.)

DOWN.—WEEK DAYS.

		a.m.	a.m.	p.m.	p.m.	p.m.	
Oswestry	...dep.	8 25	11 15	2* 5	3 55	7 45	
Porthywaen	... ,,	8 37	11 28	2*18	4 8	7 58	
Blodwel Junction	...arr.	8 42	11 33	2*23	4 13	8 3	
Llanymynech	...dep.	8 15			4 0		
Blodwel Junction	...arr.	8 25			4 10		
Blodwel Junction	...dep.	8 43	11 35	2*24	4 15	8 4	
Blodwel	... ,,	8 48	11 40	2*29	4 20	8 9	
Llansilin Road	... ,,	0	11 53	2*42	4 30	8 22	
Llangedwyn	... ,,	9 6	11 58	2*47	4 38	8 27	
Pentrefelin	... ,,	9 14	12 6	2*55	4 46	8 35	
Llanrhaiadr Mochnant	... ,,	9 20	12 13	3* 2	4 53	8 42	
Pedair Ffordd	... ,,	9 25	12 18	3* 7	4 58	8 47	
Penybontfawr	... ,,	9 32	12 26	3*15	5 8	8 55	
Llangynog	...arr.	9 40	12 35	3*24	5 15	9 5	

UP.—WEEK DAYS.

		a.m.	a.m.	a.m.	p.m.	p.m.	
Llangynog	...dep.	6*50	7 0	9 50	1 35	5 50	7*15
Penybontfawr	... ,,	6*58	7 8	9 58	1 43	5 58	7*23
Pedair Ffordd	... ,,	7* 5	7 15	10 5	1 50	6 5	7*30
Llanrhaiadr Mochnant	... ,,	7*10	7 20	10 10	1 55	6 10	7*35
Pentrefelin	... ,,	7*15	7 25	10 15	2 0	6 15	7*40
Llangedwyn	... ,,	7*20	7 30	10 20	2 5	6 20	7*45
Llansilin Road	... ,,	7*30	7 37	10 27	2 12	6 27	7*52
Llanybodwel	... ,,	7*37	7*44	10 34	2 19	6 31	7*59
Blodwel Junction	...arr.	7*41	7*48	10 38	2 23	6 38	8* 3
Blodwel Junction	...dep.	7*55		7*55	10 44	2 30	
Llanymynech	...arr.	8l 5		8l 5	10 50	2 40	
Blodwel Junction	...dep.	7*55		7*50	10 40	2 25	6 40	8* 4
Porthywaen	... ,,	7*55		7*50	10 46	2 31	6 46	8*11
Oswestry	...arr.	8l10		8l10	11 0	2 45	7 0	8*25

*† Thursdays and Saturdays only. * Wednesday only. ‡ Wednesday excepted.*

VALE OF RHEIDOL LIGHT RAILWAY.

UP.

		WEEK DAYS.								SUNDAYS.	
		a.m	9 10	a m	12	p.m	p.m	p.m	p.m	p.m	p.m
Aberystwyth	dep.	9 0	10 0	11 0	12 40	2 0	3 0	4 0		2 0	3 0
Llanbadarn	... ,,	9 4	10 5	B		B		5 50	7 5		3 5
Glanrafon	... ,,	9 10						5 55	7 10		3 10
Capel Bangor	... ,,	9 20	10 21	11 21	11 0	2 20	3 20	6 6	7 21	2 20	3 20
Nantyronen	... ,,	9 33	10 32	11 32		2 30	3 30	6 16	7 31	2 30	3 30
Aberffrwd	... ,,	9 40	10 40	11 40		2 40	3 40	6 25	7 40	2 40	3 40
Rheidol Falls	... ,,	9 46	10 46	11 46	1120	2 46	3 46	A	A	2 46	3 46
Rhiwfron	... ,,	9 53						A	A	A	A
Devil's Bridge	arr.	10 5	11 5	12 5	1140	3 5	4 5	6 50	8 5	3 5	4 5

DOWN.

		WEEK DAYS.							SUNDAYS.	
		a.m.	a.m.	a.m.	p.m	p.m	p.m	p.m	p.m	p.m
Devil's Bridge	dep.	8 30	11 15	12 15	3 15	4 30	6 7	7 15	5 0	7 0
Rhiwfron	... ,,	8 35							5 7	7 5
Rheidol Falls	... ,,	8 50	A	A	3 32	4 30	6 17	7 32	5 20	7 19
Aberffrwd	... ,,	8 58	11 40	12 40	3 40	4 38	6 25	7 40	5 28	7 27
Natyronen	... ,,	9 5	11 48	12 47	3 48	4 45	6 31	7 48	5 33	7 33
Capel Bangor	... ,,	9 20	11 55	1 0	4 0	4 55	6 40	7 59	5 42	7 42
Glanrafon	... ,,	9 30	12						5 52	7 52
Llanbadarn	... ,,	9 35	12 15		4 15	5 10	7 0	8 15	6 0	8 0
Aberystwyth	arr.	9 40	12 20	1 20	4 20	5	7 5	8 20	6 5	8 5

ALL TRAINS ARE THIRD CLASS.

A.—Stops by Signal when required to pick up or set down Passengers. ‖—Runs from July 27th to Sept. 11th. B.—Stops to pick up Passengers for Devil's Bridge only.

COAST SECTION.—PWLLHELI, BARMOUTH, DOLGELLEY, TOWYN,

UP. — WEEK DAYS.

	a.m.	a.m.	a.m.	a.m.	a.m.	a.m	a.m.	p.m.	p.m.
Pwllheli (for Nevin) dep	6 20	7 5	7 15			9 50	10 30	11 15	
Abererch ,,		R				*	*		
Afon Wen { arr	6 28	7 15			10	10 40			
{ dep	6 32				10 10				
Criccieth ,,	6 42		7 32		10 23		11 32		
Portmadoc { arr	6 52		7 42		10 33		11 42		
{ dep	5 5	6 54		7 46	10 40		11 45	1 25	
Minfford ,,	6 58		7 50		10 44			1 30	
Penrhyndeudr'th ,,	7 3				10 49				
Talsarnau ,,	7 7				10 53			1 40	
Harlech ,,	5 25	7 14	8n 6		11 0	12n 4	1 40		
Llanbedr & Pens'n ,,	7 24	8n14		11 10		12n11			
Dyffryn ,,	7 31	8n21		11 20		12n16			
Barmouth { arr	7 40	8 30		11 30		12 25			
{ dep	7 45	8 35	9 5	11 40		12 25		1 50	
Barmouth Jn. arr	7 50	8 40	9 10	11 45		12 40		1 55	
Barmouth dep	8 0		9 5	10 15		12 40			
Barmouth Jn. ,,	8 5		9 20			12 47			
Arthog ,,	8 8		9 23	E		12 50			
Penmaenpool ,,	8 20		9 35	E		1 2			
Dolgelley arr	8 35		9 40	10 40		1 7			
Dolgelley dep	7 20		8 15	8 45		10 50		11 50	1 35
Penmaenpool ,,	7 25		8 20	8 50		10 55		11 55	1 40
Arthog ,,	7 35		8 30	9 0		11 5		12 5	1 50
Barmouth Jn. arr	7 38		8 33	9 3		11 10		12 8	1 53
Barmouth ,,	7 45		8 45	9 15		11 20		12 15	2 0
Barmouth Jn. dep	7 52		8 42	9 15		11 50		12 42	1 57
Fairbourne ,,	7 55		R	9 18		11 53		B	2 0
Llwyngwril ,,	8 5		8n54	9 28		12 2			2 10
Tonfanau ,,									*
Towyn ,,	8 17		9n10	9 40		12 15		1n4	2 23
Aberdovey ,,	8 27		9n23	9 51		12 28		1n15	2 34
Dovey { arr	8 39		9 38	10 5		12 40		1 30	2 47
Junction { dep	8 45		9 53	10 14		12 55		1 50	2 55
Machynlleth arr	8 55		10 0	10 21		1 2		1 58	3 10

For Notes, see pages 8 and 9.

No Sunday Trains.

(Monday's only. Workmen's Train. — Saturday's only. Workmen's Train.)

WELSHPOOL AND

DOWN.

	a.m.	a.m.	a.m.	p.m.	p.m.
Welshpool dep	5 15	7 55	11 45	3 45	7 10
,, (Seven Stars) ,,	*				
Raven Square ,,	*				
Golfa ,,	*				
Sylfaen Farm ,,	*				
Castle Caereinion ,,	*				
Cyfronydd ,,	*				
Heniarth Gate ,,	*				
Ll'nf'r Caereinionarr	6 25	9 5	12 55	4 55	8 20

*—Trains will stop at all stations to pick up or set down Passengers.
†—Runs on Llanfair Fair Days only, viz.:—First Friday in each Month.

CRICCIETH, PORTMADOC, ABERDOVEY, MACHYNLLETH, &c.

UP. — WEEK DAYS. — SUNDAYS.

	p.m.	p.m.	p.m.	p.m.	p.m.	p.m.	a.m.	p.m.
Pwllheli (for Nevin) dep	1 40	4 0	4 20	6 55	9 15	9 0	6 4
Abererch ,,	*	*	*	*	*	*	*
Afon Wen { arr	1 50	4 10	4 35	7 5	9 25	9 9	6 4
{ dep	1 55	4 20	4 45	7 10	9 30	9 10	
Criccieth ,,	2 5	4 30	5 0	7 20	9 40	9 20	
Portmadoc { arr	2 15	4 40	5 10	7 30	9 50	9 30	
{ dep	2 20	4 45		7 40		9 33	
Minfford ,,	2 25	4 50		7 44		9 37	
Penrhyndeudr'th ,,	2 30	4 55		7 49		9 42	
Talsarnau ,,	2 35	5 0		7 55		9 46	
Harlech ,,	2 43	5 10		8 3		9 53	
Llanbedr & Pens'n ,,	2 56	5 20		8 13		10 3	
Dyffryn ,,	3 5	5 30		8 22		10 12	
Barmouth { arr	3 15	5 40		8 32		10 22	
{ dep		5 55		7 0	8 35		10 30	5 55
Barmouth Jn. arr		6 0		7 5	8 40		10 34	6 0
Barmouth dep	2 40	5 55		7 0	8 35		10 30	
Barmouth Jn. ,,	2 45	6 5		7 10	8 42		10 35	
Arthog ,,	2 53	6 8		7 13	8 45		10 38	
Penmaenpool ,,		6 20		7 25	9 0		10 50	
Dolgelley arr	3 10	6 25		7 30	9 5		10 55	
Dolgelley dep	3 25	5 20		6 35		9 50	4 25	
Penmaenpool ,,	R	5 25		6 40			4 30	
Arthog ,,		5 35		6 50			4 40	
Barmouth Jn. arr	3 47	5 38		6 54		9 40	4 45	
Barmouth ,,	3 55	5 50		7 0		9 50	4 55	
Barmouth Jn. dep		6 5		7 25			6 1	
Fairbourne ,,		6 8		7 30			6 4	
Llwyngwril ,,		6 18		7 40			6 12	
Tonfanau ,,				p.m.				
Towyn ,,		6 33		7 55	9 45		6 24	
Aberdovey ,,		6 46		8 10	9 55		6 35	
Dovey { arr		6 58						
Junction { dep		7 6						
Machynlleth arr		7 13		8 35	10 15			

For Notes, see pages 8 and 9.

LLANFAIR RAILWAY (Narrow Gauge).

UP.

	a.m.	a.m.	p.m.	p.m.	p.m.
Ll'nf'r Caereinion dep	6†30	9 40	2 0	5 25	8 30
Heniarth Gate ,,	*				
Cyfronydd ,,	*				
Castle Caereinion ,,	*				
Sylfaen Farm ,,	*				
Golfa ,,	*				
Raven Square ,,	*				
Welshpool(SevenStars) ,,					
Welshpool arr	7 40	10 50	3 10	6 35	9 40

* Trains will stop at all stations to pick up or set down passengers.
† Mondays, Tuesdays, and Wednesdays only.

COAST SECTION.—MACHYNLLETH, BARMOUTH, PORTMADOC,

DOWN. — WEEK DAYS.

	a.m.	a.m.	a.m.	a.m.	a.m.	p.m.	p.m.
Machynlleth dep		5 55		7 50	10 28	1 10
Dovey { arr				8 0	10 35	1 18
Junction { dep				8 10	10 50	1 30
Aberdovey ,,	6 15		8 27	11 4	1 47
Towyn ,,	6 23		8 37	11 12	1 57
Tonfanau ,,					B	
Llwyngwril ,,	6 35		8 54	11 24	2 10
Fairbourne ,,				9 1	11 33	2 19
Barmouth Jn. arr	6 45		9 8	11 38	2 22
Barmouth dep	8 0			9 5	10 15	12 40	2 40
Barmouth Jn. ,,	8 5			9 20	12 47	2 50
Arthog ,,	8 8			9 23	R	12 50	2 53
Penmaenpool ,,	8 20			9 35	R	1 2	3 5
Dolgelley arr	8 25			9 40	10 40	1 7	3 10
Dolgelley dep	7 20		8 15	8 45	10 50	11 50	1 35
Penmaenpool ,,	7 25		8 20	8 50	10 55	11 55	1 40
Arthog ,,	7 35		8 30	9 0	11 5	12 5	1 50
Barmouth Jn. arr	7 38		8 33	9 3	11 10	12 8	1 53
Barmouth ,,	7 45		8 45	9 15	11 20	12 15	2 0
Barmouth Jn. dep	6 46			9 10	11 45	2 25
Barmouth { arr	6 50			9 15	11 50	2 30
{ dep			8 40	9 20	12 25	2 40
Dyffryn ,,			8 50	9 30	12 35	2 50
Llanbedr and Pensarn ,,			8 56	9 36	12 41	2 58
Harlech ,,	5 30		9 6	9 46	12 51	1 55	3 8
Talsarnau ,,	5 40		9 12	9 53	12 58	2 3	3 15
Penrhyn-deudraeth ,,			9 16	9 58	1 2	2 9	3 19
Minfford ,,			9 21	10 4	1 8	2 16	3 25
Portmadoc { arr	5 55		9 25	10 8	1 12	2 20	3 28
{ dep	5 35	7 0	9 40	10 10	1 17		3 43
Criccieth ,,	5 48	7 12	9 55	10 22	1 32		3 47
Afon Wen { arr	5 55	7 20	10 5	10 35	1 40		3 57
{ dep	6 0	7 25	10 10	10 40	1 50		4 10
Abererch ,,	*	*	*	*	*		*
Pwllheli (for Nevin) arr	6 10	7 35	10 20	10 50	2 0		4 20

WREXHAM, ELLESMERE, &c.

DOWN. — WEEK DAYS. — No Sunday Trains.

	a.m.	a.m.	a.m.	p.m.	p.m.	p.m.	p.m.
Wrexham (Central) dep	8 15	9 50	11 55	1 35	4 0	6 25	8 30
Marchwiel ,,	8 20	9 55	12 0	1 40	4 5	6 40	8 35
Bangor-on-Dee ,,	8 28	10 3	12 8	1 46	4 13	6 48	8 43
Overton-on-Dee ,,	8 35	10 10	12 15	1 52	4 20	6 55	8 50
Ellesmere arr	8 45	10 20	12 25	2 0	4 30	7 5	9 0

For Notes, see pages 8 and 9.

ABERDOVEY, TOWYN, DOLGELLEY, CRICCIETH, PWLLHELI, &c.

DOWN. — WEEK DAYS. — SUNDAYS.

	a.m.	a.m.	a.m.	a.m.	p.m.	p.m.	a.m.	p.m.
Machynlleth dep	2 55	3 42	5 5	6 10	9 5	8 55
Dovey { arr	3 2	3 49	5 12	6 18	9 12	
Junction { dep	3 3	3 51	5 20	6 38	9 13	
Aberdovey ,,	3n15	4 3	5n33	6 47	9 27	9 18
Towyn ,,	3n22	4 11	5n41	6 56	9 35	9 26
Tonfanau ,,						
Llwyngwril ,,	3n31	4 22	5n51	7 7	9 39	
Fairbourne ,,	3n40	4 30	R	7 16	9 48	
Barmouth Jn. arr		4 33	6 3	7 20	9 52	
Barmouth dep	5 55	7 0	8 35	9 55	
Barmouth Jn. ,,	6 5	7 10	8 42	10 0	
Arthog ,,	6 8	7 13	8 45		
Penmaenpool ,,	6 20	7 25	9 0	10 50	
Dolgelley arr	6 25	7 30	9 5	10 55	
Dolgelley dep	3 25	5 20	6 35	9 50	4 3
Penmaenpool ,,	R	5 25	6 40		4 3
Arthog ,,		5 35	6 50		4 40
Barmouth Jn. arr	3 47	5 38	6 54	9 40	4 45
Barmouth ,,	3 55	5 50	7 0	9 50	4 55
Barmouth Jn. dep		6 5	7 25		6 1
Barmouth { arr	3 50	4 40	6 10	7 30	9 55	6 4
{ dep					10 0	6 10
Dyffryn ,,	4n8	4 55	6 25	7 45		
Llanbedr and Pensarn ,,						
Harlech ,,	4n14	5 0	6 40	7 53		5 1
Talsarnau ,,	4 20	5 10	6 48	8 11		5 2
Penrhyn-deudraeth ,,	5 22	6 52	8 16		5 4
Minfford ,,	4 36	5 28	6 58	8 22		5 4
Portmadoc { arr	4 40	5 32	7 2	8 26		5 4
{ dep	4 45	5 35	6 57	7 18	8 47		5 5
Criccieth ,,	4 57	5 47	6 57	7 18	8 47		5 5
Afon Wen { arr	4 55	5 10	6 0	7 10	7 30	9 0	9 40	8 40
{ dep								
Abererch ,,	*	*	*	*	*	*	*	*
Pwllheli (for Nevin) arr	5 5	5 20	6 10	7 20	7 40	9 10	9 50	8 52

ELLESMERE, WREXHAM, &c.

UP. — WEEK DAYS.

	a.m.	a.m.	a.m.	p.m.	p.m.	p.m.	p.m.
Ellesmere dep	9 5	11 50	2 20	3 30	5 55	7 15	9 15
Overton-on-Dee ,,	9 13	12 0	2 30	3 40	6 5	7 25	9 25
Bangor-on-Dee ,,	9 21	12 8	2 39	3 48	6 11	7 31	9 31
Marchwiel ,,	9 30	12 15	2 45	3 55	6 20	7 40	9 40
Wrexham (Central) arr	9 35	12 20	2 50	4 0	6 25	7 45	9 45

For Notes, see pages 8 and 9.

MID WALES SECTION.—RHAYADER,

UP.   WEEK DAYS.

	a.m.	a.m.	a.m.	a.m.	a.m.	a.m.	p.m.
Brecon ... dep		6 40			10 40		
Talyllyn ⟨ arr		6 50			10 50		
Junction ⟨ dep		6 51			11 0		11 40
Trefeinon ,,							
Talgarth ,,		7 4			11 13		
Three ⟨ arr		7 9			11 18		
Cocks Jun. ⟨ dep		7 12			11 20		
Boughrood ,,		7 19			11 23		
Erwood ,,		7 27			11 35		
Aberedw ,,							
Builth ⟨ arr		7 42			11 50		12 18
Wells ⟨ dep		7 45	8 45		11 55		12 23
Builth ⟨ arr		7 50	8 50		12 0		12 27
Road ⟨ dep		7 52			12 20		12 35
Newbridge-on-Wye ,,		8 0			12 28		
Doldowlod ,,		8 8			12 36		
Rhayader ,,		8 18			12 47		2 15
St. Harmons ,,							
Pantydwr ,,		8 31			1 0		
Tylwch ,,		8 41			1 10		
Llanidloes ⟨ arr		8 47			1 16		2 50
⟨ dep	6 35	8 50		11 45	1 19	1 30	
Dolwen ,,	6 40	8 56		11 50		1 35	
Llandinam ,,	6 47	9 3		11 59			
Moat Lane Jun. arr	6 53	9 7		12 5	1 35	1 50	

*—Stops to set down on informing the Guard at the preceding stopping Station, and to pick up Passengers when signalled to do so.
‡—Mondays and Saturdays only.
A—Stops for 1st and 2nd Class Passengers from or to local Stations, and 1st, 2nd, and 3rd from or to Stations on other Company's Lines. Notice to be given to Guard to set down.
AC—Stops at Borth to pick up or set down 1st Class Passengers.
B—Stops by signal to pick up or set down Passengers booked to or from Stations on other Companies' Lines. Notice to be given to the Guard to set down.
BB—Stops to set down Passengers booked from Stations on other Companies' Lines beyond Oswestry, Welshpool, and Moat Lane, on notice being given to the Guard.
C—Stops by Signal to pick up for Stations beyond Moat Lane.
D—Stops to set down from Stations beyond Welshpool, and by signal to pick up for Stations beyond Machynlleth. Also on Tuesdays stops at Carno and Llanbrynmair to set down from Newtown. Notice to be given to the Guard to set down.
DA—Stops to set down Passengers booked from Cemmes Road and Stations beyond. Notice to be given by the Passenger to the Guard at Dovey Junction.
E—Stops to pick up Passengers for Birmingham, Hereford, and beyond.
F—Stops at Arddleen on Mondays and Wednesdays only.
G—Runs via Loop at Talyllyn, and does not set down or pick up Passengers at Talyllyn Station.

BRECON, BUILTH WELLS, LLANIDLOES, &c.

UP.   WEEK DAYS.   SUNDAYS.

	p.m.	p.m.	p.m.	p.m.	p.m.	p.m.
Brecon ... dep	1 20		4 25	5 35		5 30
Talyllyn ⟨ arr	1 30		4 35	5 45		5 40
Junction ⟨ dep	1 33		4 45	5 46		5 41
Trefeinon ,,						
Talgarth ,,	1 46		5 0	5 57		5 54
Three ⟨ arr	1 51		5 5	6 2		5 59
Cocks Jun. ⟨ dep	1 55		5 10	6 3		6 0
Boughrood ,,	2 1		5 16	6 9		6 6
Erwood ,,	2 9		5 25	6 17		6 15
Aberedw ,,						
Builth ⟨ arr	2 22		5 40	6 30		6 30
Wells ⟨ dep	2 25		5 45	6 34		6 32
Builth ⟨ arr	2 30		5 50	6 38		
Road ⟨ dep	2 35			6 40		6 36
Newbridge-on-Wye ,,	2 43			6 47		6 43
Doldowlod ,,	2 51					
Rhayader ,,	3 8			7 0		7 2
St. Harmons ,,						
Pantydwr ,,	3 22					7 15
Tylwch ,,	3 31			7 20		7 25
Llanidloes ⟨ arr	3 37			7 35		7 31
⟨ dep	3 40			7 40		7 35
Dolwen ,,	3 45			7 46		7 41
Llandinam ,,	3 52			7 55		7 50
Moat Lane Jun. arr	3 56			8 0		7 55

H—Horse Boxes and Carriage Trucks are only conveyed by these trains between certain points; particulars of which can be ascertained from the Station Masters.
K—Stops to set down Passengers from Aberdovey, Llandinam, or Stations beyond. Notice to be given to the Guard at Dovey Junction and Moat Lane respectively.
M—Runs July 23rd to September 12th, inclusive.
N—Stops to set down Passengers booked from Stations on other Companies' Lines on notice being given to the Guard.
O—Stops to pick up or set down Passengers booked to or from Stations beyond Shrewsbury or Crewe. Notice to be given to the Guard to set down.
P—Stops at Abermule from July 1st to 22nd, and from Sept. 13th to 30th.
OO—Stops to pick up or set down Passengers booked to or from Stations beyond Builth Road. Notice to be given to the Guard to set down.
R—Stops to set down from Hereford, Birmingham, and beyond, on notice being given to the Guard.
V—Stops to set down on notice being given to the Guard, and by Signal to pick up for Aberystwyth.
†—Takes up or sets down 1st and 2nd Class local Passengers, and 1st, 2nd, and 3rd Class for Stations on other Companies' Lines, via Welshpool, Oswestry, and Whitchurch. Also stops to set down 1st, 2nd, and 3rd Class Passengers booked from Aberdovey, Llandinam, and Stations beyond. Notice to be given to the Guard to set down.

MID WALES SECTION.—MOAT BUILTH WELLS,

DOWN.   WEEK DAYS.

	a.m.	a.m.	a.m.	a.m.	a.m.	p.m.	p.m.	p.m.
Moat Lane Jun. dep		5 5		9 50	11 20	12 20		2 15
Llandinam ,,				9 55		12 25		
Dolwen ,,				10 2		12 32		
Llanidloes ⟨ arr		5 25		10 10		12 40		2 32
⟨ dep	5 15	5 27	8 15	10 15	11 35			2 35
Tylwch ,,		5 35	8 23	10 25				2 44
Pantydwr ,,		5 45	8 31	10 35				2 54
St. Harmons ,,				10 40				
Rhayader ,,	5 55	6 2	8 50	11 0	11 59			3 11
Doldowlod ,,		6 9	8 59	11 10				3 18
Newbridge-on-Wye ,,		6 18	9 10	11 25				3 26
Builth ⟨ arr		6 27	9 20	11 35	12 18			3 34
Road ⟨ dep		6 29	9 30	11 40	12 28		1 5	3 45
Builth ⟨ arr		6 33	9 34	11 45	12 31		1 10	3 49
Wells ⟨ dep		6 35	9 35		12 37		1 12	3 53
Aberedw ,,							1 21	
Erwood ,,		6 50	9 50				1 27	4 6
Boughrood ,,		7 2	9 10				1 40	4 16
Three ⟨ arr		7 7	10 5				1 46	4 22
Cocks Jun. ⟨ dep		7 9	10 6				1 52	4 27
Talgarth ,,		7 14	10 11				1 58	4 33
Trefeinon ,,								
Talyllyn ⟨ arr		7 27	10 23		10 20		2 10	4 45
Junc. ⟨ dep		7 35	10 50				2 15	4 50
Brecon ... arr		7 45	11 0				2 25	5 0

LLANFYLLIN BRANCH.   No Sunday Trains.

DOWN.   WEEK DAYS.

	a.m.	a.m.	p.m.	p.m.	p.m.
Llanymynech d.	8 25	11 10	4 10	6 35	8 0
Llansaintffraid ,,	8 35	11 18	4 18	6 43	8 10
Llanfechain ,,	8 42	11 25	4 25	6 50	8 18
Bryngwyn ,,					
Llanfyllin arr	8 55	11 35	4 35	7 0	8 30

UP.   WEEK DAYS.

	a.m.	a.m.	p.m.	p.m.	p.m.
Llanfyllin ... dep		7 30	10 15	1 45	5 55	7 20
Bryngwyn ,,					
Llanfechain ,,		7 40	10 25	1 55	6 5	7 32
Llansaintffraid ,,		7 47	10 32	2 2	6 12	7 40
Llanymynech ar		7 55	10 40	2 10	6 20	7 50

LANE, LLANIDLOES, RHAYADER, BRECON, &c.

DOWN.   WEEK DAYS.   SUNDAYS.

	p.m.	p.m.	p.m.	p.m.	p.m.	a.m.
Moat Lane Jun. dep		5 10	8 25	9 20		7 50
Llandinam ,,		5 15	8 30			7 55
Dolwen ,,		5 22	8 38			8 1
Llanidloes ⟨ arr		5 27	8 45	9 40		8 7
⟨ dep		5 30				8 10
Tylwch ,,		5 37				8 18
Pantydwr ,,		5 45				8 27
St. Harmons ,,						
Rhayader ,,		6 5				8 43
Doldowlod ,,		6 13				8 51
Newbridge-on-Wye ,,		6 22				9 0
Builth ⟨ arr		6 30				9 7
Road ⟨ dep	4 15	6 5	6 38			9 8
Builth ⟨ arr	4 20	6 10	6 42			9 12
Wells ⟨ dep		6 45				9 16
Aberedw ,,						
Erwood ,,		6 58				9 32
Boughrood ,,		7 8				9 43
Three ⟨ arr		7 14				9 51
Cocks Jun. ⟨ dep		7 15				9 53
Talgarth ,,		7 20				9 58
Trefeinon ,,						
Talyllyn ⟨ arr		7 33				10 11
Junction ⟨ dep		7 35				10 13
Brecon ... arr		7 45				10 23

For Notes, see pages 8 and 9.

KERRY BRANCH.   No Sunday Trains.

UP.   WEEK DAYS.

	a.m.	a.m.	a.m.	p.m.	p.m.	p.m.	p.m.
Kerry ... dep	6 50	8 40	11 20	12 45	2 45	3 50	7 0
Abermule arr	7 15	9 5	11 45	1 10	2 30	4 15	7 25

DOWN.   WEEK DAYS.

	a.m.	a.m.	noon	p.m.	p.m.	p.m.	p.m.
Abermule ... dep	7 25	9 40	12 0	1 20	2 40	4 45	8 55
Kerry ... arr	7 50	10 5	12 25	1 45	3 5	5 10	9 20

‡ Mondays and Saturdays only.   † Tuesdays only.

For Notes, see pages 8 and 9.

MAIN LINE.—WHITCHURCH AND ABERYSTWYTH.

DOWN.		Week Days										
		H							H		H	H
			Tuesdays only. Third Class only.								North Express.	London Express.
		a.m.	a.m.	a.m.	a.m.	a.m.	a.m.	p.m.	a.m.	a.m.	p.m.	p.m.
Whitchurch	dep	2 25	...	...	...	...	8 20	...	10 7	10 15	12 17	...
Fenn's Bank...	,,	*	...	...	...	...	8 27	...	c	10 23	...	...
Bettisfield ...	,,	*	...	...	...	...	8 34	...	c	10 31	...	...
Welshampton	,,	*	...	...	...	...	8 37	...	...	10 35	...	...
Ellesmere ...	arr	2 53	...	...	...	...	8 45	...	10 26	10 42	12 33	...
Wrexham	arr	...	...	...	...	...	9 35	...	...	12 20	...	...
(Central)	dp.	...	...	...	...	...	8 15	...	9 50	...	11 55	...
Ellesmere ...	dep	2 55	...	...	...	...	8 55	...	10 29	10 45	12 35	...
Frankton ...	,,	*	...	...	...	...	9 0	...	...	10 50	...	...
Whittington...	,,	*	...	...	...	...	9 8	...	c	10 58	...	...
Oswestry	arr	3 15	...	...	...	...	9 13	...	10 43	11 3	12 47	...
	dep	3 25	...	...	...	8 5		...	10 48		12 50	...
Llynclys ...	,,	...	...	...	...	8 13	...	...	10 56	...	...	...
Pant	,,	...	...	...	...	*	...	...	...	...	...	...
Llanymynech	arr	*	...	...	...	8 18	...	...	11 0	...	...	...
Llanfyllin	dep	...	...	...	...	7 30	...	...	10 15	...	...	...
	arr	...	...	...	...	8 55	...	...	11 35	...	...	...
Llanymynech	dep	*	...	...	...	8 20	...	...	11 1	...	...	...
Four Crosses	,,	...	...	...	...	8 25	...	...	11 5	...	...	...
Arddleen ...	,,	...	...	...	...	Mon	...	...	...	...	...	...
Pool Quay ...	,,	*	...	...	...	8 35	...	...	11 13	...	...	...
Buttington ...	,,	*	...	...	...	8 40	...	...	11 17	...	...	...
Welshpool	arr	3 55	...	...	...	8 45	...	...	11 22	...	1 12	...
	dep	4 12	*7 55*	...	...	8 50	...	...	11 30	...	1 14	2 15
Forden ...	,,	...	*8 5*	...	...	9 0	...	...	D	...	...	...
Montgomery	,,	4 24	*8 10*	...	...	9 4	...	...	11 41	...	1 25	o
Abermule ...	,,	...	*8 20*	...	...	9 11	...	...	*	...	...	...
Kerry ...	dep	...	...	...	...	8 40	...	...	11 20	...	...	...
	arr	...	...	...	...	10 5	...	...	12 25	...	...	...
Newtown	...dep	4 41	*8 30*	...	...	9 25	...	...	12 0	...	1 42	o
Moat Lane	arr	4 49		...	...	9 33	...	...	12 8	...	1 50	2 50
Junc.	dep	4 55		...	...	9 38	...	...	12 12	...	1 55	2 52
Caersws... ...	,,	4 58		...	...	9 42	...	...	D	...	...	...
Pontdolgoch...	,,	...		...	...	*	...	...	...	...	...	...
Carno	,,	5 11		...	...	9 52	...	...	D	...	...	...
Talerddig ...	,,	...		...	...	*	...	...	...	...	...	...
Llanbrynmair	,,	5 20		...	...	10 2	...	...	D	...	...	...
Cemmes Road	,,	5 29		...	...	10 14	...	...	12 52	...	...	...
Machyn-	arr	5 37		...	...	10 23	...	...	1 0	...	2 43	3 32
lleth	dep	5 42		8 35	9 45	10 28	...	12 20	1 10	...	2 47	3 35
Dovey	arr	...		8 43	9 52	10 35	...	12 30	1 18	...	2 55	...
Junc.	dep	...		8 48	10 10	10 43	...	12 55	1 28	...	2 57	...
Glandyfi ...	,,	5 50		8 51	10 13	D A	...	12 59	B B	...	B	...
Ynyslas	,,	...		9 3	10 24	D A	...	1 10	B B	...	B	...
Borth	,,	6 2		9 7	10 29	11 3	...	1 20	1 50	...	B	B B
Llanfihangel...	,,	...	...	9 12	10 36	D A	...	1 25	B B	...	...	...
Bow Street ...	,,	6 11	...	9 20	10 41	D A	...	1 30	B B	...	...	...
Aberystwyth	arr	6 20	...	9 30	10 50	11 25	...	1 40	2 10	...	3 35	4 20

On Newtown Fair Days, i.e., last Tuesday in each month, will be 25 minutes earlier throughout.

For Notes, see pages 8 and 9.

DOWN.		Week Days.										Sun.
		H	H									
		South Wales Express.					Third Class only. Mondays only.	☞ Wednesdays only.				
		p.m.	p.m.	p.m.	p.m.	p.m.	p.m.	p.m.	p.m.	p.m.	p.m.	a.m.
Whitchurch	dep	...	1 50	2 0	...	...	...	...	5 20	6 40	8 42	2 25
Fenn's Bank...	,,	...	...	2 7	...	...	...	...	5 28	6 48	8 49	*
Bettisfield ...	,,	...	...	2 20	...	...	...	...	5 36	6 56	8 56	*
Welshampton	,,	...	...	2 24	...	...	...	...	*	7 0	9 0	*
Ellesmere ...	arr	...	2 8	2 30	...	...	...	...	5 46	7 6	9 6	2 53
Wrexham	arr	...	2 50	4 0	...	...			6 25	7 45	9 45	...
(Central)	dp	...	1 35	...	...	...			4 0	6 35	8 30	...
Ellesmere ...	dep	...	2 13	2 31	...	...			5 50	7 9	9 8	2 55
Frankton ...	,,	...	...	2 36	...	...			5 55	7 14	9 13	*
Whittington...	,,	...	...	2 44	...	...			6 1	7 23	9 23	*
Oswestry	arr	...	2 28	2 48	...	...		...	6 6	7 28	9 28	3 15
	dep	...	2 35	2 53	...	3 45		*5 0*	6 12	7 35		6 15
Llynclys ...	,,	...	...	3 0	...	3 55		*5 10*	6 20	7 45	...	6 23
Pant	,,	...	...	3 3	...	3 59		*5 13*	*	7 50	...	...
Llanymynech	arr	...	...	3 6	...	4 3		*5 17*	6 24	7 54	...	6 29
Llanfyllin	dep	...	...	1 45	...	...		...	5 55	7 20	...	...
	arr	...	...	...	...	4 35		...	7 0	8 30	...	...
Llanymynech	dep		...	3 8	...			*5 20*	6 27	7 57	...	6 30
Four Crosses	,,		...	3 12	...	...		*5 25*	6 32	8 1	...	6 35
Arddleen ...	,,		...	Wed	...	...		*5 31*	...	...	...	...
Pool Quay ...	,,		...	3 20	...	...		*5 37*	6 39	8 11	...	6 42
Buttington ...	,,		...	3 25	...	...		*5 42*	6 47	8 16	...	6 48
Welshpool	arr		3 3	3 30	...	...	...	*5 50*	6 52	8 22	...	6 54
	dep		3 10	3 35	4 20	...	*5 30*	...	7 10	8 28	...	7 0
Forden	,,		...	...	4 28	...	*5 40*		7 18	8 36	...	7 9
Montgomery	,,		B	B	4 32	...	*5 50*		7 23	8 45	...	7 13
Abermule	..dep		...	...	4 42	...	*6 0*		7 30	8 53	...	7 20
Kerry ...	dep	...	...	...	3 50	...	...		7 0	...	...	...
	arr	...	...	...	5 10	...	...		...	9 20	...	...
Newtown	..dep	...	3 40	4 5	4 54	...	*6 10*		7 46	9 6	...	7 34
Moat Lane	arr.	...	3 48	4 18	5 2	...			7 54	9 15	...	7 43
Junc.	dep	3 35	3 54	4 23	5 7	...			8 6		...	7 48
Caersws... ...	,,	...	...	...	5 10	...			*	...	...	7 51
Pontdolgoch	,,	...	...	...	*	...			...	...	...	7 54
Carno	,,	...	...	...	5 23	...		...	A	...	...	8 2
Talerddig ...	,,	...	...	...	*	...		...	...	...	...	...
Llanbrynmair	,,	...	...	...	5 35	...		...	A	...	...	8 16
Cemmes Road	,,	4 10	B	B	5 43	...		...	8 41	...	...	8 30
Machyn-	arr	4 18	4 38	5 2	5 52	...		p.m.	8 50	...	...	8 40
lleth	dep	4 20	4 41	5 5	5 55	...		6 55	8 55	...	...	8 45
Dovey	arr	4 27	4 48	5 12	...	...		7 3	...	...	...	...
Junc.	dep	4 32	4 51	5 17	...	...		7 10	...	...	...	...
Glandyfi ...	,,	4 34	...	...	6 3	...		7 13	A	...	...	8 54
Ynyslas	,,	...	...	...	6 14	...		7 25	...	...	...	9 6
Borth	,,	4 48	B	BB	6 20	...		7 30	9 18	...	...	9 10
Llanfihangel...	,,	oo	...	...	Y	...		7 36	...	...	...	9 16
Bow Street ...	,,	5 0	...	...	6 35	...		7 41	A	...	...	9 23
Aberystwyth	arr	5 10	5 20	5 45	6 45	...	...	7 55	9 35	...	...	9 35

For Notes, see pages 8 and 9.

MAIN LINE.—ABERYSTWYTH AND WHITCHURCH.

UP.		Week Days.										
							H	H				H
			☞ Wednesdays only.					South Wales Express.				North Express.
		a.m.	a.m.	a.m.	a.m.	a.m.	a.m.	a.m.	p.m.	a.m.	a.m.	p.m.
Aberystwyth	dp	...	...	...	7 15	8 40	9 10	9 35	...	10 0	11 5	12 15
Bow Street ...	,,	...	...	...	7 25	8 50	...	oo	...	10 10	11 16	...
Llanfihangel...	,,	...	...	...	7 30	8 54	...	oo	...	10 15	*	...
Borth	,,	...	...	...	7 35	8 58	B	9 53	...	10 20	11 25	12 33
Ynyslas	,,	...	...	...	7 40	9 5	...	...	...	10 24	11 29	...
Glandyfi ...	,,	...	...	...	7 52	9 16	...	oo	...	10 36	11 41	...
Dovey	arr	...	...	...	7 55	9 19	9 45	10 9	...	10 38	...	12 49
Junc.	dep	...	...	...	8 0	9 22	9 53	10 14	...	10 50	...	12 55
Machyn-	arr	...	...	...	8 8	9 30	10 0	10 21	...	11 0	11 49	1 2
lleth	dep	...	...	...	8 15		10 4	10 26	...		11 54	1 5
Cemmes Road	,,	...	...	...	8 25	...	10 13	B	...	...	12 4	1 15
Llanbrynmair	,,	...	...	...	8 37	...	...	B	...	...	12 16	...
Talerddig ...	,,	...	...	...	*	...	...	...	...	...	12 29	...
Carno	,,	...	...	...	8 51	...	...	B	...	...	12 33	...
Pontdolgoch	,,	...	...	...	8 58	...	...	...	...	...	*	...
Caersws... ...	,,	...	...	...	9 5	...	...	...	...	...	12 45	...
Moat Lane	arr	...	...	...	9 9	...	...	11 10	...	...	12 47	1 47
Junc.	dep	...	...	6 55	9 15	...	...		...	...	12 52	1 50
Newtown ...	,,	...	...	7 8	9 30	...	11 0	...	...	...	1 5	2 4
Kerry ...	dep	...	...	*6†50*	8 40	...	...	...	...	...	12M45	...
	arr	...	...	*7†50*	10 5	...	...	...	...	...	1M45	...
Abermule ...	dep	...		7 17	9 39	...	...		...	...	1 15	...
Montgomery	,,	...		7 25	9 47	...	o		...	...	1 27	...
Forden	,,	...		7 30	9 51	...	...		...	...	1 31	...
Welshpool	arr	...		7 40	10 0	...	11 25		...	...	1 40	2 27
	dep	...		7 45	10 20	...	11 40		...	...		2 32
Buttington ...	,,	...		7 50	10 25	...	...		...	...	...	...
Pool Quay ...	,,	...		7 55	10 30	...	...		...	...	...	
Arddleen ...	,,	...		Wed	F	...	...		...	...	...	
Four Crosses	,,	...		8 5	10 40	...	...		...	...	...	
Llanymynech	arr	...		8 8	10 45	...	...		...	p.m.	...	
Llanfyllin	dep	...	7 30	7 30	10 15	...	...	...	...	1 45	...	
	arr	...	...	8 55	11 35	...	...	...	...	...	...	
Llanymynech	dep.	...	8 6	8 10	10 50	...	...	...	...	2 15	...	
Pant	,,	...	...	*	10 54	...	...	...	...	*	...	
Llynclys ...	,,	...	...	8 19	11 0	...	...	...	...	2 25	...	...
Oswestry	arr	...	8 20	8 27	11 10	...	12 10	...	...	2 35	...	2 57
	dep	6 5		8 35	11 25	...	12 15	...	1 50		...	3 2
Whittington...	,,	6 10	...	8 39	11 29	...	...	...	1 55	...	...	...
Frankton ...	,,	6 18	...	8 47	11 37	...	...	...	2 3	...	...	...
Ellesmere ...	arr	6 23	...	8 52	11 42	...	12 30	...	2 8	...	...	3 17
Wrexham	arr	...	...	9 35	12 20	...	...	...	2 50	...	...	4 0
(Central)	dep	...	...	8 15	9 50	...	11 55	...	1 35	...	...	...
Ellesmere ...	dep	6 25	...	8 55	11 45	...	12 35	...	2 10	...	...	3 20
Welshampton	,,	*	...	9 2	11 52	...	...	...	*	...	...	...
Bettisfield ...	,,	6 35	...	9 6	11 55	...	...	...	2 19	...	...	...
Fenn's Bank	,,	6 47	...	9 16	12 5	...	...	...	2 28	...	...	...
Whitchurch	arr.	6 55	...	9 25	12 12	...	12 55	...	2 35	...	...	3 40

For Notes, see pages 8 and 9.

UP.		Week Days.										Sun.
			H		H	H				H		
		Tuesdays only. Third Class only.	London Express.									
		p.m.	p.m.	p.m.	p.m.	p.m.	p.m.	p.m.	p.m.	p.m.	p.m.	p.m.
Aberystwyth	dp	...	1 0	...	2 15	2 45	2 55	...	5 40	6§25	8 25	6 25
Bow Street ...	,,	...	...	...	...	...	3 5	...	5 50	...	8 35	6 35
Llanfihangel...	,,	...	...	...	...	...	3 10	...	5 57	...	*	6 39
Borth	,,	...	B	...	2 33	3 5	3 15	...	6 10	6AC43	8 45	6 43
Ynyslas	,,	...	...	...	...	...	3 20	...	6 14	...	8 50	6 47
Glandyfi ...	,,	...	...	...	...	...	3 35	...	6 25	...	9 4	7 0
Dovey	arr	...	1 35	...	2 50	3 23	3 38	...	6 27	7§ 0	...	...
Junc.	dep		1 50	...	2 55	3 27		...	6 31	7§ 6	...	...
Machyn-	arr		1 58	...	3 10	3 34	...	...	6 38	7§13	9 15	7 10
lleth	dep		2 3	...	3 12	3 36	...	...	6 40	7§17		7 17
Cemmes Road	,,		...	...	...	...	...	...	6 50	7§26	...	7 26
Llanbrynmair	,,		...	...	...	...	...	...	7 2	7§38	...	7 38
Talerddig ...	,,		...	...	...	...	...	...	*	K	...	*
Carno	,,		...	...	...	...	...	...	7 17	7§52	...	7 52
Pontdolgoch...	,,		...	...	...	...	...	...	7 25	...	...	8 0
Caersws.. ...	,,		...	...	...	...	...	...	7 30	8§ 4	...	8 4
Moat Lane	arr	...	2 51	...	3 58	...	...	...	7 33	8§ 6	...	8 6
Junc.	dep	...	2 55	...	4 2	...	...	...	7 38	8§11	...	8 11
Newtown ...	,,	*2 20*	3 5	...	4 15	4 32	...	...	7 54	8§26	...	8 26
Kerry ...	dep	*2 5*	...	...	3P50	...	...	...	7 0	...	...	...
	arr	*3 5*	...	...	5P10	...	...	...	9 20	9 20	...	...
Abermule	. dep	*2 35*	...	...	F	...	...	...	8 3	8§35	...	8 35
Montgomery	,,	*2 42*	b	...	4 32	...	...	...	8 10	8§44	...	8 44
Forden	,,	*2 46*	...	...	...	...	...	...	8 15	...	...	8 48
Welshpool	arr	*2 56*	3 30	...	4 45	4 55	...	...	8 25	8 55	...	8 55
	dep			3 35	4 55		...	5 55	8 30	9 0	...	9 0
Buttington ...	,,	....	...	3 40	...	...	...	6 2	8 35	K	...	9 5
Pool Quay ...	,,	...	...	3 44	...	...	...	6 7	8 40	K	...	*
Arddleen ...	,,	...	...	Mon	...	...	...	Mon	...	...	...	...
Four Crosses	,,	...	...	3 52	...	...	...	6 17	8 48	K	...	*
Llanymynech	arr	...		3 56	...	...	...	6 22	8 52	9 20	...	9 20
Llanfyllin	dep	...		...	...	...	...	5 55	7 20	...	...	...
	arr	...		4 35	...	...	...	7 0	...	...	...	...
Llanymynech	dep	...		3 58	...	...	...	6 25	8 55	9 22	...	9 21
Pant	,,	...		*	...	...	...	*	8 58	...	...	...
Llynclys ...	,,	...		4 7	...	...	...	6 38	9 2	K	...	9 26
Oswestry	arr	...		4 15	5 20	...	...	6 50	9 10	9 35	...	9 35
	dep	...		4 20	5 25	...	...			9 40	...	9 40
Whittington...	,,	...	...	4 25	...	...	...	...	...	*	...	*
Frankton ...	,,	...	...	4 33	...	...	...	...	...	*	...	*
Ellesmere ...	arr	...	...	4 38	5 40	...	...	...	...	9 57	...	9 57
Wrexham	arr	...	...	...	6 25	...	...	...	...	...	...	...
(Central)	dep	...	...	4 0	...	...	...	...	...	8 30	...	...
Ellesmere ...	dep	...	...	4 42	5 46	...	...	...	...	10 0	...	10 0
Welshampton	,,	...	...	4 49	...	...	...	...	...	*	...	*
Bettisfield ...	,,	...	...	4 53	...	...	...	...	...	*	...	*
Fenn's Bank...	,,	...	...	5 3	...	...	...	...	...	*	...	*
Whitchurch	arr	...	...	5 10	6 10	...	...	...	...	10 25	...	10 25

For Notes, see pages 8 and 9.

port, Nottingham and Sheffield. However, nearly half as many went to Barmouth or Pwllheli, and there were through coaches via Bangor to Pwllheli and Portmadoc which did not run down the Coast Line further south.

No through coaches or trains were shown in the tables at this time via the Manchester & Milford Railway, though there were four with tight connections at Aberystwyth, two from Pembroke Dock and two from Carmarthen. Being realistic, one must wonder how many times, with five minutes only to make the change, passengers on the notorious M&M missed their connection.

There were also good connections at Builth Road on the Mid-Wales line, where the LNWR station was just above the Cambrian one, and from Breconshire stations excellent times could be made by this route to Liverpool, Edinburgh and many other distant places. There were two good connections off the Midland Railway in the northwards direction at Three Cocks, enabling passengers from Birmingham and Hereford to reach all parts of the system; from Hereford to Pwllheli took seven hours. People did of course take gargantuan journeys in those days in their stride; the Cambrian tables showed trains from Inverness and Aberdeen; some 12½ hours would get you from Inverness as far as Oswestry.

Only up to 1914 were there any through trains from the Great Central Railway via Wrexham to Aberystwyth. A line joining the Ellesmere branch station (Central) with Exchange (GW and WMCQ) had been open from 1895. The 11.40 am from Manchester in 1904 ran from Chester with only a stop at Hawarden on the WM&CQ and left Wrexham Central only 8 minutes after arriving at Exchange, giving an arrival at Aberystwyth at 5.20 pm and Pwllheli at 7.40 pm. Mostly the two stations at Wrexham ignored each other; in 1955 a traveller on the morning train from Chester would arrive at Oswestry at 9.18 if changing at Gobowen, and 10.32 if tramping across Wrexham to change trains.

Steamer Services

With such a long coastline, one might have expected the Cambrian Railways to enter with spirit into the shipping business; but doubtless for the first 20 years of their existence the capitalisation of any scheme would have been beyond them. However, they did rebuild the harbour at Aberdovey under powers granted in 1883 to take coastal and packet steamers, and in 1886 a service of nine sailings per month began from there to Waterford in Southern Ireland, under the auspices of the Waterford & Aberdovey Steamer Co. In 1889 the Cambrian itself obtained powers to operate (and build) steamers, and took over direct operation of the Waterford service. The same year however, it dropped out of the timetables. With its tortuous rail journey at the English end, this service can never have been a serious competitor for the Irish traffic with Holyhead or New Milford.

Accidents

Scrutiny of the Board of Trade returns reveals remarkably few accidents notified by the Cambrian, compared with other lines of similar size.

Whether this was because they did not occur, or because they were not notified, is open to conjecture. The ones which were dealt with show a fairly happy-go-lucky system in force in the early days. An accident at Carno on 8th November, 1869 was notable because Earl Vane in a saloon became detached and was carried backwards to Moat Lane. A down passenger train had hit a goods train shunting in the station; an LNWR carriage was smashed, by no means the first to suffer on the Cambrian. On 27th May, 1872 the driver of a mixed train from Oswestry got off his engine at Moat Lane to alter the points for setting back into the up line: the fireman moved the train but was unable to stop it, and it collided with another passenger train. On 16th August, 1873 a train arriving at Newtown divided, the engine running into a siding and the carriages into the platform; apparently the facing point lock had been removed and sent to Oswestry for repairs. On 1st January the same year a 16½ year-old porter turned a passenger train into a siding at Carno, where it hit a pilot engine. On 22nd June, 1881 a mixed train left the rails on the Llanfyllin branch through some coal trucks being too loosely coupled; on 22nd November the same year two wagons were blown by the wind out of a siding at Afonwen in the path of a passenger train. On 7th April, 1884 a cattle train ran away down the incline from Llanfihangel to Borth, and struck the back of a train being shunted for a special to pass. But it must be emphasized that in the 12 accidents notified between 1871 and 1884, no passenger was killed; when Cambrian trains came to grief they were never going very fast (and it was usually arranged that the rolling stock that was smashed belonged to some other line).

There were casualties among the staff, however. When in November 1861 a goods train from Newtown ran off the line at Abermule due to excessive speed, both footplate men were killed. The driver was killed, too, when an engine was derailed at Caersws in 1868, due to part of the embankment being washed away. Once again driver and fireman (both named William Davies) were killed when a landslide derailed a train on Friog rocks on 1st January, 1883. No elemental force was responsible for the next affair, in 1887, when the down morning mail ran off the line at Ellesmere. It appeared that the porter was playing cards with a postman and carelessly left a facing point wrongly set. The porter was sacked, but an agitation was made locally for his restitution, and the station master signed a memorandum on his behalf. For this the station master was transferred (and later sacked), which led to even greater agitation, rising rapidly to national levels. A Select Committee had sat on certain aspects of the matter, and as the company gave the appearance of having sacked the station master for the evidence he gave before it, the perfect Gilbertian ending to the porter's card-party was that the General Manager and a Director of the Cambrian appeared at the Bar of the House of Commons, accused of breach of privilege, and were reprimanded.

In June 1897 a Sunday School excursion from Royton in Lancashire, double-headed, was returning from Barmouth when it left the rails at Welshampton; nine children were killed. The Cambrian said it was due to a four-wheeled L&Y van 'running rough'. The L&Y for their part, said that the Cambrian's track was in a state to cause any vehicle to run rough; the truth probably lay between.

On 26th November, 1904 there was a head-on collision at Forden between a goods and a passenger train, but no one was seriously injured. It was caused by the fact that a goods train was allowed to stand in the platform, because there were horses aboard and the down line platform was higher than the up one, and more suitable for disembarking them. The driver, who had passed distant and home signals, was sacked.

An accident occurred on the Mid-Wales line at Tylwch after the CR had taken over working; on 16th September, 1899 the down Mail had arrived from Llanidloes, and was due to cross an up excursion from South Wales. This fact seems not to have been known to the staff, who failed to set the facing point; the excursion overran the home signal, which was badly sited in a cutting, and ploughed into the mail train. Photographs indicate that one van was pushed halfway through a bogie carriage; since only one passenger was killed, either the 'mail' was lightly loaded or the passengers had alighted to stretch their legs.

At Harlech in September 1911 damage to an engine and some wagons was caused by the driver of a freight train setting off as he thought on the main line, but in fact in a long refuge siding; it was dark, but nevertheless there must have been slack station working.

And so we come to 26th January, 1921, the date of the classic head-on collision that caused a great stir in those days when accidental death was rarer than it is today. A slow train from Whitchurch had duly arrived at Abermule at 11.56 am. The driver handed the tablet to a member of the station staff. Everyone chatted, and various guesses were made about the present position of the express from Aberystwyth, which was due to leave Newtown at 11.57. But when someone handed the driver a tablet and signalled him away, nobody seemed surprised. Nor did the engine crew look very hard at the tablet, or they would have seen that it was the same one they had just given up, for the Montgomery section, and not the Newtown section. A mile west of the station, the two trains met head-on, the one coming down the grade moving at a smart pace. Seventeen people were killed, including Lord Herbert Vane-Tempest, a Director of the railway.

A serious washout near Scafell station occurred at the end of June 1936, a bridge over the Dulais being washed away. Ganger Haynes's daughter walked two miles to Newtown to stop the 6.25 am mail train from Aberystwyth at Caersws. The line remained closed for seven days.

Signalling

The Cambrian possessed some curious signals; in certain cases the spectacles were located halfway down the post. There was also a characteristic double-armed post used at Halts for passengers to signal the driver to stop. In common with other earlier lines, the Cambrian originally used a white light for 'all clear', green for 'caution' and red for 'stop'. A note in an 1864 rule book added 'anything waved violently up and down is a signal of danger'. Tyer's Electric Tablet system was used throughout the Railways, except where one-engine-in-steam working was in force and on the few sections of double line. Most of the signalling was installed by the firm of Dutton of Worcester. A feature was the use of stop signals only in many cases; there were no distants, but the stop signals were set well back to avoid danger due to over-running.

An early Cambrian signal, with the lamp lower than the arm, which was still in use on the main line in 1934, as the up home signal for Weston Wharf.   *Author*

A later type of signal at Llanbrynmair; the s signal controlling the long siding was tinguishable at night by having a magenta r than red spectacle glass.   *Oakwood Colle*

Chapter Six

The Route and Stations

THE MAIN LINE

Whitchurch, the start of the Cambrian's main line, was an LNWR station; it comprised three platforms, with a goods shed west of the up (LNW down) platform, and locomotive shed (closed 1950) and turntable east of the down (LNW up) platform; a large foundry west of the station was rail-served. The North signal box was by the north points of the platform loop, and a South box by the road overbridge, beside the CR line, which branched off just south-west of the station, becoming single.

Running level for a mile and then down at 1 in 80, the line crossed into Wales just before Fenns Bank station (3 m), which had a loop and two sidings; also a siding to a brickworks, from which a narrow gauge line ran to a moss litter works. This part was known as 'the Whixall Moss' and was overcome by the Cambrian engineers in much the same way that Stephenson overcame Chat Moss. A further moss litter siding preceded Bettisfield station (6¾ m), a single platform with a loop, and a goods loop off which a spur ran to a goods shed. Welshampton (8 m) was a small station with a siding but no loop; it was on a gradient of 1 in 80 against down trains.

Ellesmere (11 m) had a large station building on the down side and a further platform with shelter on the up side. There was also a goods shed on the down side, up end, and a siding to the Smithfield cattle market; signal cabin and water tower were on the up side, and there was a turntable originally. The junction with the Wrexham branch was some way south of the station; the loop for direct running to Oswestry was sanctioned for traffic in December 1896 but was little used, and was taken out about 1910. In 1918 the War Department applied to place an ammunition depot on the 'redundant loop'.

Frankton (13 m) appeared in later tables as a Halt, being unstaffed from 1956; it lost its goods service in 1964 along with Welshampton, Bettisfield and Fenns Bank, although goods trains ran to Ellesmere until 27th March, 1965. Whittington (High Level), 16¼ m, was a small wooden station with a loop and siding, just east of the point where the Great Western line passed under, its station being to the south-east. Tinkers Green Halt (17¼ m) was opened on 16th October, 1939 for workers and soldiers at the army depot at Park Hall. In World War I a siding complex there was connected to the Cambrian line at Drenewydd. At 18¼ m the OE&WR made end-on connection with the O&NR in 1863, the Cambrian station lying just south-west of the existing GWR one. It comprised three running lines between two rows of station and office buildings, the main one on the up side.

The Oswestry Works was on the east side at the north end, a part of the town known as Shelf, with tracks entering at both ends. At its west end it had a gas-oil works and erecting shops; a stores area was followed by the carriage and wagon works and paint shop at the east end. A 2 ft gauge tramway ran the length of the carriage and wagon works and out to a timber drying store. The locomotive shed lay beside the Whitchurch line on the up side; there was a small carriage shed by the west entrance to the Works. A long iron footbridge ran from the works across all lines towards the Town.

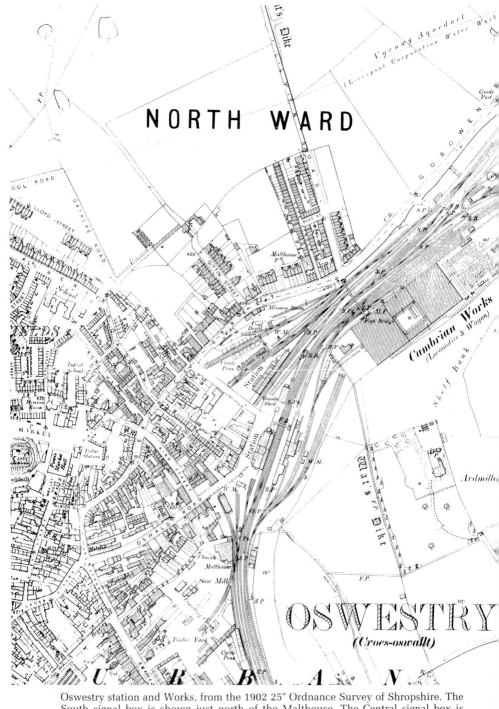

Oswestry station and Works, from the 1902 25″ Ordnance Survey of Shropshire. The South signal box is shown just north of the Malthouse. The Central signal box is shown at the junction with the GWR station, and the North box near the east end of the Works, with the GWR box nearby. Note the turntable at far right; the engine shed (five roads) is just off at right. *Reproduced from the 1902, 25″ Ordnance Survey Map*

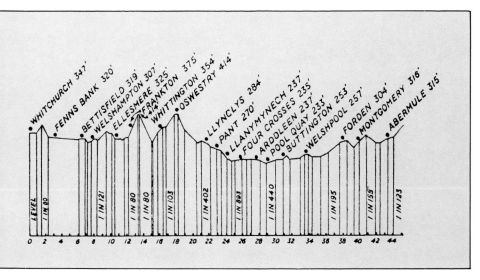

The main line gradient profile *(continued on p. 113)*.

The joint Cambrian and LMS locomotive shed at Whitchurch in July 1933, showing a Dean 0−6−0 on the turntable. *Author*

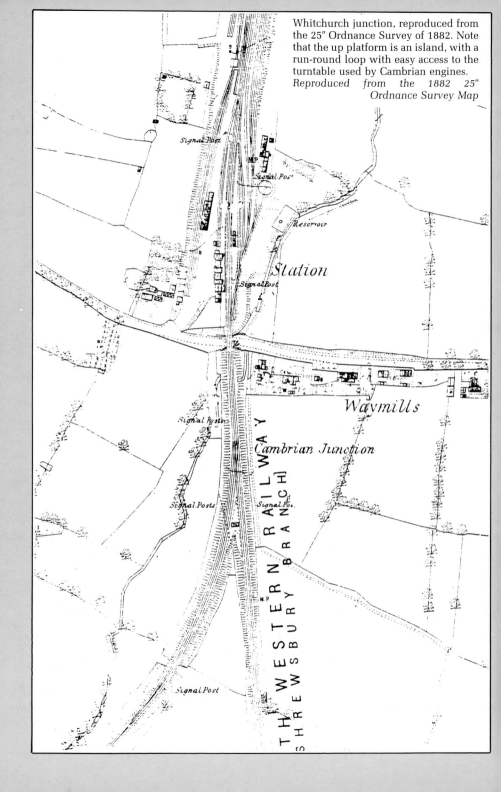

Whitchurch junction, reproduced from the 25″ Ordnance Survey of 1882. Note that the up platform is an island, with a run-round loop with easy access to the turntable used by Cambrian engines.

Reproduced from the 1882 25″ Ordnance Survey Map

Fenns Bank station; note the old Cambrian carriage body on the platform. This was one of two stations in the Welsh county of Flint before the line re-entered Shropshire.
Oakwood Collection

Bettisfield station, which had a passenger loop and also a goods loop which served the goods shed and cattle landing.
Oakwood Collection

An early photo of Welshampton; note the end of an old carriage, probably in use as a goods shed.   *Lens of Sutton*

Welshampton station later: it had no loop and now only an old gunpowder van served as a goods shed.   *Oakwood Collection*

The station building on the down side at Ellesmere, showing the original Cambrian Railways canopy still in place.   *Lens of Sutton*

Ellesmere station sidings from the footbridge looking north-east. *Oakwood Collection*

Whittington High Level station in August 1933; this was a wooden station. A permanent way man's motor trolley can just be seen by the barrow crossing.   *Author*

Llanynmech station in 1953 looking 'up' from the roadbridge; on the far right is the old Shropshire & Montgomeryshire Railway station, at this time still in War Department use.   *J. Edgington*

A 1953 view of the down end of the Oswestry complex, with the Gobowen motor train entering.   *J. Edgington*

Oswestry station from the works footbridge in 1953; on the right is the former GWR station, then in use as a goods depot.   *J. Edgington*

The long footbridge at Oswestry connecting the locomotive works with the town, seen looking in the down direction.   *Oakwood Collection*

An auto-train at Oswestry up side in 1934, with the '517' class of 0−4−2T running bunker first.   *Author*

There were three signal boxes: the North one near the north-east corner of
the Works, one called Central by the link across to the GWR station, and a
South one on the up side, at the down end of the station, near a siding to a
saw-mill. A siding and sheds west of the South box were taken over after
closure by the Cambrian Railway Society, at that time housing a 'Manor'
4–6–0 which later moved to Llangollen, and a preserved auto-trailer.

Tracks from here to Llanymynech were doubled in 1900; on leaving there
was a ⅜ mile-long stretch of 1 in 80 against up trains and goods trains from
Llynclys were banked. At 19½ m came Weston Wharf, a goods station
closed in 1961, on the up side. There had been a mile-long tramway from
near here to Sweeney Brickworks. A mile further on a skew bridge marked
the point where the Cambrian passed over an ancient tramroad known as the
Morva or Gronwen tramway, which ran from coal-pits at Coed-y-Go on
Sweeney Mountain to the 'Gronwen' wharf on the Canal near Morton, on the
section between Frankton Locks and Llanymynech.

Llynclys Junction at 22 m was where the Porthywaen branch, and later the
Tanat Valley trains also (described later) left the main line. The station, ¼
mile further on, had a loop with the main building on the up side. The line
passed under the bridge carrying the Crickheath Tramway, a mineral line of
3 ft gauge which ran from the Hill quarries to a wharf on the canal (see
description of Porthywaen). At Pant (23½ m) another narrow gauge
tramway ran in a tunnel under the station to a further canal wharf, and a
spur from it ran to an exchange siding with the Cambrian west of the station.
The line now passed over the canal to reach the original junction of the
O&NR Llanfyllin branch (see description of that branch).

Llanymynech station (24¼ m) lay between two double-line junctions; the
PSNWR main line took off at the up end, and the same company's Nantmawr
branch at the down end. There was a main platform with wooden buildings
on the down side, then across two tracks, an island platform, the outer face
of which could be used in part by the PSNWR, and across two tracks again,
the mean wooden station built by the PSNWR itself and resurrected in 1911
by the S&MR. The goods sidings were on the down side; at one time there
was a turntable on a spur northwards from the goods yard. The PSNWR had
a turntable and engine shed just north of the station but these were not
restored by the S&MR. There were signal boxes at the Nantmawr junction
and the up end of the down platform.

At Four Crosses (25¾ m) the route crossed the famous Offa's Dyke, and it
would seem that a portion of it was flattened to accommodate the goods
yard, south of the station. Arddleen Halt (27½ m) only acquired its suffix in
1954, but was a very rural small platform which was never a regular stop; in
1904 it had one train on Mondays and two on Wednesdays down, and two
on Wednesdays and three on Mondays up. Pool Quay (29¼ m) was sited at
the level crossing with the A483 road; a second platform was added in 1898.
On a gently-rising gradient the line now ran across the Severn to reach
Buttington Junction (31¼ m), a station shared with the joint GW/LNW line
from Shrewsbury, though for practical purposes Welshpool, to which the
joint line had running powers, was the junction station. Buttington station
occupied the V of the junction and latterly had four platforms; the up one on

Llynclys Junction in 1904; engines shunting the Porthywaen pits, reached by the line turning right, took water from the tank behind the signal cabin, and coal from a coaling stage by the double shunt signals. *L&GRP*

Llynclys station looking in the up direction towards Llynclys Junction, a quarter of a mile beyond. *Oakwood Collection*

Pant station looking in the down direction; in the early days a tramway ran from quarries on the right under the platform to the canal on the left.   *Oakwood Collection*

The junction at the down end of Llanymynech station; the line to the right is the former PSNWR one to Blodwell Junction, and the pair on the left ran into the PSNW side of the station, being the line to Shrewsbury (Abbey).   *D.J. Powell*

Pool Quay station, showing the wooden second platform added in 1898; the level crossing was for the A483 road. *Lens of Sutton*

At Buttington Junction the joint line from Shrewsbury came in on the right; in the 1950s the up main line had only a short wooden platform. *Oakwood Collection*

Welshpool station looking 'up', with No. 7814 *Fringford Manor* in the engine siding; the former shed lay beyond the water tower. *Oakwood Collection*

Welshpool station showing the main building on the up platform, and the bay; the left-hand platform was an island. *Oakwood Collection*

the Cambrian side however was not full-length. Beyond the station was a loop, which had a loading point for a tramway to a brickworks. Immediately south of this was a further signal box, controlling the doubled line. The bridge over the Severn was rebuilt in 1946.

Welshpool (34 m) was an important station. It had a locomotive shed at the up end, down side, with a large water tower. There were three platforms and an up bay. The buildings were on the up side, and behind them the exchange sidings with the narrow gauge Welshpool & Llanfair Railway, and its passenger terminus. While this was in operation, and the Oswestry line still open, it was a very busy station, whereas now it is just a stop on the way to Shrewsbury. The goods sidings included some timber sidings, the Midland Tar Distillers' siding, Smithfield siding, and Boys & Boden (Severn Road Siding). As related elsewhere, the W&L managed a straight transition from a BR goods line to a 'preserved' one, but since 31st August, 1963 no narrow gauge stock has been allowed into the station, due to development of the area, and the present passenger service to Llanfair starts at Raven Square nearly a mile to the west, incidentally saving the trains the agony of a climb at 1 in 33 to cross the canal.

The line (doubled to Forden in July 1925) is now running south along the Severn valley, crossing the river at 36 m. Forden station (38½ m) had a level crossing south of it and a signal box and wooden building on the up platform. A siding to Cil-Cewydd Mills came 1¾ mile further on, on the east side, with a connecting tramway. The Cil-Cewydd bridge over the Severn, of four spans, was renewed in its present form in 1922. Montgomery station (40¼ m) was over a mile north-west of the county town and never acquired the importance one would expect, though the building, on the north side, was tall and church-like; a signal box was at the down end of the up platform, with a goods shed opposite; the platforms were partly staggered.

The gradients here are easy, though a gentle climb to Newtown begins before Abermule (44 m), where the down platform had a curving extra face for the Kerry branch. Newtown (47¾ m) was the most important station on this section, the present one being the third, opened on 31st May, 1869. The lucrative Price's Stores direct mail depot was adjacent to the up platform, which had its own post office. The loop begins before the road bridge, at which the first O&N station was sited. There was a large goods shed on the up side and a siding to cattle pens; then after passing over the A483 road, there was an extensive lower goods yard on the up side, on the site of the original L&NR station. Newtown has two platforms with an extra west-facing bay.

From 1912 to 1966 the line between Newtown and Moat Lane stations was double. Scafell station (49½ m) had no loop and was not rebuilt; it could therefore only be called at by up trains, latterly two per day. It was closed from 1891 to 1913 and finally on 7th March, 1955; the goods siding, which took truckloads only, closed in 1941. At 50½ m a still very obvious curving siding ran off the down side to Penstrowedd Quarry, opened by the County Council in 1902. It was lifted in 1937, though the quarry remained working, road-served.

At Forden the station building (wooden), station master's house and signal box were all on the up platform. *Oakwood Collection*

Montgomery station looking 'up', in the 1950s, with the original Cambrian station building receiving some roof repairs. *Oakwood Collection*

Abermule station had a curving platform on the down side for the branch train to Kerry; a long face for what was always a one-coach train! *Oakwood Collection*

The important station of Newtown had its buildings on the up platform and a bay in the down platform. The extensive sidings are behind the camera. The main road crosses over just round the curve. *Oakwood Collection*

The main line side of Moat Lane Junction, showing the island up platform and the down-facing bay; the Mid-Wales line platform was on the left out of the picture; the line to the locomotive shed can be seen beyond the down platform.

Oakwood Collection

Caersws had only an up platform, though there was a loop; note the small signal cabin; the crossing gates were later made iron ones, and are still in use.

Oakwood Collection

Moat Lane Junction (52½ m) served only for exchange purposes between the O&N and N&M railways; the former had put up a Moat Lane station (the remains of which could be seen by the first level crossing on the Mid-Wales line), but it really served the large village of Caersws; when the N&M was built, a Caersws station was put up less than a mile further on, in the village. Moat Lane had a large signal box in the V of the junction and station buildings, including a refreshment room, on a triangular platform. There was no down platform on the Mid-Wales side, but on the main line there was an extra island platform and a down-facing bay on the main one. Once the Mid-Wales was closed there was no purpose for the junction station and it was closed on 31st December, 1962.

The locomotive depot here was entered from points on the main line facing down; originally there was a two-gable wooden shed, but this was damaged in a gale in 1955 and a metal structure put up, which still exists in agricultural use. About six engines were usually stabled here, from 1922 including a light engine for working the Van branch after the original Van shed at Caersws went out of use.

Caersws (53½ m) had a loop; there was no down platform but trains were often crossed here. There were sidings and a goods shed at the up end. On the south side lay the small station of the Van Railway, a short platform, engine shed and loop. In Great Western days, and indeed until 1984, it was used by the Bridge Engineers for stabling service stock. In 1990 it was sold for commercial engineering work. There was a level crossing at the main station and also just beyond the Van station.

Pontdolgoch (55 m) came after three-quarters of a mile of 1 in 71, where the drag up to Talerddig eased somewhat. There was a solid building on the down side; there was no loop, though it was for a time a tablet station. Later a loop was put in at Clatter (56 m) to facilitate working over the six mile section between Caersws and Carno. Carno station (59¼ m) had two platforms with the building on the down side and a goods shed adjacent; the signal box was on the down side of the level crossing.

After a final ¾ m of 1 in 80 comes the short level stretch on which Talerddig station was set in 1896, followed immediately by three miles down at 1 in 52/6. The station had two platforms, a short siding and a signal box on the east side. The famous cutting here was up to 115 ft deep, and a wonder considering it was cut by men with primitive tools between 1860 and 1862. Llanbrynmair (64¾ m) was also on a short level piece where the down gradient eased to 1 in 60; it had a loop, station house on the down platform, and signal box opposite. There were four sidings to the south on the down side, and a notable long refuge siding at the down end, down side, which was built level although the line itself was dropping. The down platform had been lengthened and was thus intersected by a foot crossing.

Although from here to Commins Coch the gradients are nowhere worse than 1 in 78, the approach to Talerddig was more arduous for engines in the up direction, being a climb of 13 miles with the worst at 1 in 56 (3 miles) against a climb of 9 miles with the worst at 1 in 80; Moat Lane, where the climb starts for down trains, is much higher than Machynlleth, where the up 'collar' work begins, albeit mildly, at Cemmes Road. Commins Coch Halt, opened 19th October, 1931 was at 68¼ m.

The separate Van Branch station at Caersws in 1976; it had not been used by passengers since 1893. *Author*

Pontdolgoch was once a tablet station and the vacated signal box can be seen in this 1950s picture beyond the platform looking 'down'; there was a short siding behind it. *Lens of Sutton*

Carno station had its buildings on the down side; note that the platforms have been lengthened and raised at the up end. *Oakwood Collection*

Talerddig station, showing the signal box on the down side and short siding on the up side. *Oakwood Collection*

Part of the famous Talerddig cutting, looking 'down' near Pandy Bach.
Oakwood Collection

Llanbrynmair looking 'up'; the platforms appear staggered because the GWR extended the down platform beyond the walkway (towards the camera) and the up one at its up end. Note the token picking-up and setting-down posts at the left.
Oakwood Collection

Cemmes Road was the junction for Dinas Mawddwy; the original Mawddwy Railway had its own station north of the Cambrian one, an island platform and a simple office. The Cambrian station comprised a loop with two platforms, a large goods shed east of the up platform, and a signal box on the up platform. The connection with the Mawddwy branch was an awkward one, running off the up end of the up loop line and round the back of the goods shed, calling for a train running through to reverse twice.

Machynlleth station (75¼ m) was not especially pre-possessing in itself, with a small but solid building on the down platform and only a shelter on the up. However, its locomotive sheds south of the station played an important part in the working; the smaller two-road shed is believed to be that built in 1863; the larger, three-road one to the west of it was added in 1891. The turntable has been in various places in the yard; the last one was of 55 ft capacity. There were two signal boxes, the east one near the entrance to the locomotive yard, and the west one on the down platform close to the building. However British Rail combined the work of both in a central box of hideous design, at the end of the up platform.

There was a lower goods yard north of the station, a curiosity of which in later years was that the buffers were provided by buffer beams bolted to the bodies of old iron covered vans. To the north again there was the Corris Railway station, which still stands, and exchange sidings between narrow and standard gauge wagons. There was no narrow gauge engine shed, as this was at Maespoeth Junction near the top end of the line. The top goods shed, near the locomotive shed, was let out to industry when goods service ceased, but has now been reclaimed for railway engineering use. Right under the cliff of the gouged-out rock where all this was set, is at present the siding for oil wagons serving the diesel train depot; one of these is mounted on the frame of a McConnell tender of about 1853, and has not moved for some 20 years. In 1990 BR opened a new station building, very basic, next to the old one which was scheduled to become a museum; this scheme fell through and its future is uncertain.

The bridge across the main road over which the west ends of the platforms run is of interest because it formed the start point of the Aberystwyth & Welsh Coast Railway (the Newtown & Machynlleth ended at the road); also because it had to have a small arch at its west side to accommodate the horse-worked portion of the Corris Railway on its way from Machynlleth yard to the Dovey wharves at Derwenlas and other nearby slate-loading points.

The line now followed the south bank of the Dovey estuary, resulting in a somewhat tortuous progress; at 77½ m came the site of the crossing on the level of the Corris tramroad, at Derwenlas. This horse-worked section of the Corris was known to have reached Quay Ward and probably continued to Llandyrnog though physical traces are few. This crossing was not a great embarrassment as traffic on this lower part of the tramroad soon dropped off. Dovey Junction (79¼ m) is one of the country's remotest stations, having no road access. It was simply the place where the line to Aberdovey took off after the great bridge idea had failed. The station lies below the level of the flood plain, and though this was acceptable in steam days, it gave more

The Machynlleth breakdown train in the depot there in 1934; it comprised a six-wheeled hand-operated crane with match wagon, and a four-wheeled riding and tool van. *Author*

The motive power depot at Machynlleth in the 1950s; a Collett 0–6–0 No. 2244 is on the table and 'Dukedog' No. 9000 is in the siding, with former CR 0–6–0s standing on the back road. *Oakwood Collection*

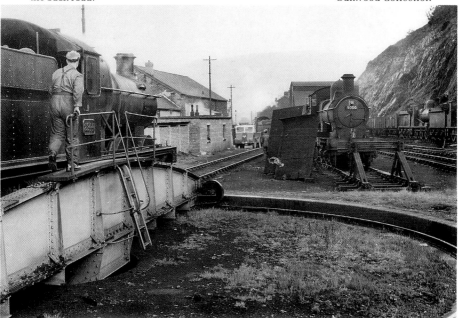

trouble with dmus, and when re-signalling came in in 1988, it was simply not feasible to have the points operating under water, so the two loops each side of the island platform were singled, and the only remaining point moved east to higher ground. Originally called Glandyfi Junction, it had a signal box at the point of junction on the south side; this was replaced about 1958 by a flat-roofed affair on the platform. Also on the platform was a very large refreshment room, replacing one opened in 1881, later simply a waiting room. On the up side at the up end of the layout was a set of sidings; no delivery was possible and they were used only for goods trains up or down the coast to form up or await a path. There was a notable four arm signal on the down approach to direct trains to either side of the island platform or to the loops. The up starter had three arms, with an additional signal post for the north side loop. From the early 1980s passengers were encouraged to change at Machynlleth and not Dovey Junction when going from Aberystwyth up the Coast line, thus having to cover a 4-mile stretch twice. Few trains now had advertised connections there and the station became deserted; though occasional trains did stop at suitable times there was no-one there to supervise them. In the 1990 tables three trains each way were shown as stopping.

Gladyfi or Glandovey station, only 53 chains from the junction, was adjacent to the main road, and had a large station building on the down side and some sidings. It lost its goods service on 19th August, 1963, and passengers on 14th June, 1965. The building was purchased by an absentee owner in Buckinghamshire, son of its last station master, but was allowed to fall into ruin.

Ynyslas (85¼ m) was a small station with crude buildings on the down platform, by a level crossing over the Trer-ddol road; later an up platform was built and an extension of the down one; there were two sidings and the body of a former GWR 4-wheeled coach has been there for many years. The story of the two spurs to the Leri cut, the formations of which are clearly visible, has already been told. Although Savin had ear-marked Ynyslas for a holiday village and port, this did not happen; however a shipyard has recently been opened on the former west-side wharf, no longer rail-served. Some interest attaches to the large walled nursery garden south of the timber bridge across the Leri Cut, provided by Savin to produce vegetables and fruit for his Cambrian (Grand) Hotel at Borth.

Borth station (87½ m) is a large building in brick and stone 200 ft long, its style matching Cambrian Terrace (a row of lodging houses) and the large hotel recently demolished, which stood on the corner between the railway approach and the front (the present Grand Hotel has no connection). There were latterly (from 1912) two platforms, the down one being wooden; a short bay was used for camping coaches, and there was also a siding. The loop line was also extended into sidings at each end, that at the up end being used to accommodate banking engines required to assist trains up the severe (1 in 75) bank to Llanfihangel (Llandre). The signal box was on the up platform, down end; a concrete footbridge was a GWR addition. In the 1970s the down platform was removed and the shelter sold; the loop line had been taken out previously. Chapel Crossing, ¼ m west of the station, was one of the last

Dovey Junction in the 1950s with (*left to right*) the Aberystwyth side passing loop, platform line, Coast Line platform line and passing loop. The sidings are behind the camera; the signal box (also behind) was later moved on to the platform.
Oakwood Collection

Gladyfi station seen here in 1963 was only three-quarters of a mile from Dovey Junction station; its building still stands, for it was bought by the son of its last station master, but is falling into ruin.
R.M. Casserley

At Ynyslas the old low level part of the platform on the down side contrasts with the later extension with signal box beyond; the wooden up platform at the left was a later addition. *Oakwood Collection*

The up platform at Borth, showing the up bay in which camping coaches were placed; the wooden down platform was a later addition; the signal box was on the main platform behind the camera. *Oakwood Collection*

The up end of Bow Street station in BR days, with a 'Manor' class 4−6−0 about to leave for the climb to Llandre. *Oakwood Collection*

The second locomotive shed at Aberystwyth, with the water tower and coaling plant at the right, and Carmarthen line tracks going off in the foreground. A turning loop was put in by the GWR, passing behind the water tower.　　　　*Oakwood Collection*

The main line gradient profile (*continued from p. 87*).

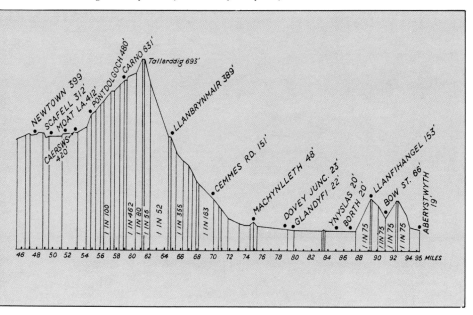

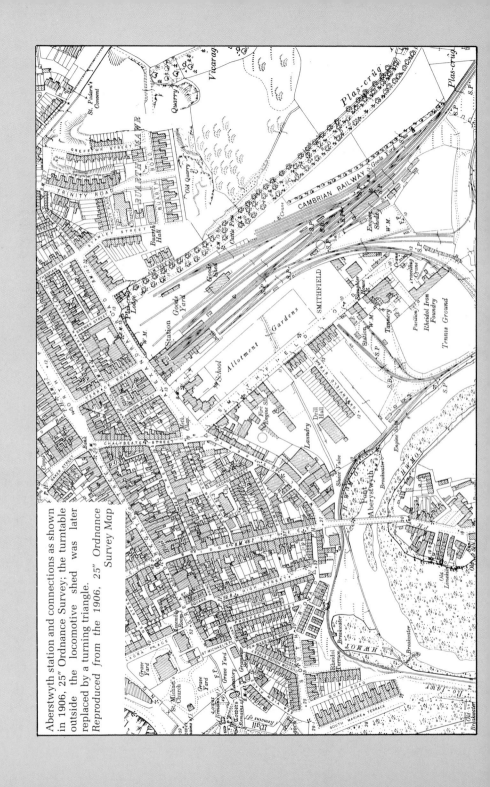

Aberstwyth station and connections as shown in 1906, 25" Ordnance Survey; the turntable outside the locomotive shed was later replaced by a turning triangle. Reproduced from the 1906, 25" Ordnance Survey Map

gated crossings, removed at the end of 1988; it was operated from a nearby cottage. A bridge across a marshy valley a quarter of a mile further on is still a timber one.

Llandre (89¾ m) was called Llanfihangel until 1916. The slate station building differed in style from most others, having a bow front in the centre, with clock. The signal box was on the up platform, down end; a wooden down platform was added in 1910, and there were sidings, goods shed and cattle ramp between it and the road. Double lines ran across the level crossing, that on the east side having been used for a loading platform serving the Hafan & Talybont Tramway, which climbed across the Borth road just before the road bridge. Owing to road engineering, the present position makes this look improbable, but it was so; the tramway crossed the road and ran up the north side of Glanfread Lane. The exchange platform, put in in 1897, was stated to be 300 ft long. The station was closed on 14th June, 1965 and some time later the signal box also closed, a ground frame with metal hut being set up by the crossing gates. This was removed after radio-signalling came in.

Bow Street (91½ m) had a loop, second platform (buildings were on the down one) and extensive sidings between the station and street, on the area now occupied by a builders' merchant. Somewhat unusually, the sidings were connected to the up line, though they were on the down side; however a short siding also came off the down line, fitted with a trap point; the signal box was at the down end of the station.

Aberystwyth (95¾ m) was by far the largest station on the system, though it began as a single platform, the canopy of which still exists (former No. 4 platform); another platform was soon added, with four lines in between. Later this platform was widened and the lines reduced to three. It continued to build up, embracing from August 1867 the Manchester & Milford Railway platforms on the south-west side. Ultimately, after the station frontage had been completely rebuilt by the GWR, it comprised two island platforms; that on the western side was combined with the southbound M&M platform, which was much shorter, as was the second M&M platform against the boundary wall, which was curved at the end to follow the tight curve of that line on to the Rheidol bridge. There was a large locomotive shed on the down side, up end, with turntable; on the other side of the layout were a goods shed, further turntable, cattle pens, carriage sidings, and a large signal box standing near the end of the up platform. In 1935 the locomotive shed was rebuilt and the turntable removed; a turning triangle was made by a spur across from the M&M line, in the middle of which stood the large water tank and coaling ramp which are still a dominant feature of the station skyline after almost all the lines have gone.

The narrow gauge Rheidol branch trains have since 1968 occupied the former M&M platforms. This railway had its original terminus and engine shed between Park Avenue and the river, the site now occupied by a bus depot. In 1925 the passenger terminus was moved to a position outside the west wall of the main line station. In 1968 the former main line engine shed was passed over to the narrow gauge, and the latter's former shed demolished.

A general view of Aberystwyth station in the 1950s: *left to right*, Platform 1 for Carmarthen, Platform 2 serving both the M&M line and the Cambrian, Platform 3 and 4 used for main arrivals and departures; Platform 5 (unroofed) was out of the picture right.   *Oakwood Collection*

The grand façade of Aberystwyth station put up by the GWR in 1924/5; the station itself is due to be demolished, but this façade may be retained for a shopping centre.
Oakwood Collection

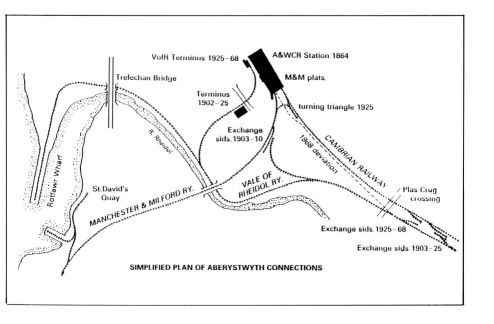

SIMPLIFIED PLAN OF ABERYSTWYTH CONNECTIONS

The following are the Circular Routes

(a) By **G.W., L. & N.W.**, and **Cambrian**, *via* Chester, Ruabon, Llangollen, Bala, Dolgelley, Barmouth, Aberystwyth, Portmadoc, Carnarvon, Bangor, Chester; or *vice versa.*

(b) By **G.W.** and **L. & N.W.**, *via* Ruabon, Llangollen, Bala, Blaenau Ffestiniog, Bettws-y-Coed, Llandudno Junction, Rhyl, and Chester; or *vice versa.*

(c) By **L. & N.W.**, *via* Shrewsbury, Welshpool, Machynlleth, Aberystwyth, Barmouth (Dolgelley), Portmadoc, Carnarvon (by Afonwen or Beddgelert and Llanberis), Bangor, Chester; or *vice versa.*

Circular Tickets are also issued by the Great Western and Cambrian Co.'s in conjunction, embracing Aberystwyth, Barmouth, Bettws-y-Coed, and Carnarvon (L. & N.W.), Dolgelley, Llandudno (L. & N.W.), Tenby, Welshpool, etc.

Passengers may break their journey at the above-mentioned places; also at Oswestry, Gobowen, Corwen, Bristol, Birmingham, Wolverhampton, Oxford, Ludlow, Leamington.

THOUSAND MILE TICKETS.

The Cambrian Railways Company issue first class 1,000 and 500 mile tickets, the coupons of which enable the purchasers to travel between stations on the Cambrian railways during the period for which the tickets are available, until the coupons are exhausted.

The price of each ticket is £5, 5s. 1,000 miles and £2, 17s. 6d. 500 miles, being about 1¼d. per mile.

Application for these 1,000 or 500 mile tickets must be made in writing, giving the full name and address of the purchaser, and accompanied by a remittance, to the General Manager, Cambrian Railways, Oswestry (cheque to be made payable to the Cambrian Co. or order), from whom also books containing 100 certificates for authorizing the use of the tickets by the purchaser's family, guests, or employees can be obtained, priced 6d. each book, remittance to accompany order.

Extract from Baddely & Ward's 'North Wales Part 2', 1912.

An oil depot was set up on the site of former carriage sidings, taken up before the final clearing of 1982, which saw the end of the signalling and the removal of all remaining sidings except three on the east side of the station, now all removed. The layout now (1991) consists of one platform (the western one of the original pair) with a crossover positioned to allow two large diesel locomotives to run round a train; the other end of this loop is by the oil depot, and the single line into the depot comes off this loop, which continues as a siding across Plascrug crossing to a buffer stop. The line from Aberystwyth to Llanbadarn road crossing was double for many years, and off the up line there was a gasworks siding 300 yards beyond Plascrug crossing. Here also, off the down line, was a siding which included a mixed gauge portion for transfers to the Rheidol line. When this was taken up, transfers of narrow gauge stock from maintenance at Crewe was effected by a work train crane on a siding (now removed) which ran on the east side of the engine shed. Up to 1987 this had a short siding off it running to a ramp on which there was narrow gauge track, to allow same-level end-on transfers.

There have of course over the years been many changes to the Aberyst-wyth layout, and this account is only a summary. Now all is flattened, old engine slag, bits of masonry and all sorts of rubbish ground flat by heavy bulldozers; what will occupy the space has been discussed by the local Council for a decade. The former carriage sidings on the east side are also a wasteland, the only remnants being a number of iron lids sunk in the ground labelled 'GWR Gas Oil', being the points on the underground tanks from which carriage gassing-up was done before all lighting was electric.

The platform numbering under the GWR and BR has been: 1, Carmarthen, 2, Carmarthen and main line, 3, main line, 4, main line, 5, relief platform (outside canopy). No. 3 is at present used; No. 5 was still there until 1991 used for parking engines or stock when there are two trains in the station area. There are ground frames half way up the former platform 4 (no rails), and beside the oil siding, plus a third at the end of former No. 1, controlling Rheidol line points.

The Cambrian had not proceeded with its harbour branch here because it wished such traffic to go via Aberdovey. The narrow gauge branch to Rotfawr Wharf saw little traffic after about 1920 and was lifted in 1930. The Manchester & Milford Railway harbour branch was never much of a threat; it seems to have been closed before the 1903 edition of the Ordnance Survey, although the buffer stops on St David's Quay were still in position in 1962. The goods shed there was knocked down later and flats built on the site.

THE COAST LINE

The first section of the line, the deviation built after the idea of a bridge near the river mouth was abandoned, has all the appearance of an after-thought. Dovey Junction itself (4 m) is on an unsuitable site, and the coast line on leaving it had to cross the river abruptly on an unimpressive bridge, which until 1914 had an opening span for the benefit of barges sailing to Derwenlas. Mileages are reckoned from Machynlleth; Gogarth Halt, at 5½ m was a short wooden platform on the muddy edge of the estuary, on the up side; it was opened on 9th July, 1923 and closed in September 1984, though

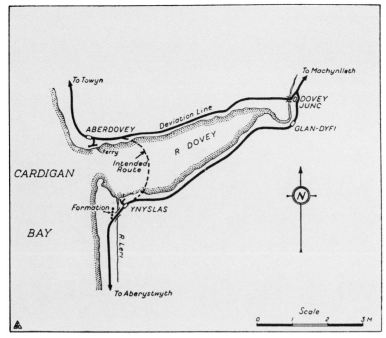

The viaduct across the Dovey would have left Ynyslas and run on a curve to what is now Penhelig Halt. During the years that the railway was open to Borth but not to Aberdovey, an extension of the siding on the west side of the Leri carried passengers and construction materials to Penrhyn Point, opposite Aberdovey Ferry.

Aberdovey looking in the up direction about 1910, with the canopy from the old Pwllheli station re-used here on the up platform; note the small bay for loading horses just beyond the level crossing. *Lens of Sutton*

Another view of the up end of Aberdovey, showing the harbour branch running straight ahead while the main line climbs to the left.   *Oakwood Collection*

The up end of Towyn station in BR days, showing the signal cabin and lay-by on the down side.   *Oakwood Collection*

The extensive sidings at Towyn in the 1950s. The right-hand track led back to the exchange siding with the Talyllyn Railway wharf. The 88½ milepost (*right*) is measured from Whitchurch. *Oakwood Collection*

A picture taken from the road bridge at the up end of the Towyn layout; the exchange siding with the Talyllyn Railway (note the engine *Dolgoch*) has now been removed. *Oakwood Collection*

its last train had stopped there well before. The course of the line is
serpentine as it tries to follow the north side of the estuary; at 6 m is
Frongoch tunnel, through a rocky outcrop and with an old quarry behind it;
near Abertafol Halt (7¼ m) opened on 18th March, 1935 and also closed in
1984, there is another short tunnel, Morfor.

The next halt, Penhelig, opened on 8th May, 1933, is really in the village
of Aberdovey, and at the point where the bridge, if it had been built, would
have met the present course. Two tunnels, Penhelig and Craig-y-don, are
needed to take the line on a raised level round the back of Aberdovey, to
come down to a junction with the sand siding and wharf branch. It would
have been more convenient and much cheaper to stay by the water and build
in front of the village, but fishing and boat-building were the only
occupation the villagers had, and the railway would have interfered with
both. Had Savin been able to face the expense of the bridge in 1863 it would
have much reduced the cost of running the line; on the other hand the
stretch between Gogarth and Penhelig is one of the most scenically perfect
on the whole railway.

Aberdovey station (9¾ m) is beyond the junction with the harbour branch
and well out of the village; it had two platforms and sidings at the down end,
up side, including one to a mill disused from about 1900. There was a
livestock siding and ramp on the up end of the up platform, where there was
also a tunnel for passengers to walk to the beach. The main platform (up
side) canopy came from Pwllheli old station; it was sold on to the Bala Lake
Railway for use at Llanuchllyn. The station building is now private and the
loop lifted, but the main platform is still in use.

Towyn (now Tywyn) station (13½ m) had sidings and a goods shed on the
up end up side; two sidings ran south to the Wharf station of the Talyllyn
Railway for loading slates from Brynyglwys quarries at Abergynolwyn. This
traffic ceased in 1950 when the narrow gauge line closed; however it was
taken over next year by a preservation society and when it reopened 'Wharf'
was its main station; previously Pendref station at the back of the village had
been the main one, and trains were sometimes unwilling to proceed to
Wharf. The exchange siding remained in use for supplying locomotive coal
but this ceased in the seventies. The siding alongside the TR 'wharf' is now
lifted, but the other is in place.

This part of the line is not 'holiday coast'; just beyond Towyn was the
large Morfa army camp and beyond that a branch line to Tonfanau quarries;
this replaced an earlier narrow gauge line, worked by a locomotive, which
had an exchange siding on the Coast Line at 15¾ m. The area around the
Dysynni cut was a firing range, and around Tonfanau station (16 m) there
were further army camps. This is an untidy station, more a halt, with one
wooden platform disfigured by various small buildings, and had little life
apart from the camps. For some years only one train each way has been
permitted to stop. There were now two miles of inhospitable coast before
Llangelynin Halt (18¾ m), opened on 7th July, 1930, a short wooden platform with an iron shelter.

Tonfanau station was not opened until 1895 and was little used; note the six temporary buildings on the platform, probably due to uses at different times by the nearby army camp. *Oakwood Collection*

Llangelynin Halt was little used, and in 1992 has no trains, closure having been applied for. *Oakwood Collection*

Llwyngrwil station, with the building on the up platform; the water tank is a legacy from the period when it was a terminus; the signal cabin was on the down platform behind the camera. *Oakwood Collection*

Winding track as the line begins the climb up to Friog Rocks on the way to Fairbourne.
Oakwood Collection

The main line side of Barmouth Junction (Morfa Mawddach); the Dolgelley branch runs to the right of the main building. The down platform (*left*) was a later addition.
Oakwood Collection

Llwyngwril (20 m) besides being the hardest name to pronounce, was also the terminus of the service from Aberdovey begun on 24th October, 1863; for this reason it had a large water tank and water points on both platforms. At the down end the track was tiled for drainage of water from standing engines. Its short siding at the down end, up side, had a camping coach from the 1930s. The train now embarks upon a breath-taking ride along a shelf in the cliffs, the sea edge below strewn with all kinds of objects to break the force of the tide; the disasters here, and the steps taken to make the line safe, are described elsewhere. Nervous passengers may well be relieved as the train coasts down the 1 in 55 towards the flat land of Fairbourne. This station (22¾ m) was opened on 6th June, 1899, and is of poor construction. A 2 ft gauge horse tramway which had been carrying bricks from a yard just north of the station was adapted to carry passengers to the ferry at Penrhyn Point, using two improvised bogie carriages with canvas covers and open sides. Passengers had used the ferry in the period 1865–7 before the Bridge opened, but either walked or used a horse carriage kept at Penrhyn. In 1916 the horse tram was replaced by a 15-inch gauge miniature railway; this has undergone several changes of management, and was closed from 1939 to 1946. Recently the original railway has been removed and replaced by one of even narrower gauge. Some confusion is caused by the fact that in many guide-books pre-1914 it is marked as 'electric tramway' – it never was. The ferry station has at various times been at both sides of Penrhyn; it runs to the Quay at Barmouth which is 500 yards from the station; for many years a steamer ran from there to Penmaenpool.

Morfa Mawddach (24 m) was 'Barmouth Junction' until 1960; there was a triangular layout, but no platform was ever built on the south curve, for direct running from Machynlleth to Dolgellau. This curve was singled around 1900 and used as a siding; it was originally opened to traffic on 3rd July, 1865, for trains from Aberdovey; the west curve would have been laid at that time for construction of the bridge, but was not open for traffic until 1867, at the same time as the north curve. The station originally had three platforms, two on the main line and one on the branch, but about 1890 a down platform on the Dolgellau line was added. There was also a bay platform at the end of the up Dolgellau platform, used from 1934 for camping coaches. There was a large signal box at the north end, up side, and smaller ones at the east and south junctions. As the Barmouth turntable would not take all types of engines working through from Dolgellau (which was less restricted than the main line) the triangle was sometimes used for turning engines.

At the East Junction there was, in the early days, a crossing on the level of a narrow gauge tramway built by Soloman Andrews from quarries to the south providing stone for the Bridge abutments and for the building of The Crescent development at Arthog; a branch ran to the east side of the station; much of the formation can still be seen.

The Barmouth Bridge (it would have been called a viaduct in England) was the Cambrian's biggest engineering feature: 113 wooden spans and eight in iron at the north end, with a sliding span (converted to a swinging bridge in 1900) for navigation, which was sparse. The whole was 800 ft long and there is a footpath alongside the railway.

Barmouth viaduct as rebuilt with a swinging rather than a sliding span for navigation, looking south.
Oakwood Collection

The extra platform south of the road crossing at Barmouth station, put in by the GWR, looking south; in some years there were no Sunday trains north of Barmouth and they terminated here.
Oakwood Collection

Barmouth station looking in the up direction from its down end, with a two-coach train in platform No. 3.
Oakwood Collection

Llanaber Halt was a wretched wooden affair put up by the Cambrian and never rebuilt by the GWR; note the sea defences on this stretch of line.   *Oakwood Collection*

Talybont Halt looking south; the GWR improved this Cambrian halt by lengthening the platform and removing a siding.   *Oakwood Collection*

Talwrn Bach Halt is of Cambrian design although it was opened in 1923 shortly after the GWR took over. *Lens of Sutton*

Llanbedr & Pensarn, once plain Pensarn, had a loop but no second platform. Note that the signal cabin is in the centre of the platform some way from the level crossing gates.
Oakwood Collection

Llandanwg Halt was opened by the GWR in 1929 but could not have been more basic; for years it was just a foot-note in 'Bradshaw'; later it became a booked stop, but is now again conditional. *Lens of Sutton*

Barmouth (25½ m) is in effect two stations, since the GWR in 1923 built a platform and booking office south of the level crossing; this was to increase capacity, but proved useful later when the line north of Barmouth was closed on Sundays, since a train could be run without opening the level crossing. Latterly road traffic across this became so dense that the signalman had difficulty getting the gates open for the train. On the north side there is a wide island down platform and a narrower one on the up line having the station building on it. There were several sidings north of the station on both sides, including one for the local gasworks; also a large goods shed; a water tank was located in the goods yard. The main signal box was beyond the island platform, down end; there had been a turntable at the up end of the down side.

Llanaber Halt (27 m) and Talybont Halt (29¼ m) were both erected at the end of the pre-grouping period; the latter had a siding originally, but was rebuilt by the GWR with no siding but a longer platform. Dyffryn Ardudwy (30½ m) was renamed twice, being plain Dyffryn until 1924 and then Dyffryn-on-Sea to 1948. It was probably changed again as it was a mile walk to the sea. A camping coach was in the siding from 1934. The brick station building was a replacement for an early wooden one. Goods services ceased in 1963; there had been a crane and livestock facilities, the siding being on the east side facing south.

Talwrn Bach Halt, a Cambrian-style one opened by the GWR on 9th July, 1923, is at 32¾ m in Llanbedr village, and only ¾ m from Llanbedr & Pensarn station (originally plain Pensarn), which had a loop, plus a siding loop, signal cabin and level crossing; it stands at the mouth of the Atro River and close to 'Shell Island'. The line leaves the coast briefly but hastens back to it at Llandanwg Halt (34 m) opened on 18th November, 1929. At Harlech (36 m) we are only 5½ miles from Black Rock Halt in a straight line, but the railway takes 12 miles, as it now diverges north-east. Harlech is an important station; the up platform, added later, has a GWR 'pagoda' shelter. Two grounded bogie coach bodies decorated the siding on the landward side. There was at one time a horse-tram to the beach a mile away.

Tygwyn Halt was opened on 11th July, 1927; one can understand why the name of the village nearby was not used; it is Llanfihangel-y-traethau. The line is running straight and level; Talsarnau (39½ m) had a goods yard on the east side boasting a crane. Landecwyn Halt (40½ m), opened 18th November, 1935, is at the water's edge as the line turns north and then west to cross the Traeth Bach by a wooden toll road bridge. Penrhyndeudraeth (41½ m) was notable for the sidings containing gunpowder wagons, though the siding did not actually run into the Cook's (ICI) Works; this traffic was killed by the closing of the Barmouth Bridge for a period in the 1980s, and subsequent banning of locomotives. The signal cabin was at the up end; the unpretentious station building has recently been put up for sale. The Festiniog Railway station here is half a mile to the north. However the Coast Line now swings round in a half circle to cross under the Festiniog at Minffordd (43½ m), where the narrow gauge station is immediately above the cramped Cambrian one, which has sidings on two levels for loading slate from the narrow gauge wagons. A short distance on there was a siding on the up side for a granite quarry.

A livestock train in the up platform at Harlech in the 1950s; note the two grounded bogie coach bodies used as stores in the sidings, and the spacious sheep-loading platform, in use on this Sale day.   *Oakwood Collection*

Penrhyndeudraeth in the 1950s: a train for Pwllheli is entering hauled by a 2–6–2T, and in the siding on the right is a train of gunpowder wagons, headed by a Collett 0–6–0. The old-established gunpowder factory was across the road from the sidings and no rails actually ran into it.   *Oakwood Collection*

There is now a level stretch for 2 miles, across the Traeth Mawr marshes, made reasonably firm by Mr Madocks's embankment across which the Festiniog Railway runs closer to the sea. At 44 m came the level crossing with the Croesor Tramway and shortly after that of the Gorseddau Tramway; the latter ceased to be used about 1892, but the former became part of the Welsh Highland Railway (WHR) in 1923, for which the GWR built a small signal box at the crossing. From 1931 WHR trains from Beddgelert terminated north of the crossing when possible, to avoid paying dues to the GWR.

Just before the level crossing at Portmadoc station (44¾ m) a short branch goes off to the north, the points facing the station; this was the 'Beddgelert Siding'. It probably started as the course of the abortive Beddgelert Railway, but it was used as an exchange siding for slate traffic from the Croesor Tramway. It was lifted in 1973 and the Welsh Highland Railway (1964) Ltd obtained a light railway order in 1980 to use its bed as part of their line, intended to reconstitute the former WHR as far as Beddgelert. Some track had been laid and used alongside the siding in 1978, together with a depot for acquired stock.

The Cambrian station covered a large area; there was a locomotive depot on the up side, down end, and sidings for timber and slate on the down side. A granite quarry tramway down the face of Moel-y-Gest ran alongside the line just west of the goods yard and into an exchange siding; for a period it was also connected to the Gorseddau Tramway. The level crossing was an extremely busy one; not only were there many extra trains in the summer, but also short trips to Minffordd quarry and slate sidings, ballast trips to Wern from Machynlleth and working the Beddgelert siding.

There was a long shunting neck on the down side, down end, from which goods trains could run direct to the up line. The refreshment room became a public house which lasted long after all other glories had departed. Portmadoc has had a remarkable number of stations; the Festiniog Railway one was always called Harbour, and there was High Street Halt on the connecting line to the WHR. This company called its station 'Portmadoc New', and used the same name when it was moved north of the GWR crossing. When the new WHR started public trains, it laid down a station just east of the BR level crossing simply called Portmadoc; a further station called Pen-y-Mount, ¾ m away, was the end of the line in 1991. This totalled seven stations in all.

Because Portmadoc was so fully developed before the Cambrian arrived, it was forced to run round the back of the town, and this in turn made it necessary to pass on the landward side of Moel-y-Gest, instead of the flat coast the other side; the result was three-quarters of a mile at 1 in 50 for down trains, and a similar distance at 1 in 54 in the up direction. A banker from Portmadoc helped out, being attached to an up train at Criccieth for the return. At 46½ m came Wern Siding, under Portmadoc control, a Cambrian Railways ballast quarry. Black Rock Halt (48½ m) was opened on 9th July, 1923; originally a small wooden platform with black iron shed, it was later enlarged with a more handsome shelter, but weather damage finally forced its closure on 13th August, 1976 (official date was 27th June, 1977).

This view of Minffordd station shows the bridge over which the Festiniog Railway runs, and on the right the curved siding on two levels which was used for exchange of slate traffic.   *Lens of Sutton*

Portmadoc station from the level crossing, looking in the down direction, with the engine shed beyond the footbridge; the extensive goods and slate sidings were to the left, behind the goods shed visible above the down platform shelter.

Oakwood Collection

The line was now back on the foreshore, where it would stay, but a rock outcrop at Criccieth (49¾ m) forced a gradient each side of the station, which for many years had the importance of being used by Lloyd George and his family; there was a large goods shed and a building which did not disgrace this town of up-market boarding houses.

Afon Wen Junction (54 m) was used in common with the LNWR (later LMS) whose line from Bangor came in from the north, the last 13 chains of this branch being Cambrian-owned. There was nothing at all at this beach location except a three-platform station and a large water tank on steel legs. The footbridge arrangement was unusual; one from a path gave access to the down end of the island platform on the up side of the station, but that leading to the down platform was at the other end. The signal cabin was at the down end of this, with the water tower and engine siding beyond it. LNW engines had to cross the CR to water and coal; other than that, LNW trains normally had the use of the outer face of the island platform, but in GW days the pointwork was altered so that GW trains could also use this platform.

At 54¼ m is Penychain Halt, opened on 31st July, 1933. On the seaward side here Butlins built a large holiday camp in 1939; just as it was being finished, it was taken over by the Navy as 'HMS Glendower'. After the War some further work needed doing, and the Camp did not open until the 1947 season. A camp station somewhat detached from the halt was built on the seaward side, with brick waiting rooms and wooden platform; the old halt platform was also refurbished, and the line doubled to Afon Wen, since most of the Butlins traffic would be coming via Bangor and the LMS. For a time in the summer Pwllheli trains used the Butlins platform for down trains (if not occupied) and the old one for up trains, but by the 1970s the camp station had fallen into disuse as most campers came by car. The pressure of camp traffic in the 1950s made necessary some alterations at Pwllheli engine shed.

Abererch Halt (55¾ m) was opened by the Cambrian, a solid stone platform with signal post in the centre carrying two arms to give notice to trains to stop. In 1933 it was upgraded to a station and given a short siding for a camping coach, becoming unstaffed in 1956; it is now a halt again.

At 57¼ m came the original Pwllheli terminus station; the main building was on the down side, and a locomotive shed and carriage shed on the up side. After it was closed in 1909 the locomotive shed was moved to the down side and the carriage shed demolished.

The present station (57¾ m), features an island platform of considerable length, each face with an engine release road beside it. A large one-storey wooden building spreads across the concourse, with a wide yard for buses outside. The old station retained its sidings on the down side; the station canopy was moved to Aberdovey. The new station was built adjacent to a 2 ft 6 in. gauge horse tramway opened by the Corporation in 1899 running to the new promenade. Another horse tramway, this time 3 ft gauge, ran from the Post Office, a short distance away, to Llanbedrog on the Lleyn peninsular, though passengers had to change cars at the beach end of Cardiff Road, as this tramway was operated in two sections. All closed by 1929.

Afon Wen Junction, c.1935, showing the ex-LNWR 'coal' tank engine working the line to Bangor using the water-tower, which was on the edge of the beach; there were no houses nearby. The left-hand side of the island platform was normally used by LMS trains. *Author*

Black Rock Halt, in the sand dunes of Morfa Bychan, was at one time a crude platform with a black hut; it was improved in GWR days (it was planned but not opened before 1923), but nevertheless by 1977 more or less fell down before being officially closed. *Lens of Sutton*

A view from the coal; a Dean 0-6-0 ready to take a train out of Pwllheli in August 1931; the single platform had a line each side, both with engine-release roads.   *Author*

Cambrian motor-bus No. 1, a two-cylinder Orion, put on in June 1906 between Pwllheli and Nevin.

GWR buses parked on the north side of Pwllheli station: Maudslay No. 1565 and Morris No. 1665; next year (1931) all appeared in Western Transport red livery.   *Author*

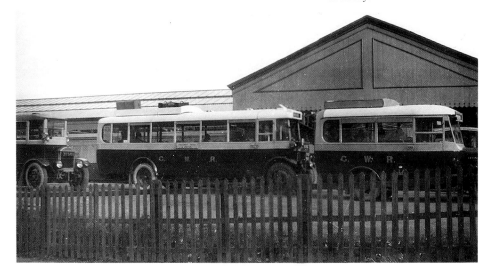

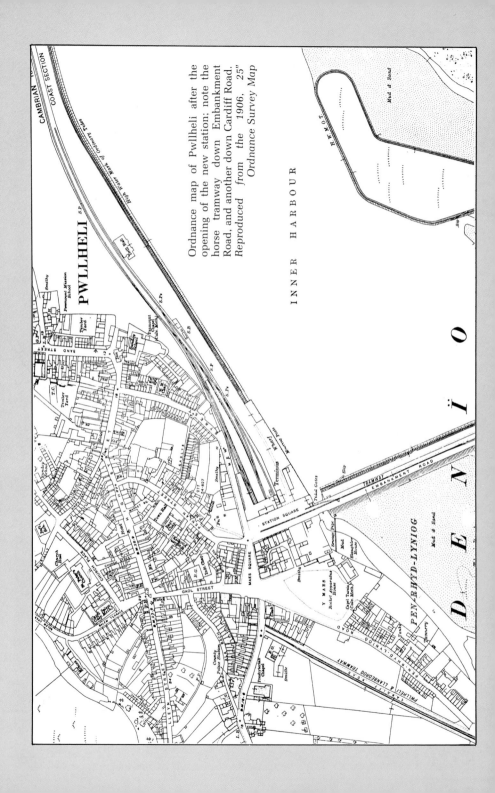

Ordnance map of Pwllheli after the opening of the new station; note the horse tramway down Embankment Road, and another down Cardiff Road. Reproduced from the 1906, 25" Ordnance Survey Map

Though now a bleak ending to what is virtually a siding from Portmadoc, Pwllheli was once very busy; the track from the old station was doubled in 1923. In the early 1930s long trains from Paddington mingled with short trains of four-wheeled carriages for Barmouth or Machynlleth; there were the observation cars to be detached and run round; in a short siding off the upside release road a gas-container wagon was kept. Outside, buses of the GWR, LMS-Crosville, Tocia Motors, Nevin Blue and other fleets waited, many with chalked excursion boards propped against them. By the 1970s, the buses had gone and the station forecourt was a car park.

THE MID-WALES LINE

(No pictures of this section are included as they are fully covered in the author's 'The Mid-Wales Railway' also published by The Oakwood Press.)

Moat Lane Junction, where this line joined the main line has already been described; the level crossing a few hundred yards on is the site of the original Llanidloes & Newtown Railway station, and the next two stations, Llandinam (2 m) and Dolwen (5 m) were both single-platform affairs built by the L&N; the former, which adjoined the large house of the famous David Davies of Llandinam, had sidings. These stations remained open for freight until 2nd October, 1967 to service the building of the Clwedog dam. At Llanidloes the early L&N station was on the Newtown side of the large joint station (7¾ m) erected in 1864 to serve three railways: the L&N (Cambrian), Mid-Wales, and Manchester & Milford, though no trains of the last-named ever appeared. The large brick building had two wings; the down platform was an island, and at the up end were two engine sheds, one for the L&N and one for the Mid-Wales, though this latter was later taken down and the turntable moved to its site. There was a goods shed, sidings and cattle pens at the north end, west side. The Thomas Ironworks was adjacent to the sidings. The north signal box was by the engine shed, the south one at the down end of the up platform.

Nearly two miles on comes the site of Penpontbren Junction, where the Mid-Wales Railway tracks joined those built, but not used by, the L&N. Here the formation of the Llangurig branch of the Manchester & Milford Railway can be found across the Dulas; rails were laid but never used (unless one believes the local story that one goods train did run). Tylwch Halt (11 m) was a station until 1939, and lost its down platform and goods yard some time before it closed; goods working ceased in 1953. The station building on the up side is now a house called 'Tylwch Halt'. This stretch of line, with its rock cuttings and glimpses of the rushing river, hints at how difficult railway-building would have been in the Cambrian Mountains to the west, through which several early railways were routed on paper.

Glan-yr-afon Halt (12½ m) was near an existing siding of that name, but was put in by the GWR in 1928. The line is climbing at rapidly-varying grades, the last three miles to the summit near Pantydwr being at 1/77 to 1/111; the descent on the other side is less steep. Pantydwr station (14¾ m) had a short siding with cattle dock at the up end of the down platform, and a signal box on the up platform. The line now left the Dulas valley and cut through ground to reach the valley of the Marteg; St Harmons (16¼ m) had

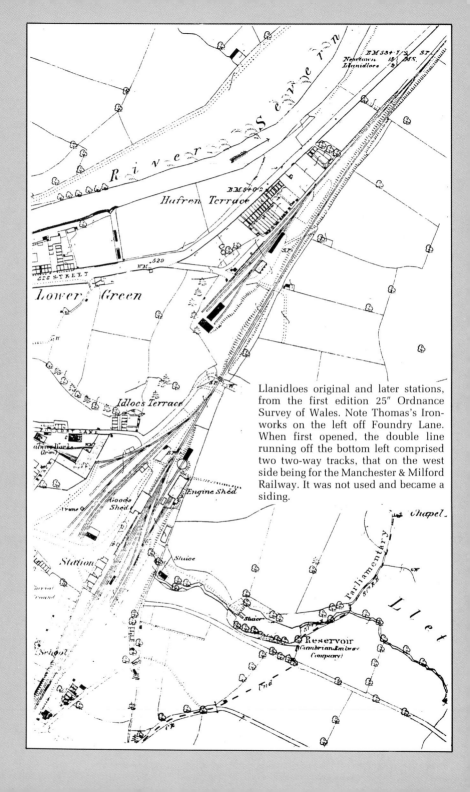

Llanidloes original and later stations, from the first edition 25″ Ordnance Survey of Wales. Note Thomas's Ironworks on the left off Foundry Lane. When first opened, the double line running off the bottom left comprised two two-way tracks, that on the west side being for the Manchester & Milford Railway. It was not used and became a siding.

no loop, but a siding across the road beyond the level crossing. It was opened in 1879 and saw little traffic, being unstaffed from 1936, but not called a halt.

The Marteg or Gilfach tunnel is 372 yards long; originally it was bare rock but was later lined. Half a mile further on, where the line passed under the A479, was Marteg Halt, opened on 18th May, 1931, a wooden platform approached by a long flight of wooden steps. Here the line comes into the wide valley of the Wye; had a branch to Trawscoed and Aberystwyth planned in 1864 been built, it would have used the upper part of this valley. There was a high bridge, the pillars of which still stand, over the river at Cwm-Coch, known as the 'M' bridge; the Mid-Wales lettered its major bridges from A (at Penpontbren) to T at Trefeinon.

The line now stays on the west bank into Rhayader (14 m), an important station with stone building, water tank and signal box on the down platform, and large goods shed on the up side; these remain today in other use. The main sidings on the up side formed two loops; but though one had a platform face, it was not so used. A half-mile further on, having passed through a 271-yard tunnel, came Elan Junction, where the Waterworks railway of the Birmingham Corporation took off to the right for its six-mile climb into the mountains. A signal box and loop were put in at the junction, but all wagon-exchanging was carried out at Noyadd just up the branch, where there was more level ground. From the junction there is nearly a mile of 1 in 60 falling, an impossible task for up goods or through trains without the help of bankers, which were stationed at Doldowlod (24¾ m), an otherwise featureless station, now a caravan site. There were two platforms with a signal box on the up platform; the sidings at the down end, down side, were closed in January 1962 for goods, though retained for banking engines, which had a slip crossing to the up line, until the line closed at the end of the year.

At 26¾ m came Watts Siding and at 29 m the station at Newbridge-on-Wye, the most important on the Mid-Wales both for local passengers and tourists. It comprised a long up platform and a shorter down one, with the signal box at its north end and a goods shed behind it.

The line now crossed its highest viaduct, over the Ithon near its junction with the Wye. All Mid-Wales Railway high bridges were built cheaply using cast-iron pillars with cross-bracing; later it was necessary to enclose these in stone or concrete, but even this did not prevent severe engine weight restrictions and a ban on double-heading. Beyond Thomas's siding comes the spur from the Mid-Wales to the Central Wales line (CWR) at Builth Road. This was built by the Mid-Wales but soon after sold to the LNWR; it was very seldom used for passenger trains. It joined the CWR well west of the station near the locomotive shed. The Mid-Wales station (32¾ m) lay below that of the CWR, with a footpath and later luggage lift connecting them; the former was named Llechryd until 1889; the apellation of 'High Level' and 'Low Level' was not applied until 1950. The Mid-Wales had two signal boxes, one at the spur junction and another at the down end, down side.

It was now only a short run down to Builth Wells (34½ m) which was an important centre in pre-Cambrian days, with locomotive shed and carriage shed and repair facilities. The station building was on the up platform, with a water tank, beyond which was a level crossing and north signal box beyond that. All the facilities and goods arrangements lay in a triangle of land at the down end, up side, occupying a considerable area. The south signal box was beyond the down platform.

Past the Llanelwedd stone quarries siding was Llanfaredd Halt (36½ m) opened in 1934; Aberedw (38 m) was a single platform with no loop, built on a gradient rising for down trains of 1 in 112, which increased to 1 in 75 past Tyr Celin, a small private platform. Erwood (41¾ m) was somewhat separated from its villages by the fact that the line kept to the east side of the Wye; it had staggered platforms with a signal box on the down one. Llanstephan Halt (43½ m) was a tiny wooden platform with a large name-board proclaiming 'Llanstephan Radnor Halt'; it was opened on 6th March, 1933. The other halt of the same name, with which confusion was avoided, was Llanstephan Crossing at the Welsh Agricultural Show ground.

Boughrood & Llyswen (45½ m) acquired its second name in 1912, no doubt because that village, though on the wrong side of the Wye, was the larger. It was a rather decrepit station, with a small waiting room at the down end of the up platform, a signal box at the up end, and a level crossing a considerable distance to the north with the station master's house beside it. As the Wye turns east, the railway crossed it on a viaduct, 150 ft long but not high, and then across the smaller Afon Llynfi to enter Three Cocks Junction (48¼ m). This was intended as a triangular junction, but the north spur was never completed. The station lay in the south apex, with four platforms, those to the east being used by the trains of the Hereford, Hay & Brecon and later Midland Railway; the signal box was between the lines at the south end of the centre platform. Here the Mid-Wales met the old Hay Tramroad, whose wayleave they would use (with some deviations) to Talyllyn Junction; the tramroad ran east of the later station. This is now a Calorgas depot, but a concrete memorial to its former status has been put up. The first 29 chains of the line to Hereford had been Cambrian property. There was a chemical factory at Pontithel.

Talgarth (50½ m) was a major station, with water tank on the down platform and a large goods shed south of the station on the down side. Trefeinon, a small station with level crossing, was not an original station, and the second platform and loop were added later. Llangorse Lake Halt (54¾ m) was added in 1923, a wooden platform with corrugated iron shelter.

The end of the Mid-Wales Railway came half-way along the East and North loops of the Talyllyn Junction layout (56 m). The Mid-Wales Railway had its original station at the north junction of this triangle, and the Brecon & Merthyr had theirs (called Brynderwen) at the West junction. They were 600 yards apart, and a joint station was obviously called for. This was opened by the B&M more or less on the Brynderwen site in 1869. The Mid-Wales station had platforms on both the north and east loops, the latter being necessary for trains to and from Newport and beyond running through to Aberystwyth, and it seems this station remained open for such trains until 1878; it later became a bungalow and trains stopped in the loop to change engines, without passengers being able to alight. There was an engine shed within the triangle, but it was for the B&M shunter.

On B&M metals, the Mid-Wales trains continued through the ancient tunnel at Talyllyn, built in 1818 for the Hay Tramroad (but much altered) to Brecon (60 m). The Watton station, which was first used, lay near the Abergavenny Canal basin, and had two engine sheds, one for the MWR, and one for the HH&B and B&M. The Mount Street station of the Neath & Brecon Railway used as a terminus by the MWR from 1868 to 1871, was just beyond the Free Street bridge; the 'joint' station opened in 1871 was off Free Street, and comprised three platforms and a bay for Hereford trains. The engine shed and goods facilities remained at Watton, and there was a spur line from this low level station up to Free Street, which was on a higher level line built from Heol Lladron (or Brecon) Junction to a junction with the Neath & Brecon Railway.

THE LLANFYLLIN BRANCH

Perhaps the least interesting of Cambrian branches, this one, opened on 17th July, 1863, originally left the main line just north of Llanymynech; the process by which it later left from south of that station has been detailed. From the old junction, it was only a short distance to Rock Siding, which sought to serve the narrow gauge tramways coming down Llanymynech Hill, one of which ran under the Cambrian (as two branches) to wharves on the Shropshire Union Canal.

The branch in its final form had a halt (opened on 11th April, 1938) at Carreghofa (¾ m) beside the road and canal overbridges. At Wern Junction the new spur to join the old branch ran to the left; the line straight ahead was the Nantmawr branch under lease from the Shropshire Railways, and to the right could be seen the lifted part of the old branch between Wern Junction and Rock Siding. Llansantffraidd (3 m) had a single platform and three sidings, with an overhead mobile crane straddling the siding for lifting timber. Llanfechain (5 m) was also a single platform.

Bryngwyn (6¾ m) was shown in the 1866 'Bradshaw' with one train on Tuesday and one on Wednesday. Later it was called a 'flag station'; a signal post with slotted arms was placed in the centre of the platform. It was approached by a long wooden staircase on its south side; the original wooden shelter was replaced by a corrugated iron one; Bryngwyn Hall, for which it was no doubt built, lay half a mile south. Llanfyllin (8½ m) comprised a single platform on the south side, with a goods shed opposite, and a rather long run back to the locomotive shed (closed in 1951) and turntable, on the south side.

THE TANAT VALLEY BRANCH

The Tanat Valley Light Railway included a piece of line from the Porthywaen branch west of Llynclys Junction, which ran parallel with that branch for a short distance, parting from it at Porthywaen signal box; a halt here was used as a ticket platform for Oswestry as there was no further stop; this was 4¾ m from Oswestry. Shortly after, the former Nantmawr branch of the PSNWR was joined, east of the old Llanyblodell station, now renamed

The terminus at Llanfyllin, showing the signal cabin on the platform and the goods shed opposite; the engine shed is behind the camera. *Oakwood Collection*

Bryngwyn station as rebuilt by the GWR; it was originally a wooden 'flag station' with a passenger-worked signal in the centre. *Oakwood Collection*

Llanfechain on the Llanfyllin branch had only one platform, but a substantial station house. *Oakwood Collection*

Blodwell Junction (6 m). The old brick platform was used, and a signal box built at the west end. The 2½ m line to Llanymynech now diverged left and the main new construction curved right, to a new Llanyblodwell station (6¾ m). As befitted a light railway, all stations had ash platforms and iron buildings.

Glanrafon Halt (7¾ m) was built around 1905 at the request of Mr J. Harmer, who partly paid for it; its platform was only 75 ft long against the 170 ft of the others. It was regarded as a 'flag stop' until GW days. Llansilin Road (9¼ m) had a single platform with a loop siding on the south side. Llangedwyn (10¾ m) had two platforms, a cattle siding, water-tank and ground frame by the level crossing. Pentrefelin (12¾ m) was a single platform with ungated crossing. Llanrhaidr Mochnant was another two-platform affair with a goods shed on the north side; Pedair Ffordd (15¼ m) was a single platform. At Penybontfawr there was only one platform, but a loop, and at one time two siding loops, one of which may only have been used during the building of the second Vrynwy aqueduct. Just beyond the line passed over the aqueduct by a series of low bridges; it was here in pipes, not open.

Llangynog (19½ m) had a single platform with engine release road and on the south side a water tank and engine shed (closed 1909). On the north side was an exchange siding with the narrow gauge incline coming down from Craig-Rhiwbarth quarries. In 1910 the platform line was extended across the road to a siding serving the Ochr-y-Craig lead mine, and here also granite chippings were loaded from the Ochr-y-Craig and Makers granite quarries. Chippings from the Berwyn Granite Quarry, Cyrniau, were loaded in the station yard from lorries. All this traffic began to die in the 1950s and the branch west of Llanrhaidr was closed in 1952, the eastern part remaining open for freight until 1964.

THE WREXHAM BRANCH

This branch left the main line at Ellesmere, the junction having been already described. Owing to the decision of the Cambrian to work it push-pull, and the Great Western's introduction of steamcars, there were a remarkable number of halts. The first, Elson Halt (1¼ m) opened on 8th February, 1937, later had a Royal Ordnance Depot adjacent. The second was Trench Halt (2¾ m) opened in December 1914. Overton (4¼ m) was a station, but was followed by Cloy Halt (5¼ m) opened on 30th June, 1932; Bangor-on-Dee was a two-platform affair, with wooden buildings, and was followed by two halts very close together, Pickhill (8¾ m) opened on 30th May, 1938, and Sesswick (9¼ m) an earlier Cambrian one, opened in October 1913. Between Elson and Trench the line crossed over the Lake Vyrnwy aqueduct.

Marchwiel (10½ m) also had an ROD; the wooden station building was on the down side and the signal box on the up platform, down end, with sidings opposite. A girder bridge on five stone piers carried the line over the Clywedog Valley. Hightown Halt (12 m) opened on 1st October, 1923, was the last before Wrexham; however first came the Adenbury Brickworks siding on the up side (12¼ m), the formation on the down side of an earlier

Llanginog station looking 'up'; there was originally an engine shed where the locomotive (2−4−0T No. 1197) is standing. *W.A. Cranwell*

Lady Margaret, a former Liskeard & Looe Railway engine, shunting at Llanginog in
1934; behind can be seen the incline to the Craig Rhiwbath quarries. *Author*

A Llanginog train at Penybontfawr about 1904, Tanat Valley Light Railway. There are coal wagons in the station loop, and timber trucks and a mobile crane in the siding. A later goods loop followed the line of the boundary hedge; the small hut by the cart is a weighbridge.   *Author's Collection*

Llanrhaiadr Mochnant station on the Tanat Valley Railway seen here as opened; all the stations had corrugated iron buildings and ash wood platforms.   *E.C. Burns*

Llangedwyn station had two platforms; note the ground frame without any cover at right. *D.J. Powell*

Llanyblodwell (Tanat Valley) station; the former PSNWR station of the same name was rebuilt as Blodwell Junction. *D.J. Powell*

Marchwiel station looking in the up direction; the wooden station building had a canopy over the platform and over the entrance from the station approach road.

Oakwood Collection

Marchwiel on the Wrexham branch looking 'down'; note that the slip crossing provides an extra run-round, and that up goods trains can leave direct without a reversal.

Oakwood Collection

half-mile branch to the Barracks, and at 12½ m the Caia goods station.
Wrexham Central (12¾ m) was a joint station with the WM&CQR (later GCR and LNER) which made an end-on connection via the WMCQ-owned spur through the town from its Exchange station, lying beside but a bit below the GWR's Wrexham station, later called General. The Central station had two platforms and a bay on the north side, west end. There was a turntable on the down side, down end and a goods shed on the up side. A small engine shed (closed 1922) was built at Caia; the GWR shed was at Croes Newydd and the WMCQ one at Rhos-ddu. Following the passenger closure on 10th September, 1962, Overton and Bangor goods sidings closed on the same day, but Wrexham Central lost its goods service on 7th December, 1964 and Marchwiel on 4th September, 1972. Pickhill siding closed in 1941, but the Cadbury siding nearby lasted to 27th March, 1965.

THE KERRY BRANCH
Leaving the platform at Abermule, at ¾ m came Middle Mill Siding, on a tortuous curving section with five bridges after which was the tiny halt at Fronfraith, 27 ft long, with a siding disused early on (1¾ m). Goitre (2¾ m) was near the top of a 1 in 43 gradient. A siding to a brickworks was at the level of the platform top with a point trailing for down trains. The summit at 3 m had a stop board. Kerry station (3¾ m) was spread over a large area, with the engine shed first (closed 1931), on the up side, then several sidings, and a platform with large station house at the far down side end. The 1888 1 ft 11½ in. gauge Kerry Tramway had an exchange siding at the back of the platform; there was some 5 miles of track, serving woodlands and timber works; it was closed down in 1895, but some parts re-opened in 1917 worked by German prisoners. Kerry station had ground frames at both ends, and in early years used a sector table for running round rather than points. The Kerry branch had a long period of goods-only use (1931–56) during which the track became very weed-grown; it was finally lifted in 1958.

THE NANTMAWR BRANCH
As already stated, this was a branch of the Potteries, Shrewsbury & North Wales Railway, taken over by the Shropshire Railways and leased to the Cambrian. It ran from the south-west end of Llanymynech station, a double line junction, via Rhydmerydydd Siding (1¾ m) and Llanyblodwell to the quarries at 3¾ m, Nantmawr. At ¾ m it passed under the canal and road, and it also passed over the Llanfyllin branch, at what became Wern Junction when, under the re-arrangement described in that section, a spur went off westwards to Llanfyllin. After Blodwell Junction was built for the Tanat Valley Light Railway at the former Llanyblodwell station, the Nantmawr branch joined the Tanat Valley at its west end and left again at the east end, curving round to Nantmawr, with a siding first at the Llanddu quarries, which had a narrow gauge line from the siding passing over the main road to the quarries, and this was in use up to the late 1980s. The quarries at Nantmawr latterly operated by BQC, also had a ¾ m tramway running north. Traffic here ceased in the 1970s.

THE PORTHYWAEN BRANCH

This branch, built by the O&N in 1860/1, tapped at Porthywaen the same
stone deposits as did the PSNW Nantmawr branch. It left the main line north
of Llynclys station, with a double-line junction, sidings on each side, signal
box, water tower and coal stage. Beside it on the south was the 3 ft gauge
Crickheath Tramway which carried stone to a wharf on the Shropshire Canal
and was still in place in the 1930s. After a siding connecting to the narrow
gauge track of the Dol Goch quarry, the route of Savin's private line to his
New British Coal Pit at Coed-y-Go (about 2 m) went off to the north; this is
said to have worked only from 1861 to 1869 and was derelict before 1880; it
began with a very steep gradient. A siding then diverged and burrowed
under the branch to enter Whitehaven pit; as it did so it ran as a three-rail
track; the western rail for both standard and narrow gauge and the centre rail
for narrow gauge only; this rail had chairs on every second sleeper only. In
the pit, the Crickheath tramway diverged right from the Cambrian sidings.
The pit covered a wide area and included the Pear Tree pit (east), Hunt's and
Little Rock centre, Cooper's and Joey's, west. The branch proper continued
climbing to some sidings and lime kilns fed by a double tramway incline up
the hill at Porthywaen (1¾ m), 300 yards east of the nearest part of the
Nantmawr branch.

When the Tanat Valley branch was built it diverged from the Porthywaen
branch not far from Llynclys Junction and ran beside it, crossing the Crickheath Tramway on the level by the signal box opposite Porthywaen Halt; the
TVR ran south of the box and the Porthywaen branch north of it. There were
some alterations to track over the years; a siding serving Pear Tree Quarry
was taken off the branch before it began climbing over the old siding
entrance to Whitehaven pit; also a crossover was put in just east of the box
enabling trains from Llynclys on the TVR track to run into the Whitehaven
complex, or to the works sidings which replaced the former timber siding at
Porthywaen village.

THE VAN BRANCH

By the time the Cambrian took over the Van Railway in 1896, passenger
traffic had ceased; however the stations were still there, as they are today,
used as houses. On leaving the separate station at Caersws with its short
platform, run-round, goods shed and engine shed (down end, up side) the
line crossed the R. Carno and the road (level crossing) and at 2 m reached
Trewythen Siding, which had no platform or building. Red House (2¼ m)
was the same. Trefeglwys, the first real station (4¼ m) was sometimes called
Pwll-glas; it was some way from Trefeglwys village, the birthplace of the
Piercy brothers. Here there was a level crossing, station house, sidings and
coal stage; at Cerist (5¼ m) the layout was similar. After crossing the
Llanidloes road, Garth & Van Road, the passenger terminus appeared;
station master's house, platform and short siding; there was probably a run-
round originally. The line carried on some 300 yards to points where the
Cambrian Railways' ballast siding ran off to the down side, while the other
line curved right into the Van Mines complex, ending in a run-round with
no extra sidings. Many of the buildings and chimneys here still stand,

The Van Mines about 1900, with Manning, Wardle 0−4−0ST No. 22 shunting in the loop; the double gravity narrow gauge incline can be seen to the right of the nearest chimney. *Author's Collection*

Kerry terminus in 1934; *left to right*, the passenger station, single platform and station building (now a house), weighbridge hut, sidings, and one-engine locomotive shed at the right, which still stands in 1991. *Author*

Blodwell Junction station in 1934, with a rebuilt 'Queen' class 0–6–0 No. 900 setting off for Nantmawr; note that Tanat Valley line trains from the far right line are not able to use the loop.   *Author*

A later view of Blodwell Junction from the Llanginog end; beyond the bridge the Nantmawr line went straight on and the TVR line to Oswestry swung right. *D.J. Powell*

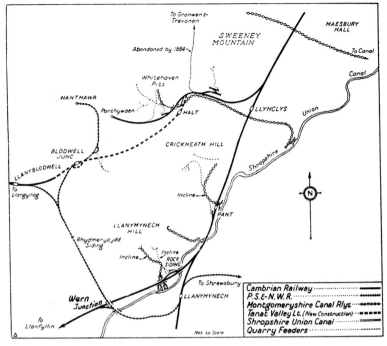

A map of the lines in the Llanymynech area.

'Lady Margaret' came from the former Liskeard & Looe Railway to Oswestry in 1923, at a time when the 'Seaham' on the branch was under repair; she worked the Porthywaen and Llanginog branches for many years, mainly on goods workings; seen here at Porthywaen in 1935.   *D.J. Powell*

Wern Junction in 1937 from the canal overbridge; the right-hand line is the old one to Blodwell Junction, and the left the spur which enabled trains to run direct to Llan-fyllin without reversing at Rock Siding.
R.S. Carpenter

This goods train from the Porthywaen branch is at the point where the track of the Crickheath Tramway, gauntleted with the standard gauge, is about to cross the Tanat Valley Line on the level; note the trap-point.
Lens of Sutton

Whitehaven pit on the Porthywaen branch. The photographer is standing on the bridge which carries the branch proper over the siding, which burrows under it; at centre right there is a square crossing of the GWR track with that of the narrow gauge Crickheath tramway. *Author*

A Llanginog train near Porthwaen Halt in 1947, with 2–4–0T No. 1197; this was always an ungated crossing and taken very cautiously. *W.A. Camwell*

though the double self-acting narrow-gauge railway incline to quarries above has gone, also the long launder which fed the water-wheel until steam was introduced.

The line was not worked between 1893 and 1896. Some mining continued until 1920 and the CR and GWR ran some goods, timber and ballast. The tracks beyond the ballast siding junction were lifted by early 1939 and all had gone by summer 1941; the official closing date was 4th November, 1941.

THE DOLGELLAU BRANCH

When what became the south loop of the Barmouth Junction triangle was opened on 3rd July, 1865 there was no station there, the Barmouth Ferry station being to the south; presumably there was a siding to serve the Bridge works. The arrangements at this station, now Morfa Mawddach, have already been described. Arthog station (1 m) (opened March 1870) had a siding but no loop, and did not offer goods facilities; it was unstaffed from 1955. At 3 m there was Garth Siding, which connected with a narrow gauge tramway to some quarries. Penmaenpool (5¼ m) was a curious station, on a thin strip of land beside the Mawddach estuary. Opposite the station was a wooden bridge, later purchased by the Cambrian Railway and 300 yards west beyond the George Hotel was a locomotive shed, closed in 1965. Dolgellau station (6¼ m) was the Great Western one, though it is thought that the Cambrian had a temporary station for a few months where the two companies' metals joined west of the present station; the GW station had a turntable at the east end, south side. Barmouth to Dolgellau was 'up' in 'Bradshaw', so a through train from Machynlleth at the south junction changed from 'down' to 'up'.

SHREWSBURY JOINT LINE

Since this joint GW/LNW line is now seen as the main line for what is left of the Cambrian, it merits a short description. From Buttington Junction the first station, Breidden (3 m) was called Middleton up to 1912 and Middleton Hill to 1918. Plas-y-Court Halt (5¼ m) was followed by Westbury (6 m) a normal passing place, and then Yockleton Halt (9¼ m) and Hanwood (12¼ m). This was the junction for the Minsterley branch. A mile and a half further on the joint line passed under a brick bridge carrying the Shropshire & Montgomeryshire line from Llanymynech, which continued alongside on the south side, with an exchange siding at Hookagate (no station on the joint line). The large Hookagate PW depot, once a feature on the down side, has now virtually disappeared. There was also a WD depot from 1941 to 1960. Meole Brace was an S&MR halt, and soon after this the line ran off right, across the GW Worcester line, to Abbey Foregate station in Shrewsbury. At Sutton Bridge Junction the joint line met the Worcester line to run into Shrewsbury (17 m), passing Coleham Goods station and Severn Valley Junction, where the former line of that name took off. Cambrian line trains had the opportunity to by-pass Shrewsbury station by using the Abbey Foregate Loop, which passed south of the gigantic signal box to give direct running to Wellington.

All stations and halts were closed to passenger traffic on 12th September, 1960.

Penmaenpool station building (*left*), the George Hotel (*centre*) and the engine shed beyond. A wooden bridge, at one time owned by the Cambrian, ran to the right across the river to the main Dolgelley to Barmouth road. *Oakwood Collection*

The Penmaenpool engine shed lay some way west of the station itself; the engine in residence is Standard class 2–6–4T No. 80080. *Oakwood Collection*

THE DINAS MAWDDWY BRANCH

Starting from its separate station at Cemmes Road, one platform with booking shed, the line crossed the R. Twymyn on a timber bridge, rebuilt in 1911; the first station, Cemmaes (1¾ m) had a small wooden platform with a long siding sweeping round the east side to a track from the village (now a through road); a timber bridge across the Dovey followed. There were two sidings north of here, one called Dol-y-Fonddu at 2¾ m and the Nantcliff Silica Siding at 3½ m; neither was used for very long. Aberangell (4¾ m) was notable for two things; a wide arched bridge over the R. Angell south of the station, and a long raised loading ramp on the down side beyond the single platform, for loading slate from the Hendre Ddu Tramway. This 2 ft gauge line ran some 4 m into the mountains to the west, having several branches. It was very active in the 1892–1914 period; some traffic continued up to the late twenties, including during World War I some timber felling. In 1893 transport of tourists to the quarry was advertised.

Staying close to the west side of the Dovey, the line reached Mallwyd (5¾ m), a short platform on the down side. Bullock's Siding was just before the terminus on the down side, comprising two lines, the westmost one having transhipment arrangements with a 2 ft 2 in. gauge railway running down from quarries in the mountain, a line half a mile long with two inclines. Dinas Mawddwy station (6¾ m) was in Minllyn rather than the main village, and had a platform and house on the west side; this line had no loop, but had points running into the engine shed, closed 1931, the run-round being at the up end of the layout; from the loop line of this a siding ran through a goods shed to the station wall, an unusually splendid one.

Much of the terminal area has been given over to the Meirion Mill premises, but the station building is a tea-house and the engine shed is in use as a store, with outside water-crane still in place. In 1975, 600 yards of 2 ft track with a steam engine *Trixie* were put down by the Mill for visitors, but it has now gone, apart from a few yards with wagons on display.

Only Aberangell among the intermediate stations was kept open after the passenger closing in 1931, until 30th June, 1951.

THE WELSHPOOL–LLANFAIR BRANCH

The Llanfair railway now starts outside the town, but in Cambrian days it ran from the station yard, and the locomotive shed and sheep and cattle docks were located where the line, having left the passenger station, took a turn to the west; a carriage shed was adjacent to the engine shed. The Stondart Quarry Tramway, laid about 1818, had started at the canal basin at Pont Howell and passed through the town on a narrow wayleave, which though the tramway ceased working in 1854, was still available 50 years later. Part of this was used by the Welshpool & Llanfair (W&L) on its way to Seven Stars Halt and Raven Square (1 m), the end of a sharp climb at 1 in 33/36. The quarry tramway had taken a route along Brook Street but the W&L took a more northerly route, passing the terminus of the tramway at the quarry at Dol-y-felin. Some relics of this tramway have been preserved, including some three-ribbed rail from a road crossing which suggests that double-flanged wheels may have been used; the gauge is given as 2 ft 6 in. but was more likely to have been 3 ft.

Cambrian livery again, at Capel Bangor on 17th October, 1987; Rheidol Branch No. 8
carried this livery from 1986 to 1991, when it reverted to its former name 'Llwelyn',
but still in black livery.   *Author*

The station at Dinas Mawddwy was entered through an attractive wall with pillars
for the double gates; the building on the left is now a café.   *Oakwood Collection*

Although not pictured by most people as a heavily graded line, probably because its trains were never heavily-loaded, in fact the first five miles was very much a switchback, with half a mile of 1 in 29 starting a mile beyond Raven Square, with some 1 in 42 (also up) beyond Golfa (2¾ m) and some up and down at 1 in 32/33 through Sylfaen Halt (3¾ m), (opened in 1913 as the Sylfaen Farm Siding) to Castle Caereinion (5 m) after which the descent through Cyfronydd (6½ m) was quite mild; from Heniarth (7¾ m) to Llanfair (9 m) it was almost level. Between Cyfronydd and Heniarth there were two rivers to cross, the Cwmbaw by a six-arch stone bridge, and the Banwy by a steel girder viaduct of three spans. Castle Caereinion had a loop and signal box; Llanfaircaereinion had a loop, two sidings for coal traffic, and a goods shed.

After being taken over by the Preservation Society, the railway ceased to affect the Cambrian station at Welshpool, though some narrow gauge track remained in place until recently; the terminus for the Llanfair line became Raven Square and the engine shed facilities moved to Llanfair.

THE VALE OF RHEIDOL RAILWAY

This narrow gauge branch line has been described in detail in many books, and only a summary is needed here. It was opened for passenger traffic on 22nd December, 1902, and absorbed by the Cambrian in 1913; it was sold by British Rail in 1988. The Aberystwyth terminus was off Smithfield Road (now Park Avenue); a two-line station, with carriage sidings, and a double engine shed by the river, where a harbour branch diverged. In 1925 the line was extended to end outside the GWR station, and in 1968 it was re-routed from Plas-Crug crossing to run into the former Manchester & Milford platforms within the station, the former GWR engine shed being taken over also.

After passing under the M&M, with a siding on the north side to the former M&M sidings, there was a transfer siding with the CR at Plas-Crug, later (1925) moved closer to the station by the GWR. Llanbadarn (1¼ m) had a siding and level crossing; Geufron ballast siding was by the timber bridge over the Rheidol, the subject of weight and speed restrictions. Glanrafon Halt (2¼ m) was opened on 7th May, 1904; Lovesgrove Halt (3¼ m) was used by the Volunteers' summer camps from 1911 to 1913. Capel Bangor (4½ m) had a carriage shed on the riverside, entered from the loop by a reverse from a siding; this slipped into the encroaching river. Nantyronen (6¾ m) became a water point in 1982 (but had no loop); previously water was taken by up-valley trains at Aberffrwd (7½ m), opened on 27th April, 1904, which had a loop, sometimes clipped for periods, taken out in 1963 and restored in 1990. Rheidol Falls (9¼ m) was a halt opened in March 1904; half-a-mile further came the famous Erwtomau curve; at its apex was a lead mine, but there was no siding, loading of wagons being carried out as they stood on the main line. Rhiwfron (10¾ m) had a siding for a lead mine. Devils Bridge station (11¾ m) had two main lines and three sidings; the water-point was below the station, on the far side of the sheer cutting through which trains spectacularly entered. The layout here has been simplified.

This is a very heavy line to work, the strain of gradients being compounded by severe curves, mostly with check rails. Climbing starts at 5½ m with some 1 in 50, then after half a mile of level ground, it is climbing all the way except for level ground at stations, 5½ miles of 1 in 50 right to the terminus; there is no break for Rheidol Falls halt. Down-valley trains have some severe checks at curves and an hour is allowed each way. Since 1990 trains can pass at Aberffrwd; though this is not the middle of the line geographically, it is so time-wise, owing to climbing. No passing loop anywhere was in use from 1963 to 1990.

THE CORRIS RAILWAY

Although the Corris Railway was never part of the Cambrian, its presence at Machynlleth cannot be ignored; indeed today (1992) as the Corris station there still stands, together with some small station shelters up the valley, Maespoeth Junction engine shed and parts of Corris station, it is far from forgotten. Some track has been re-laid between Maespoeth and Corris, and working occasionally takes place.

The horse-worked section west of Machynlleth is not easily followed, though the gate through which it left the road near Derwen-las to cross the Cambrian is still in place, as is the small arch in the overbridge of Machynlleth station; after passing through this, oddly enough the horse tramway had a loop in the roadway as it turned to enter the yard area, which was on the north of the presently surviving station.

After leaving the Machynlleth terminus, the line ran north-west to cross the Dovey River on a timber viaduct, rebuilt in iron about 1900. There was a halt at Fridd Gate (½ m) closed early, and another shortly after at Doldderwen; Lliywdy was at 1½ m, Llwyngwern 2½ m, junction for a short branch to a slate works to the east, now used as an experimental wind power centre. All the time the line is climbing the Dulas Valley with the road on its left, with some short sharp gradients, but the only long one is a quarter of a mile of 1 in 60 before Esgairgeiliog (3½ m). At Maespoeth Junction (4½ m) there was no station, but the engine shed and water point for the railway (there was no locomotive shed at Machynlleth or Corris). The main line turned north-east, while the Upper Corris branch followed the road. This 2-mile branch was worked only by horse and mainly laid in light flat-bottom rail; some original bridge-rail could be found on branches, of which there were several, the chief slate workings being at Braich Goch and on both sides of the valley at the end of the line; recent landscaping has made these difficult to follow.

Returning to the main line, Corris station (5 m) was a large loop with a carriage shed in the centre; the line went on to Garneddwen station (closed early) and Aberllefeni (6½ m) beyond which were extensive quarries still working until recently, after the railway had closed. Beyond these again, the Ratgoed Tramway continued another 2 miles to the remote Ratgoed Quarry, this private section being horse-worked.

Chapter Seven
Under the Great Western

The Great Western was not like the other three 'big four' railways after Grouping. It did not need breathing space to sort out its identity, since all the companies it had been amalgamated with were so much smaller than itself. So without delay the Great Westernisation of the Cambrian began, with an infusion of locomotive power, which while better than most of the existing stock, was not at all modern. Another GWR feature was the lavish provision of halts; the Cambrian had just opened a few, but the new management might be said to have 'over-egged the pudding', putting down platforms at most unlikely places. Gogarth Halt (1933), for example, just north of Dovey Junction, was called after a local farm because there were no houses there. The next one down the line, Abertafol (1935), was at least in a very attractive place; Penhelig (1933) was closer to the centre of Aberdovey than the station was, but never attracted much traffic. And so on up the Coast Line; Llangelynin (1930), Llandanwg (1929), Talwyn Bach (1923), Tygwyn (1927), Llandecwyn (1935), Black Rock (1923), and Penychain (1933). They were wooden, with small square corrugated iron shelters, unlike the splendid 'Pagoda' shelters used on the GWR's early halts in England.

The Mid-Wales line acquired Glan-yr-afon Halt in 1928, Marteg (1931), Llanfaredd (1934), Llanstephan (Radnor) (1933), and Llangorse Lake (1923). On the Wrexham branch, which already had two halts, new ones were added at Elson, Cloy, Pickhill and Hightown. On the Whitchurch line Tinkers Green Halt was put up in 1939 for the army at Oswestry Camp. Carreghofa Halt appeared in 1938 close to the beginning of the Llanfyllin branch, and the main line got one, at Commins Coch in 1931.

The Great Western policy in England had been 'put up the halts, then bring on the steamcars'. However it was different in Wales; although steamcars were duly introduced from 1922, apart from the Wrexham branch they did not serve halts, their main duties being between Barmouth and Dolgellau. They were a mixture of 70 ft and 60 ft cars, and it was found that the longer ones were not suited to the Penhelig tunnels; some 60 ft cars were sent to Machynlleth, but they mainly worked from Moat Lane to Llanidloes, though there were trips up the Coast Line as far as Criccieth. From 1927 they began to be replaced by auto-trains.

The Cambrian atmosphere began to evaporate, as big brother put up its preferred type of signals and used the branches to find work for its last non-bogie stock. By 1930 only 50 Cambrian carriages remained in service, many with iron sheet panelling. Another custom previously alien was the siting of Camp Coaches in suitable sidings; they were to be found at Borth, Bow Street, Towyn, Fairbourne, Barmouth Junction, Dyffryn on Sea, Talsarnau, Afon Wen, Abererch and Aberdovey.

It was still a glorious area for the railway enthusiast however; more or less a working Great Western Museum. There were 'Barnums' and 'Dukes' aplenty, and little tank engines from English branch lines, plus a few from South Wales; and some of the new signalling was a modeller's delight. Perhaps there was an excess of zeal here; the fixed distant for down trains near the top of Llandre bank must have seemed ironic to a driver slogging up at a snail's pace.

An auto-train for Dolgelley in the bay platform built by the GWR on the up side of the level crossing at Barmouth. *Lens of Sutton*

Peckett 0–6–0ST No. 680, formerly of the Alexandra Docks & Railway, at Oswestry in 1934 having banked a mineral train up from Llynclys Junction. *Author*

The Great Western made some improvements on the narrow gauge Rheidol branch, providing two new engines (Nos. 7 and 8) in 1923 of a similar design to the original ones, and in 1924 No. 9, officially a rebuild of a Davies & Metcalfe engine, but in fact another new one almost similar to Nos. 7 and 8. Also it built new carriages, including 'summer coaches' with unglazed sides. At Aberystwyth, the line was extended from the old terminus (on the site of the present bus garage) to the street outside the main station; there was a run-round here, but the engine shed and carriage sidings remained west of Smithfield Road (now Park Avenue). The GWR also officially recognised that the Harbour branch was closed; this ran behind the engine shed to Rotfawr Wharf and had been little used.

The GWR was now very interested in motor buses, and soon their chocolate and cream livery was seen in many areas, not least the Lleyn Peninsular where the Cambrian had made its rather puny efforts. The buses parked beside the station at Pwllheli were a mixed bunch; small Thornycrofts, large Guys and Maudslays mainly. They were in competition on the Edeyrn route with the long-established Tocia Motors and other local operators. By 1930 it had been decided that for railways to run buses under their own name was not a good thing, and the routes and vehicles were hived off to new companies, that covering the northern area being Western Transport, the routes in the south part of the former Cambrian mainly went to Western Welsh.

One innovation had been the operating of a railway-owned Morris half-track 'bus', which ran trips from Aberystwyth station to parts of Plynlimon which were beyond the road.

As part of its bus expansion, the GWR had taken over Bristol Tramways Group, and with its bus services in the Machynlleth area came the Corris Railway. This had been opened as a horse-tramway in 1859, from the slate quarries at Aberlefenni and Upper Corris to the River Dovey at Derwen-las. It became a passenger line (apart from the Upper Corris branch) in 1883, working to a large station built beside the CR lower sidings at Machynlleth. .Unlike other narrow gauge lines, it had little tourist traffic, and the GWR closed the passenger service on 1st January, 1931; slate carrying continued until 1948; a description of the route is given in Chapter Six. Two of the three engines, and one carriage, survive today running on the Talyllyn Railway.

The Great Western enforced severe speed restrictions on parts of the lines, and also maintained the 14 ton axle weight restriction from Moat Lane to Three Cocks on the former Mid-Wales line, which meant in effect that this became a preserve of the Dean 0–6–0s; however elsewhere locomotive power was increased, with virtually no restriction for trains to Barmouth via Ruabon and Dolgellau, which bore the brunt of the post-Great War holiday boom.

Trains were now heavier and in summer more frequent than in Cambrian days; the GWR was heavily dependent upon the skill of seasoned operating staff in keeping the banking engines and pilots, now so often needed, in the right place at the right time. The Cambrian had been generous in the provision of loops, some such as Talerddig strategically-placed with banking engines in mind.

A steamcar for Aberdovey entering Barmouth Junction in 1929; these were more frequently seen on the Dolgelley service. *Rev. B. Edmonds*

Light pannier tank No. 2054 at Oswestry in 1934; this class, originally saddle-tanks, could operate on all branches. *Author*

One of the liabilities taken on by the GWR was the maintenance of the portion of line which ran down a shelf at Friog Rocks south of Fairbourne station. This shelf was well above sea level, but needed continual protection if it were not to be undermined. The Cambrian had done what they could, but not enough; the GWR engineers decided in 1930 upon a radical programme of dumping thousands of tons of rocks, each weighing 6–10 tons, at the foot of the old Cambrian sea-wall, which although 33 ft high at the Barmouth end was only 25 ft above Ordnance Datum at the north end of its half mile stretch. The work was carried out on Sundays, when there were no trains; a crane was located at the site, and two engines used to bring stone both from the south and north ends of the site to feed it. It is worth mentioning here that the process had to be repeated in 1955; on this occasion a different method was used, a rake of loaded wagons being propelled from Barmouth to the crane, which lifted each wagon after it was unloaded and placed it on the track behind it, until all wagons were discharged. There is of course no room for a temporary siding on the shelf.

This was only an extreme case of a larger problem of sea protection; at many places on the Coast and along the Dovey Estuary the introduction of quantities of quarried rock or pre-cast concrete blocks has been needed over the years.

Friog came into the news on 4th March, 1933, when a landslide came down and dashed ex-Cambrian 0–6–0 No. 874 down on to the rocks 190 feet blow, totally destroying it. In 1936 concrete arches supported on substantial piers on the cliffside and skewbacks into the rock were erected to carry any landslide over the line.

In the early 1930s the through trains from London, from Euston at 10 am and Paddington at 11.10 am both arrived at Pwllheli at 7.8 pm; there was the luxury of a buffet car on the Aberystwyth portion from Whitchurch. Four out of six trains on the Dolgellau branch were now advertised as one-class motors; the Kerry branch had three trains; Llangynog had an extremely complex table: of the down trains, one was Monday, Tuesday, Friday only; one Wednesday, Thursday, Saturday, one not Saturdays, one Saturdays only, and one on the first Wednesday in the month! Llanfyllin got five trains, and the Wrexham branch eight, seven of them motors.

The passenger service on the Dinas Mawddwy branch was discontinued as from 1st January, 1931; as regards the goods service, this is known to have ceased finally in 1951, but a notice published in the *Montgomeryshire Express* on 1st March, 1930 announced that the railway goods service would be replaced by a road motor on that date; only Aberangell and Dinas Mawddwy would remain open for the road motor service.

The Talerddig 'summit' has always been a factor in planning engine workings. It is not an even climb; for westbound trains the steepest part is a short piece of 1 in 71 near Pontdolgoch; however for trains going east there is a very hard pull, with three miles of 1 in 52–62 at the end of it. Some trains were able to do without pilots going west, but the other way double-heading was usual and often a banker also. There was another problem; the loop at the summit could only take an engine and ten coaches. When the summer loading had risen to 13 coaches on occasion, care had to be taken that two

No. 98, a '94 class' 4–4–0, seen here at Oswestry in 1937 as GWR No. 1043; one of the few Cambrian engines superheated by the GWR. *H.C. Casserley*

At Aberystwyth in July 1934; the bowler-hatted station foreman discusses the problem of having three 'Dukes' and a pannier-tank stuck in Platform 3. The train in Platform 2 (*right*) is for Carmarthen and in Platform 4 is a London train. *Author*

such trains did not arrive at Talerddig together, not easy in the boom years before 1939, and just after the last War. The Collett 0–6–0s and small 2–6–2Ts usually acted as banking engines, though the former were quite capable of running the train on from Talerddig, if it so happened that two of them had brought the train up from Machynlleth. Though double-heading was used on passenger trains, banking was invariably applied with goods trains, in case of a broken coupling.

There were of course other banks requiring assistance; for example from Doldowlod up to Rhayader on the Mid-Wales. Here double-heading was forbidden between Three Cocks and Llanidloes, and banking engines used to come out of the sidings at the south end of Doldowlod and couple on the rear of northbound trains if at all heavy. The Aberystwyth line also had its minor summits; that at Llanfihangel (Llandre) required a pilot to be added at Borth to down trains, and because of a further mile of 1 in 75 west of Bow Street the pilot often continued to Aberystwyth. Up trains had 2½ miles of climbing almost from the start, and could not 'rush' the Llanfihangel bank, even after a mile at 1 in 75, because almost all trains stopped at Bow Street, with a start straight on to the 1 in 75 up. Nevertheless, the up trains always seem to make easier work of it than the down ones, where the curve under the bridge at Llandre carrying the Borth road saw engines near their last gasp.

A train which intrigued railway enthusiasts in the late 1930s was that from Barry to Llandrindod Wells, the only regular service using the Builth Road spur. What interested them was the fact that in both directions the train had to be propelled along the spur; and that as there was no turntable at Llandrindod Wells, the engine had to work tender first into Builth Road. Here the return train met a local from Builth Wells, with a Cardiff engine, also running tender-first, and the two trains exchanged engines. One enthusiast described the trip on this train southwards, three coaches with a '23XX' 0–6–0, logging a start-to-stop speed to Talgarth of 40 mph, and 'all but 60 mph between Philips Siding and Boughrood'.

The late 1930s were the best years for holiday traffic on the Cambrian. The recession over, there was money to spend, and not very many families yet had cars. The Mid-Wales share was of course small compared with the stream coming via Shrewsbury or Oswestry or Ruabon, but there was enough LMS red to enliven the scene, and it was in the middle of the best year of all that War came again.

World War II affected the Cambrian lines less than most others; the Camp at Oswestry produced some traffic for the halts on both lines adjacent to it, and there were many other War establishments, such as the Navy at the new unopened Butlins Holiday Camp at Penychain, Pwllheli. However, the gunpowder factory at Penrhyhdeudraeth remained small. It was the Wrexham branch which saw most military activity and this was closed from 10th June, 1940 to 6th May, 1946 to passenger traffic, so as not to hinder traffic to a large ROF at Marchwiel, and military stores elsewhere on the line. Workmen's trains were run from Oswestry to Elson Halt, calling at Tinkers Green Halt.

No. 57 as GWR No. 1192 in 1926 filling its tanks at Oswestry preparatory to working a
train to Llanginog; with its prominent GWR boiler fittings this engine shows little of
its Cambrian origin.   *H.C. Casserley*

No. 63, one of the 1893 4—4—0s, seen here on shed at Oswestry in 1926 differs only
from its earlier form in having GWR boiler fittings and smokebox and raised tender
sides in place of coal rails.   *H.C. Casserley*

After the War the tens of thousands of workers ready for a holiday responded to the call from Butlins, whose Pwllheli Camp released from Service use in 1947, saw a great flood of customers, which in turn called for an enlargement of Penychain Halt and the doubling in 1947 of the line from there to Afon Wen. Passengers came from all over, but more often from the Midlands and North, and special trains ran via Bangor, reversing at Afon Wen. However many also came from South Wales, and a Saturday train was run from Swansea via the former M&M line to Aberystwyth, reversing there and at Dovey Junction.

Aberystwyth also got its share of holidaymakers, and for them the Rheidol branch was re-opened on 23rd July, 1945, with two trains each way. Ticket issuing was limited to the capacity of seven coaches, which was the limit even with expert driving. Double-heading was not allowed. The engines had spent the War in the recently-enlarged shed at the junction with the wharf branch in Aberystwyth, and the coaches either in the Capel Bangor shed or sheeted at Aberystwyth. At the end of the season all three engines went to Swindon for overhaul in preparation for heavier traffic to come.

LOCOMOTIVES UNDER THE GWR

The immediate 'first aid' to the Cambrian locomotive department provided by the new owner comprised 'Barnum' and 'Stella' and '3232' class 2-4-0s, 'Duke' 4-4-0s, a few 'Aberdare' 2-6-0s, but chiefly the Dean '2301' class 0-6-0, the first of which had actually arrived on the Cambrian in 1920, and which would be the mainstay on almost all sections for 30 years. Some specific requirements were met from the Great Western's now large stud of non-standard absorbed engines; ex-Brecon & Merthyr 0-6-0ST No. 20 (GWR 1677) was sent for shunting at Machynlleth; two ex-Alexandra Docks Railway Peckett 0-6-0STs (Nos. 18, 19, GW 679/680) took turns at Oswestry on the Porthwaen traffic. Ex-Culm Valley branch 0-6-0T No. 1376 and ex-Liskeard & Looe Railway 2-4-0T *Lady Margaret* were on the Tanat Valley line.

Not that the Great Western massacred the Cambrian stock out of hand; much of it was allowed to go on for 10 years and more. The most remarkable case is that of the 'Queen' class 0-6-0s, the original Sharp, Stewarts. By 1928 there were still four of them at work, Nos. 14, 45, 48 and 51 (GWR 898, 900, 908, 910). Nos. 45 and 51 were at Portmadoc, mainly on short trips to Minffordd and ballast duties; the other two were at Oswestry working local goods trains including trips to Nantmawr and Llanddu quarries. No. 908 had a four-wheeled tender, though it had acquired a six-wheeled one at its 1896 rebuilding, and a similar one was restored when it was transferred to the Lambourn Valley branch in 1932 (rebuilt in 1927 as stated earlier). The life span of these four engines was remarkable: 898, 72 years; 900, 81 years; 908, 65 years; 910, 70 years. No doubt good workmanship played a part, but the main reason for their longevity was their light weight (28¼ tons) which gave them the entrée to parts of the Cambrian denied to the more modern engines.

Until 1932 no engines were seen north of Barmouth other than the Dean and Cambrian 0-6-0s and the '3521' class 4-4-0s, also both classes of 2-4-0, though the 'Stellas' went very soon. In 1926 the Great Western had

Great Western Railway

Radnorshire Agricultural Society's Show at Llandrindod Wells.

Wednesday, August 20th, 1930

CHEAP TICKETS

TO

Llandrindod Wells

(Via BUILTH-ROAD and L. M. & S. RAILWAY).

FROM	Times of Starting				Third Class Return Fare.	
	a.m.	a.m.	a.m.	p.m.	s.	d.
Llanidloes	—	8 0	10 18	12 54	3	11
Tylwch	—	8 5	10 25	1 1	3	6
Pantydwr	—	8 15	10 33	1 10	3	0
Rhayader	—	8 30	10 49	1 25	2	2
Doldowlod	—	8 40	10 57	1 37	1	9
Newbridge-on-Wye	—	8 53	11 5	1 47	1	3
Brecon	7 15	—	10 40	1 20	4	2
Talgarth	7 40	—	11 10	1 47	3	0
Three Cocks	7 47	—	11 15	1 54	2	9
Boughrood and Llyswen	7 53	—	11 22	2 0	2	4
Erwood	8 2	—	11 30	2 9	1	10
Aberedw	8 8	—	11 40	2 15	1	6
Builth Wells	8 18	9 40	11 50	2 25	1	0
Llandrindod Wells arr.	8 58	10 4	12 45	3 5		

Passengers return from Llandrindod Wells same day at 6.0 p.m.

CONDITIONS OF ISSUE.

Children under Three years of age. Free ; Three and under Fourteen. Half-price.
Excursion and other tickets at fares less than the ordinary fares are issued, subject to the Notices and Conditions shown in the Company's current Time Tables.

LUGGAGE ARRANGEMENTS.

CHEAP DAY TICKETS.—Passengers holding Cheap Day Tickets may carry with them 60lbs. of marketing goods at Owner's Risk, free of charge, all excess over that weight to be charged for. Passengers returning from Shopping Centres may take with them, free of charge, at Owner's Risk, articles not exceeding in the aggregate 120lbs. (First Class) or 60lbs. (Third Class) which they have purchased for their own domestic use. Furniture, linoleum, musical instruments, cycles, mail carts, typewriters and other articles of a similar character are excepted from these arrangements.
Dogs accompanying Passengers are charged for at the single fare for the double journey, tickets available on day of issue only.

For any further information respecting the arrangements shown in this Bill, application should be made at any of the Company's Stations or Offices ; to
Mr. H. WARWICK, District Traffic Manager, G.W.R., Oswestry ; or to
Mr. R. H. NICHOLLS, Superintendent of the Line, G.W.R., Paddington Station, W.

Paddington Station, August, 1930.　　　　　JAMES MILNE, General Manager.

No. 275 (1,500) Oswestry 31/7/30.　　　　Printed by Joseph Wones, West Bromwich ; also Birmingham and London.

taken a close look at operating restrictions, which under the Cambrian had been rather rule-of-thumb. GWR engines carried on their cab-sides a classification letter set in a coloured disc; a red disc implied the heaviest engines, blue less so, then yellow, and 'uncoloured' much lighter. From 1929 the line from Dolgelley to Barmouth was rated a blue route, and soon 'Bulldog' 4–4–0s and 2–6–0s were seen. However much of the system was rated 'uncoloured', including that part of the Mid-Wales between Three Cocks Junction and Llanidloes; here only Dean and Cambrian 0–6–0s were seen, apart from the odd visit by a '517' class 0–4–2T. On the main line, 'Duke' class 4–4–0s began to appear in considerable numbers; double-heading 'Dukes' were not uncommon, or a 'Duke' with a 'Barnum'. On parts of the line a banker also was required in summer time. Much use was made of the frequent loops for handling light engines, so that a heavy train coming down to Machynlleth might have a single 'Duke', but a similar train heading the other way for Talerddig might have three.

Of the local services, only the Dolgelley–Barmouth and Wrexham–Ellesemere trains regularly used Great Western steamcars, though they did run to Machynlleth from Barmouth or Criccieth at times. Later many 0–4–2T engines were fitted for auto-working, and the services north of Oswestry were worked by these. The Tanat Valley line remained a preserve of the 'Seaham' 2–4–0Ts, assisted by *Lady Margaret*, a 2–4–0T transferred from the Liskeard & Looe line. The ex-LVR 0–6–0Ts were off the Kerry branch by 1930 and a 'Dean' took over. A number of '4500' class small 2–6–2Ts were now available, but mostly seen on light goods and piloting on the Coast Line. While the passenger service lasted on the ex-Mawddwy Railway, the trains were mostly worked (mixed) by an early GWR 0–4–2T with open-backed cab.

By the mid-1930s the 'Duke' 4–4–0s were wearing out, and were gradually replaced by 'Dukedogs', basically a 'Bulldog' lightened and with a 'Duke' boiler. The larger ('7400') 0–6–0PTs were now allowed, as well as the lighter class seen earlier, and '2251' class Collett 0–6–0s. In the last years before the War, traffic was very heavy and locomotive power not really sufficient, so when the first 'Manor' class 4–6–0s appeared, from 1938, there was much relief, though they were at first restricted to the Ruabon–Barmouth run.

During the War, a number of 'outside' engines appeared from time to time, but the Dean 0–6–0s still took the brunt. A total of 280 of these had been built from 1883 to 1899, but of 50 loaned to the War Department in 1914–18, seven did not return; in 1939 too the War Department requested them, and a few working on the Cambrian had to go. Several were lost at Dunkirk, but in the main they stayed in the UK. The War certainly prolonged the life of the remaining ex-Cambrian 0–6–0s; only No. 88 went, in 1944. Thus it was that by the time of Nationalisation fourteen were still serving, along with two 'Seahams' (1196/7). Holiday traffic built up fast after 1945; to cope with it there were five 'Manors', the last four 'Dukes', 19 'Dukedogs' (or 'Earls' as they preferred to be called), and 23 Dean 0–6–0s assisted by 16 Colletts, and the ex-CR 0–6–0s.

Aberystwyth engine shed in 1934; an ex-Cambrian 0−6−0 is under repair; a train from London is entering with a 'Duke' 4−4−0, and on the left is an LMS train of ex-LNW corridor stock. *Author*

'Barnum' 2−4−0 No. 3217 on a down Coast Line train at Barmouth in 1934; the first vehicle is an LMS mail van. *Author*

At Cemmes Road the driver of the pilot engine of a non-stopping train, hauled by a 'Duke' and a 'Barnum', gets ready to pick up the token from its post, July 1934. *Author*

Former Cambrian 0−6−0 No. 45 near the end of the Nantmawr Branch in 1934; it will pick up the loaded BQC wagons; nobody will be surprised if instead of running round, it returns brakevan-first to Blodwell Junction for the return to Oswestry.

Author

There had always been a need for a light locomotive to be shedded at Moat
Lane, to work the ex-Van Railway, still laid with flat-bottom rails. For many
years this was ex-Mawddwy Manning, Wardle No. 824, heavily Great-
Westernised, but in 1939 ex-LVR No. 819 was there. 824 was officially
withdrawn, at the age of 76 years, in 1940. In November of that year the Van
was officially reported as closed, though the portion between Garth station
and Van Mines had been lifted by 1939.

The Great Western had inherited two small studs of narrow-gauge
engines, from the Cambrian, and acquired another in 1930 when the Corris
Railway was taken over. The two 0–6–0Ts on the Welshpool & Llanfair
were given Swindon-type chimneys and safety-valves. On the Corris, which
had two Hughes 0–4–2Ts, built as 0–4–0Ts in 1878, and a 1921 Kerr,
Stuart 0–4–2T, no 'Great Westernising' was done; within a few weeks of
Nationalisation the whole line was closed.

The engines of the LMSR using the Mid-Wales Railway between Talyllyn
and Three Cocks changed before the War from Johnson 0–4–4Ts of the old
Midland Railway to 0–6–0s of the former Lancashire & Yorkshire. At Afon
Wen station, which was also used by the LMS, the rather grand Whale
4–6–2Ts which shared the working with old Webb 'Coal' tanks were taken
off in 1936; the Webbs continued for some years being gradually replaced by
standard 2–6–2Ts.

During the Wartime period, 1939–44, there was a regular freight working
from Dolgellau to Barmouth Junction hauled by a GWR '28XX' 2–8–0, from
Wrexham. It is recorded that for a time this train was worked by an LNER
0–6–0, No. 1963.

In 1947 Brecon and sub-sheds had 11 engines, six of them Dean 0–6–0s;
Machynlleth and sub-sheds had 54, including two ex-Cambrian and 16
'Dukedogs'; Oswestry and sub-sheds housed 58 engines, 12 of them
survivors from the Cambrian, eight 'Dukedogs' and 11 Dean 0–6–0s. This
made a total for the Mid-Wales Division of 123 machines, excluding narrow-
gauge ones, an increase of about 20 on the number taken over in 1922;
however, the Brecon shed serviced, as well as the Mid-Wales, two lines
which had not been part of the Cambrian.

For a few years after the War things hardly changed but in 1946 the last
'Aberdare' 2–6–0 left, and the 'Dukes' became rather scarce; by 1949 there
were two on Coast Line passenger work and two on goods, and one in store.

CARRIAGE STOCK
The Great Western scrapped four-fifths of the Cambrian carriage stock
between 1922 and 1930; those that survived included the two saloons Nos. 1
and 9, the observation cars 176 and 178, four 6-wheeled thirds, and a
number of bogie carriages, most of which had steel sheeted panelling sides.
Only seven (Nos. 20, 271, 285, 306/8/9, 314) lasted into BR days; No. 238
was converted to a wireless van and later a Mess & Tool van for Wolverhampton having put in 74 years of service when withdrawn in 1969.

The replacements from the GWR were four-wheelers for the branches and
main line 'locals', some in four-coach close-coupled sets, followed by non-
corridor bogie clerestory stock and a few other short bogie items, and by the

mid-1930s some fairly new steel stock; a pair of these, a brake 3rd and a compo. was for the Llanfyllin and LLanymynech branch, carrying this information painted on the end of the compo. An early motor-train set was put on to the Wrexham branch, and later single auto-train coaches appeared on the Dolgellau service, sometimes one each side of the engine. The through trains as the years went by exhibited all generations of GWR corridor stock, from the clerestory stock to the flush-sided steel design.

The GWR four-wheelers included some fascinating items; No. 6792 working on the Llanfyllin branch was a five-compartment compo. with one end compartment altered for the guard's use with double doors; compo. No. 7865 on the Pwllheli–Machynlleth service with four wide compartments was a reminder of former luxury. Six-wheeled saloons Nos. 9310 and 9359 also were noted in 1930 in the short siding at the north-west corner of Pwllheli station which also housed the oil-gas container wagon for supplying gas-lit coaches.

Carriage stock on the narrow gauge Rheidol line was strengthened in 1924 by four more 'summer coaches' with wire mesh sides very similar to the original ones, and in 1938 a clean sweep was made of old stock; 12 new bogie carriages were provided, including two 3rd brakes, and three additional 'summer coaches' built on original frames. The three four-wheeled brake vans were also replaced. The GWR fitted steam heating to several of the original coaches, but the winter service was soon abandoned (in 1931); first class had been abolished at the end of the 1926 summer season.

Cambrian 0–6–0 No. 45 of 1864, now with GWR fittings and numbered 900, waits at Portmadoc in August 1930 to return a ballast train to Machynlleth.   *Author*

An up 'Cambrian Coast Express' at Portmadoc in 1965, headed by 4−6−0 No. 75004. Just visible on the left are the Moel-y-Gest granite quarries from which a narrow gauge line ran into the yard in earlier days.   *T.J. Edgington*

A down freight on the Mid-Wales line at Builth Road in 1957; note the Central Wales Line goods train crossing over the lower station; the light 2−6−0 No. 46520 was one of several working the restricted-weight line from Brecon to Moat Lane.   *T.J. Edgington*

Chapter Eight
British Railways in Charge

The whole of the former Cambrian became, on 1st January, 1948, part of the Shrewsbury District of the Western Region, in which it was to remain until 1963. The case for including it in the Midland Region would have been stronger but for its connections to South Wales, with the former Mid-Wales Railway and former Manchester & Milford still operating. In fact things changed little; the first closure, of the goods service on the Mawddwy branch on 1st July, 1950 (official, last train earlier), was brought about mainly by flood damage.

It was not long, however, before rumours were flying of other closures, one obvious choice being the narrow-gauge Welshpool & Llanfair line, which had not carried passengers since February 1931. There had been a great change in railway enthusiasts since the War; there were many more of them, and they no longer took it for granted that every railway would stay open for ever. There was particular nostalgia for the W&L, especially from the close-by Midlands, and many enthusiasts' specials were run over the line, using open wagons, in spite of British Railways' protests that the track was unsafe owing to its weed-infested condition. Closure came on 5th November, 1956, but a Preservation Society was immediately formed, and the western part of the line was running again by the spring of 1963, using the original engines; the passenger stock alas had gone.

The Kerry branch goods service was terminated on 1st May, 1956; this coincided with the last few months of the last three Dean goods 0–6–0s, which had been sharing a roster comprising a thrice weekly pick-up goods trip from Oswestry to Newtown, a trip up to Kerry, and then a working to Brecon.

The timetables for the former Cambrian lines were still delightfully old-fashioned. For example, the 9.55 am from Aberystwyth would call at Talerddig on Tuesdays only and only to pick up; the 9.28 am from Oswestry to Whitchurch would call at Welshampton on Saturdays to pick up; the up 'Cambrian Coast Express' would call at Llandre, Llanbrynmair and Montgomery only to pick up passengers travelling beyond Shrewsbury; and so on. Scafell, the up line-only platform on a double line between Moat Lane and Newtown, was not in the 1955 timetables; it had in 1954 two advertised trains, but it is uncertain when a passenger last used the platform; there was also a goods siding, advertised in the RCH Handbook as for wagon loads only, said to have been last used about 1941.

This was quite a happy time on the former Cambrian, the lull before the storm of closings in the 1960s. Diesels were still on the horizon; holiday trains were streaming in from all over the Midlands and North to Pwllheli Holiday Camp; the newly-doubled line between Afon Wen and Penychain was magnificent on a summer Saturday with trains in Midland Region livery joining the 'GWR' ones from Birmingham and London. Even in winter there were four through coaches per day from Bangor to Pwllheli, and 15 trains per day through Barmouth Junction in both directions, only three each way being motors. The mix of engines was enormous; though the last original Cambrian engines had gone in 1954 there were exciting visitors; the 1955

Talyllyn Railway Special was hauled by an ex-LSWR 'T9' 4–4–0 assisted by an 'Earl' as the 'Dukedogs' were also known (13 had carried names of Earls until losing them in 1937).

There were many notable special trains; the 1951 'North West Land Cruise' train, Rhyl–Barmouth–Caernarvon–Rhyl, had a restaurant car; the 1960 one included an ex-Devon Belle observation car; the 'Radio Cruise Train' of 1956 from Llandudno waited at Aberdovey for two hours and returned via Dolgellau. In 1959 the 'Welsh Chieftain' was started (summer only) running between the Coast and Rhyl via Dolgellau, Corwen, and Denbigh.

The Tanat Valley branch was closed temporarily on 15th January, 1951, but in fact the closure became permanent; goods service ceased beyond Llanrhaiadr Mochnant on 1st July, 1952, and the remainder on 5th December, 1960; however a short section between Porthywaen and Blodwell Junction remained in place for access to Llanddu stone quarries. The siding at Llynclys Junction also remained, as the weighbridge was used to check the stone in the 20-ton hopper wagons.

The first of the 'Beeching' closings on the Cambrian was the Ellesmere–Wrexham branch, on 10th September, 1962; however, Marchweil station stayed open for goods until 4th September, 1972. The last train also ran on the Mid-Wales line on 30th December, 1962; the Brecon & Merthyr line south from Talyllyn and the Hereford line east from Three Cocks were closed also; the Neath & Brecon line west from Brecon had already closed on 15th October; a town which formerly had three railway stations and a canal now had nothing. The former Cambrian station at Talgarth remained open for non-rail goods delivery until 9th November, 1964. The part of the Mid-Wales line which was originally L&N also remained until 2nd October, 1967 to serve the construction of the nearby Clwedog dam; Dolwen was closed entirely but Llandinam and LLanidloes were open for wagon load goods.

The famous Beeching Report of March 1963 painted a gloomy picture for Wales; even the Coast Line was under threat but political pressure staved this off. The Llanfyllin branch went on 7th December, 1964, so did the former LMS service from Afon Wen to Caernarvon, leading to the closing of the junction station, which served no village. That part of the main line between Buttington Junction and Whitchurch closed on 18th January, 1965, including Buttington station.

Trains from Barmouth to Ruabon did not run from the 13th to the 17th of December, 1965 due to floods east of Dolgellau. The part of this route from Llangollen Goods Junction to Bala Junction never re-opened; the Barmouth line did but was finally closed from 18th January, 1966. The track was not lifted until 1968; the local council requested it be left 'for possible use by mono-rails or hover trains'. In 1966 also the double line from Aberystwyth to Llanbadarn crossing was singled, and Newtown–Moat Lane.

In 1965 Aberystwyth lost its line south to Carmarthen, the old Manchester & Milford (which had never been part of the Cambrian), and there was now no railway from North Wales to South Wales that did not run through England.

The situation at Oswestry, once the hub of the Cambrian Railways, after

This train from Oswestry to Welshpool is headed by 2−6−0 No. 46513; it stands on the 'Cambrian' side of Buttington station, the Joint line to Shrewsbury being on the other side. Note that the up platform has been shortened; note also the curious signal controlling the loop.
Oakwood Collection

A good view of the south end of Oswestry station; 2−6−0 No. 46509 has brought in a long Society Special and left it in the up platform before running to shed.
H.C. Casserley

A Welshpool train stopped at Oswestry down platform in 1955 is hauled by 'Dukedog' No. 9012; this combination of the 'Duke' and the 'Bulldog' performed valuable service on the Cambrian lines. *T.J. Edgington*

Dolgelley was a GWR station though the Cambrian metals began only a few hundred yards towards Barmouth. This service along the north bank of the Mawddach was mainly worked by railmotors; in this case one of the '58XX' class of 0–4–2T supplies the power. *Oakwood Collection*

January 1965 was ironic. The great station remained open only for the ex-GWR shuttle to Gobowen, though the tracks carried a couple of stone trains a day to Porthywaen and Llanddu, and lifting trains from the Llanfyllin branch. The locomotive shed was finishing a few repairs, but the Works itself had been sold. Then on 7th November, 1966 the Gobowen service went, and soon track-lifting began, leaving only a single track between the cliff-like station buildings, to wander through Llynclys and Porthywaen junctions to a reversal just short of Blodwell Junction giving access to Llanddu quarry siding. A small part of the north-west corner of Oswestry station was taken over by the Cambrian Railway Society in 1972, with a locomotive being rebuilt and a preserved railmotor trailer. The official date for closing Oswestry shed (6E) was 18th January, 1965, and on the same date Penmaenpool, a sub-shed of Croes Newydd (6C) shut.

One closure which had nothing to do with Beeching occurred on 20th March, 1960, when the last War Department train ran to Llanymynech over the former S&MR. This had been owned jointly from January 1948 by the Western Region and the WD, although all trains had been of WD stock; the last train was hauled by a standard 0–6–0ST with ex-Caledonian Railway carriages. The official closing dates were: Criggion branch (not WD) 4th January, 1960, main line 29th February, 1960. The Army had erected a new engine shed at Kinnerley and this saw further use by industry, as did the Abbey Foregate station sidings, now an oil depot and reached by a new spur from the Severn Valley line.

The Beeching 'Axe' did not, of course, slice off only complete lines; it also closed stations on lines left open, and all those on the former Cambrian between Welshpool and Machynlleth except for Caersws and Newtown were closed on 14th June, 1965, as well as Ynyslas, Llandre and Bow Street; Glandyfi had already closed on 19th August, 1963. As a similar process had been applied to the joint line to Shrewsbury in September 1960, this meant that there were only six stops on the 81½ miles from Shrewsbury to Aberystwyth. However, there were passing places, notably Westbury and Talerddig, where a lengthy stop not indicated in the public timetables was the rule rather than the exception; even after the closings the 'Cambrian Coast Express', which did not stop at Caersws, could only manage an average of 30 mph.

May 1964 saw the official closing of the Aberdovey wharves, though the rails had been partially lifted for some time. The local authority had been petitioning for the removal of the sidings, which occupied much valuable estuary frontage, since 1923, but the problem had seemed a long way from Paddington. The Act of 1883 had required the Cambrian to remove the west wharves 'when no longer used'; this imprecise term had given trouble elsewhere. It was probably the request by 'Outward Bound' to use the wharf which triggered action; so it is still there but no longer carries rails.

In 1967 the 8.20 and 10.10 am through from London (Paddington) trains for Pwllheli on summer Saturdays were not re-instated after last runs on 3rd September, 1966; these were good trains, reaching Pwllheli in 8 hours 12 minutes; the first one ran non-stop from Machynlleth to Harlech apart from Barmouth. In March of this year the London services were switched from

The daily goods trip to Aberystwyth is down to one wagon on 25th April, 1974; note the exchange siding for locomotive coal for the Rheidol engines at right.   *Author*

Well into the season, some Rheidol stock returns from repainting; here one of the brake vans is being lifted back to its own rails by the Crewe crane, on 17th June, 1976.
                                                                                                      Author

Birmingham Snow Hill to New Street, and Euston instead of Paddington.

For the summer of 1970 the Stoke Division of LMR, now in charge, decided to reinstate Sunday trains, which had not been a regular feature on the lines for 50 years. It was an ambitious programme; a train from Shrewsbury to Aberystwyth, two from Aberystwyth up the Coast, plus an evening one to Barmouth; even a trip up the Rheidol. Later the Shrewsbury train was extended back to Wolverhampton and Birmingham. On the first day, Sunday 5th July, there was also a nine-coach dmu excursion to Pwllheli, six cars from Birmingham plus three from Chester, and 'foreign' excursions from Liverpool, Rotherham, Derby and Nottingham. On the next Sunday the LNER Society ran a 12-coach train hauled by '24/2' class engines Nos. 5135 and 5145 from Euston to Welshpool via the Abbey Foregate curve.

Diesel multiple-unit trains began running in January 1965, though diesel locomotives did not arrive for another 14 months. The initial supply of units was sparing; two two-coach sets for the Coast Line and Aberystwyth locals, and one six-car train for the Birmingham service. At first the livery was dark green, but later dark blue, or for the through stock, blue and cream. In the 1970s some refurbished 'blue trains' appeared in the two-tone livery, and it was not long before sets were appearing in mixed liveries. The Coast trains were extremely crowded in summer, though there was often a spare set at Machynlleth which could be added if a train arrived already full. In the timetables there was an increasing pressure for passengers to change at Machynlleth rather than Dovey Junction if travelling from Aberystwyth up the coast, and this station became more and more forlorn, the Refreshment room long closed and used as a very dirty waiting room, and the ugly new signal box on the platform unwilling to respond to passengers pleas for news of a train. Some of this was undoubtedly latent hostility to the far-off controllers; 'Ask them at Stoke' was a cry from the heart of a signalman who knows the down London train ought to be there, fears it has stalled on Talerddig bank, and has not been told anything.

Freight traffic was running down, but had occasional spurts; in 1971 there were some ICI specials from the Penrhyndeudraeth powder works to Longtown in Cumbria, and in 1984 there were three trains a week of timber for Welshpool, five wagons from Perth and five from Dundee.

An exciting train in May 1975 carried the LMS Pacific *Princess Margaret Rose*, set between two bogie bolster wagons, away from Butlins Camp at Penychain and down the Coast on the way to Derby; she had been at the Camp since May 1963.

The type of multiple units seen varied over the years, and included most types of 2- and 3-coach sets of Metro Cammell, Gloucester RCW, Derby BR and Park Royal design.

Camping Coaches which had been a feature of the Coast Line for more than thirty years now disappeared; those at Aberdovey were scrapped on site as the siding they stood on was cut off from the running line.

Black Rock Halt, on the sea-marsh near Portmadoc, had its closure notice issued in October 1976; in fact it had already been closed as unsafe on 13th August, and the official closing date after procedures had been gone through was 27th June, 1977!

A Saturday train from Euston drawing forward at Borth; the 10 coaches of mostly NSE stock are too long for the platform; two class '37's are in charge.   *Author*

Two class '20's haul the weekly Stanlow oil empties train near Borth, 29th April, 1988.   *Author*

The greatest crisis for the Coast Line was the discovery in 1980 that the teredo worm had made the footings of the timber Barmouth viaduct unsafe, leading to a weight restriction from April. All trains were withdrawn from 12th October and there were fears that BR would baulk at the cost of making it safe. Meanwhile, six two-car dmus were sent north of the viaduct to maintain a service between Pwllheli and Barmouth; from the south trains ran to Morfa Mawddach, and an express bus was put on from Machynlleth to Barmouth via Dolgellau.

In the event BR did face the political problem which withdrawal of services permanently would pose, repairs were carried out, and on 22nd May, 1981 a formal re-opening train crossed the Bridge. Special Welcome Back tickets were issued for unlimited travel for £1. However, locomotives were not yet allowed, and the explosives traffic from Penrhyndeudraeth was never restored. There had of course been no locomotive on the north side, and such ballast work as was needed was carried out by a DMLV (No. 55995) propelling wagons.

The Welsh Development Board laid on a Special on 7th July, 1984 from London Victoria to Newtown, and in the same year the Coast Line Action Group tried to counter BR cuts on Sundays north of Barmouth by running Specials from Pwllheli to connect at Barmouth; Sunday trains at that time ran from the 'excursion' platform at Barmouth to enable the crossing to stay shut.

Much of the blame for unsatisfactory running was placed upon the use of old dmu trains, and indeed some were very much out of breath at the summit of Talerddig. The coming of Sprinter trains was signalled in 1985, after some fears of rail-buses, but the first Sprinters did not in fact run until 17th March, 1986; they enabled the next summer timetable to show a reduction in running time from Aberystwyth to Shrewsbury of up to 20 minutes. It was two years however before the last of the 'door-banging' dmus departed. The basic livery of the new Sprinters was dark blue upper parts with a pale blue line below the windows, though some had pale blue uppers and a dark blue (broader) line below; sets in a buff livery also appeared at times. Collections of five or even six Sprinters were seen at Aberystwyth, and of course more often east of Machynlleth. However later the normal thing was two coaches in winter and three in summer, the latter not too sanitary when, as was bound to happen, a train had only one lavatory-fitted coach and was full to standing, all passages blocked by back-packs.

Two trips by the preserved Pullmans of VSOE (Venice Simplon Orient Express) included the Cambrian lines in July 1988; of these the second on the 10th had the passengers detraining at Machynlleth to explore the countryside and rejoining the train the next day at Newtown, to return to Victoria. However, BR was busy lifting loops and let it be known that it would be difficult if not impossible to fit Specials into the summer workings.

During 1987 there was much uncertainty in the air; the 8.18 am from Barmouth to Machynlleth was withdrawn, but on finding many school-children disadvantaged, BR reinstated it but only to Tywyn. The October timetable came out with the 3.25 pm from Barmouth to Pwllheli covered by black blocks, and the same for the 3.51 pm from Harlech to Barmouth; the journey of the 3.00 pm from Pwllheli seemed inexplicably to end at Tygwyn.

During 1988 final preparations were being made for the introduction of radio signalling, replacing the actual token by electronic ones displayed on a box in the driving cab, and all controlled from Machynlleth. Suitable radio masts were erected in various places, including one on Glanrafon station on the Rheidol line, to cover Aberystwyth. This one gave trouble; often the train had to shunt out to the engine shed to get its signal; the signal at Westbury Loop was also very poor. The system came into operation in November 1988, and did not settle down until nearly a year later, when the frequency was changed. Trains ran very late; on one occasion an official from Machynlleth had to motor out to Borth to release a train which could not get a signal. Delay built up as the day went on, and on occasion the last train of the day left Aberystwyth at 1.00 am, next day. Only three class '37' engines were fitted and one was not always available, so a portable box was made up for unfitted locomotives or old type dmus. Some highlights of this period included a Sprinter running out of cooling water at Ynyslas and calling the fire brigade, and the crossing keeper at Llandre despairing of the last arrival and shutting his box, requiring a bus to run from Machynlleth.

The plan was to release the few remaining signalmen and crossing keepers. Some crossings were fitted with remote-controlled barriers, but most were simply given lights, flashing red ones facing the road, and white ones facing the oncoming train to show that the system was working. Unguarded crossings were not popular, and two years later the railway was forced to put in barriers at Ynyslas. At Llanbadarn keepers were retained for some time; there was a problem here in that the standard gauge and narrow gauge tracks crossed the road close to each other but not adjacent, and in theory traffic could be trapped between the two, possibly fouling the track as the barriers came down. The solution was to order that a Rheidol train could not cross the road when a main line train had just left Aberystwyth or Llandre. The Rheidol train had to stop at its Llanbadarn station and telephone Machynlleth; often the 11.00 am narrow gauge train would leave late and not clear the crossing before the next arrival on the main line had left Llandre. As it sat there quietly, the driver strolling about kicking stones, heads craned from windows inquiring why the train did not proceed; the same problem of course arose with trains coming down the valley.

The actual dates for radio signalling coming into action were: Shrewsbury–Machynlleth 20th October, on to Aberystwyth and Barmouth 21st–22nd October, and to Pwllheli 22nd–23rd of the same month.

By 1988/9 the loading of the through summer Saturday trains to and from Aberystwyth had become very poor. There were two: the 9.32 am into Aberystwyth went out as the 10.10 am to Euston, a motley collection of Mk. 1 coaches bearing the letters of all Regions apart from the Southern, double-headed by two '37s'. Then there was the 9.40 am from Euston due at Aberystwyth at 2.56 pm. This became a legend for lateness; it was a Network SouthEast train normally used in the week for commuters from Northampton and mainly good condition stock; it was almost always hauled by two '37s' and did not lack power, so the late running was no doubt due to

Two class '25's head an up Sunday excursion train near Llandre, on 3rd September, 1978. *Author*

Aberystwyth station on 24th April, 1982, the day before all the signals were removed; now only the platform the train is entering remains in use, apart from the Rheidol trains in the old M&M platforms at right, which actually load from ground level. *Author*

'Manor' class 4–6–0 No. 7819 *Hinton Manor* is given a welcome by local people at the old Llandre station, on a steam working to Aberystwyth on 16th August, 1987; as the Aberystwyth turning loop had gone, the return was tender-first. *Author*

main line troubles, and also 'drawing forward' at a number of stations. It could sometimes be an hour late (and once or twice did not arrive at all) and after the 1.09 pm Sprinter from Aberystwyth had passed him, the signalman at Llandre Crossing sometimes sat in his little steel hut for almost three hours with nothing happening, until a tinkle told him that the train had finally reached Chapel Crossing at Borth. Except at the height of the season, it reached Aberystwyth with only a handful of passengers, mostly railway enthusiasts. Both trains were axed at the end of the 1989 season.

The Llanddu quarry traffic ceased from 28th October, 1988, though it was thought that some future traffic, perhaps of rubbish trains, was possible.

LOCOMOTIVES

This tale is necessarily one of progressive withdrawal. The last of the Cambrian Railways' own 0−6−0s (No. 855) went in October 1954, though No. 844 was left as a stationary boiler at Oswestry. Next year the last three of the once so numerous Dean 0−6−0s went in turn (Nos. 2516, 2538, 2301); 2538 assisted with the Talyllyn Railway Special in 1956. Much thought had been given at Swindon to the replacement of these engines; it had to be something light enough to work over the weak viaducts of the Mid-Wales line. A light version of the Collett 0−6−0 was considered, but in the end the choice was the LM Standard class '2' 2−6−0 with some 'Great Western-isation', and trial runs were made on the Mid-Wales in 1949, though it was several years before this class took over completely at Brecon.

An unusual visitor in 1949 was a GWR diesel railcar; this was working a Society special to Welshpool, and as no such car had ever been on the Cambrian before, a special test run took place to check clearances.

The locomotives sheds at this time were: Oswestry 89A, sub-sheds Llan-fyllin, Llanidloes, Moat Lane, Welshpool and Whitchurch. Builth Wells was 89B, and Machynlleth 89C, sub-sheds Aberystwyth, Portmadoc and Pwllheli. Builth Wells was closed in 1957, and the two engines transferred to the ex-LNW Builth Road shed.

There were five 'Manor' 4−6−0s on the lines at the end of the War, and this class was increased to 14. The Standard '75000' class 4−6−0s began to appear from 1951, and these in fact continued after many of the 'Manors' went in the early 1960s. There were of course a number of '4300' moguls in service, though they and the Collett 0−6−0s were on the way out and were replaced on the Coast Line by BR '78000' class moguls, a development of the Ivatt LM2 referred to above. There were also three classes of Standard tank engines, the '82000' 2−6−2T, '80000' 2−6−4T, and '84000' class 2−6−2T, a suitable replacement which arrived in 1963 for the small GWR tanks of the same arrangement, which had for 30 years performed all kinds of tasks from running empties from Portmadoc to Minffordd quarries, to taking on the Pwllheli section of the 'Cambrian Coast Express' from Machynlleth.

The last of the 'Dukedogs' (No. 9015) had left Aberystwyth MPD for the scrapyard in 1960. Though this was a bastard type and not actually very pretty, it had continued the honourable history of the real 'Dukes' and was very much part of the Cambrian scenery; thus there was only six years or so when no engine of Cambrian flavour was to be seen. By 1966 the only steam

The end of the line from Oswestry in June 1976 was just short of the shored-up bridge at Blodwell Junction; trains still working to Llanddu were reversing short of this point from the Tanat Valley line and up the Nantmawr branch. *Author*

Many Cambrian stations made excellent houses; this is Llynclys in 1976. *Author*

was on the 'Cambrian Coast Express' and some goods workings. Already some class '24' diesels were at work, and class '25' from 1967; oddly, a class '37' appeared on the 'York Mail' on 25th June, 1966, but it would be more than 10 years before this type, so much superior in looks and performance, was working regularly.

By the summer of 1965 all local workings were dmus; a few class '4' 4−6−0s were still in steam, and Nos. 75002 and 75039 ran the 1966 Talyllyn Railway Special; there was even a shortage of engines at the end and Nos. 75033/5 were borrowed from Croes Newydd. There was still an 0−6−0PT working the Nantmawr Quarries run.

In the 1970s pairs of class '25' diesels handled the excursions and through trains, with class '24s' on the pick-up goods trips. The '25s' became increasingly unreliable; there was some improvement in the mid-1980s when class '37s' from Cardiff shed took over, also in pairs; this class had appeared earlier but not regularly. The weekly oil trains from Stanlow to Aberystwyth (usually, but not always, on a Wednesday) was handled by a pair of class '20s', though on a few occasions in 1988 a pair of class '31s' appeared on this working, and it then became a class '37' duty, sometimes a Railfreight engine.

In September 1987 the last class '40', No. 40122 (D200) was given a run on the Saturday afternoon train from Euston; it did not do very well, being on its own and carrying a heavy load of railway enthusiasts. This was also the year in which *Hinton Manor* and class '2' No. 46443, based at Machynlleth, ran steam services on Sundays to Aberystwyth and Barmouth, necessarily running tender-first half the time. A water-tank was provided at Machynlleth at the west end of the former locomotive sidings.

On 23rd September, 1989 the class '37s' working the morning Saturday train from Aberystwyth to Euston carried a small headboard reading '125 years 1864−1989', to signify the ending of the MPD at that station, which had latterly consisted only of stabling the engine of the 'Cambrian Coast Express' overnight. From now on that engine would return each evening, with its train, to Machynlleth MPD.

Carriage stock under BR differed little from that on other lines, the ever-changing liveries being added to when the Saturday morning train from Euston was from 1988 made up from Network SouthEast stock. DMU stock was varied; the last of the 'door-banging' kind was noted on the Aberystwyth service in May 1988. Although Sprinters came in various liveries, the arrival of 'Centro' sets in 1991, with their mostly bright green colour, was something of a surprise.

For many years the late George Dow, well-known railwayman and author, kept his private carriage at Machynlleth. This was No. 2233, the coach portion of a Midland Railway steam railcar.

In September 1991 there was a minor derailment on the Dovey bridge at Dovey Junction, and locomotives were temporarily banned from the Coast Line. The Saturday through train for Pwllheli was diverted to Aberystwyth, and so too were steam excursions planned for Barmouth on two Sundays. Thus it was that *Hinton Manor* and 75069 appeared unexpectedly to make use of the layout there, only weeks before all sidings other than that to the oil depot were disconnected. On the second Sunday, the giant old water tank ran dry after filling the Black Five, and the 'Manor' was only readied for the return by half a dozen visits from the local fire-tender. These scenes, with two engines lining up for the stand-pipe and eager enthusiasts roaming freely over all the lines, will not be seen again at the sanitised Aberystwyth layout now taking shape.

THE RHEIDOL RAILWAY

This was the only narrow gauge line operated by British Railways and its history under its aegis from 1948 to 1988 is a complex one. After its re-opening on 25th July, 1945, very little happened for some time apart from changes in livery; the GWR coat of arms on the coaches was replaced by the GWR 'totem'. The Western Region applied a livery of maroon and cream with no totem, but in 1956 all stock was repainted in chocolate and cream; however in 1964 a drab green livery was applied. In 1956 all the engines had been repainted Great Western green with the 'Lion' logo, and given names: 7 *Owen Glyndwr*, 8 *Llywelyn* and 9 *Prince of Wales*. In 1966 however, when the Midland Region Stoke Division took over, they were repainted in unlined blue, and the carriage stock also became blue. Threat of closure was always in the air, and in 1969 a consortium of private persons contemplated trying to buy the line, even purchasing two East German 60 cm gauge 0–8–0 engines to work it (one of these spent some time at Littlestone, RH&DR, though being of differing gauge it could not run). This fell through, and a Vale of Rheidol Supporters Association (VoRRSA) was formed in 1970 to promote the line. Its various initiatives had some effect, and fortunately the rising tide of tourism succeeded in nearly doubling passenger journeys and closure became less likely.

In 1968 when the former Manchester & Milford line was closed, platforms 1 and 2 at Aberystwyth had been given over to the Rheidol line, together with the locomotive shed. In practice, because of their low floors the trains load from ground level from two lines set between the platforms with a footway in between. In 1972 the woods by the line above Aberfrwd were hung with fairy lights and night trains run there from Aberystwyth; as the Aberfrwd loop had been taken out, they had to operate with an engine at each end. From 1983, GWR livery returned for the carriages.

The Welsh Tourist Board was now putting its publicity behind the narrow gauge lines; in 1983 the Board sponsored a new type of carriage, the Vista-car. This was a summer car with the valley side entirely of glass, and one long seat, everyone facing across the valley. However this coincided with a period when would-be passengers were being turned away from full trains, and the Vistacar had few seat places; it was little used until 1989 when it re-appeared with normal seats taken from scrapped dmus.

Between 1978 and 1981 all three engines were converted to oil firing, due to complaints from the forestry authorities about sparks. Also in 1981–6 all engines were repainted, first No. 8 in GWR green, then No. 9 in LBSC orange (said to have been the line's first livery) and finally No. 9 in Cambrian black, without its name.

The intermediate stations became irrelevant, though Llanbadarn was kept in the timetables for some time. Capel Bangor station had its original wooden building removed (the carriage shed had fallen into the river decades earlier) and a new stone station building put up in 1989, with picnic tables. Some passengers do occasionally join here, as all the best scenery is above it, and it makes the trip less costly.

In 1988 the timetables announced that Saturday trains would be diesel-hauled; but in fact the diesel engine, a six-wheeler of Brecon Mountain Railway design, did not arrive until the end of the season and was rejected by the drivers. It could however take three coaches to Devil's Bridge and on occasion did so when no steam engine was available. A similar thumbs-down had been awarded to the Festiniog Railway's Alco 2−6−2T *Mountaineer* which came as a guest in 1986, though in public it was said to have 'done well'. The fact is that the Rheidol makes very heavy demands on engine, driver and shed staff; its rising curves with their check-rails are too much for a machine not built for it or inexpertly driven.

In 1983/4 first class returned, for those travelling in the observation car end of the brake coach, which was at the tail (going up) of each set. A supplement was also charged for the Vistacar.

Somewhat unusually, two carriages on the line carried nameplates: No. 4734 (10) was *Myfanwy* and No. 4146 (4) *Lowri*.

British Rail had now decided to divest itself of this line and offered it for sale by tender. The choice in the end was between a buy-out by the staff or a late bid from the Brecon Mountain Railway, a much shorter line built on part of the former Brecon & Merthyr Railway between Pant and Pontsticill. The latter won, and it was not a popular decision. At the 1988 autumn open day the train ran with black flags and a notice 'sold down the Rheidol' on the smoke-box. Most of the shed people resigned, a sad loss for a line needing skilled fitters to keep engines in top trim for work that was at their limits in high season. The new owners did not want the VoRRSA and in due course it transferred itself to the Welshpool & Llanfair Railway.

There was little change on the railway; No. 9 went to Pant, where the BMR workshops were, and stayed there. The management took the chance of starting both 1989 and 1990 seasons with only two engines; they were lucky, except for one time when No. 8 broke a spring and for a day or two the diesel engine No. 10 was dispatched up the line with its puny three coach load. For a while tickets were issued from the remaining 4-wheeled van at the buffers, but later an office was built on the platform.

The Aberffrwd loop, taken out in 1963, was restored in 1990, allowing a more balanced high season service, although the actual number of trains run was less than under BR. The loop has electric points and various flashing light signals, run off a portable generator, but the peace of this remote mountain station is only broken for 45 days in the year; for the rest of the time all trains use the down-valley side. For the 1991 season, No. 9 returned in red livery and with a plate on the cab-side stating that it was built at Swindon in 1924, a final acceptance that it is not really No. 1212 rebuilt. The engine bearing the 'Cambrian' title had this removed and its name *Llywelyn* restored. Carriages as they were repainted lost their GWR logotype and 4-figure number, the actual running number, previously on the end, being painted on the side. No. 9 and its train-set are air-braked, not vacuum-braked.

TODAY

It is true that much of the old Cambrian has gone back to nature, and many stations on lines still open have disappeared. However it is still a wonderland for enthusiasts because so many station buildings have been converted to houses with very little alteration. Those on the Van branch have not seen a passenger train for over a century but nobody could mistake them. Penmaenpool on the Dolgellau branch is a particularly good piece of preservation, with its signal box made into a nature centre. Rumbling across the old wooden toll-bridge from the north it is easy to imagine the branch train running past the George Hotel (still there) and the engine shed (alas not there) and along the superlative estuary to what is now Morfa Mawddach. At Kerry beyond the neat station house one can still see the engine shed standing. Also, because some of the closed lines ran through very harsh surroundings, there are stretches, especially on the Mid-Wales line, where the embankments, cuttings and bridges remain in pristine condition. It must be said too that there has been a conscious effort by new tenants; the water-column at Dinas Mawddwy is still there, an added attraction to the car park of the woollen mill. At Doldowlod new signals have been put up by the caravan park owner; nobody is going to forget the Cambrian Railways.

However, British Rail did take one more small bite in the 1992 summer tables; Llangelynin Halt has been 'temporarily closed' pending application under the 1962 Act; a small loss compared with the triumph of the Coast Line's survival to reach its 125th anniversary.

An up train slows for the 'gas-bag'-operated points at the end of the Tywyn station loop on 23rd August, 1989.   *Author*

'Rationalisation' is still proceeding, with the large station at Welshpool knocked down and replaced by an island platform in the former timber yard. At Aberystwyth there are pegs in the ground for a new platform at the up end of the complex; the present station is to become a shopping centre, but it is hoped to preserve the 1864 canopy of platform 4, and perhaps the 1920s front façade.

The class '150' Sprinters have mostly been replaced by '156' and '158' sets; the '153' car intended for single-car operation also appears on the Aberystwyth service. The summer season of 1992 saw a return of the class '31' locomotives, double-headed on a Saturday Coast Line train, and the same train appeared at Aberystwyth in Eisteddfod Week. On the other hand, steam specials booked for Towyn were not allowed beyond Machynlleth. There is life in the Cambrian yet, but it is not time for those who care for it to relax.

The shape of the 1990s: a single-operating car 153384 is attached to a class '156' pair at Aberystwyth's only platform in use (the old No. 3) to strengthen the 11.00 for Birmingham in June 1992. On the right is the canopy of the original station.   *Author*

One of many colourful 'first sod' ceremonies on Cambrian lines; this one for the Tanat Valley Railway was performed on 12th September, 1899 by Lady Powis in a field attached to Porthywaen school; the line actually joined the old Porthywaen branch at a timber yard somewhat to the left. *Author's Collection*

Camping coach No. 9982, originally a broad gauge carriage, in the bay on the Dolgelley side at Barmouth Junction in 1934. *Author*

Appendix One

The 'Cutting of the First Sod' Ceremonies

Not all the constituent Companies of the Cambrian had ceremonies attending the cutting of the first sod of earth for construction work to begin. Those recorded are as follows:

Oswestry & Newtown, on 4th August, 1857, by Lady Williams Wynn of Wynnstay, at the Buttington end of Welshpool station, then a field.

Llanidloes & Newtown, on 3rd October, 1855, by G.R. Whalley, Chairman, at the site of the first station at Llanidloes.

Newtown & Machynlleth, on 27th November, 1858, by Countess Vane at the site of Machynlleth station.

Mid-Wales Railway, on 2nd September, 1859, at Rhayader by Mrs Pyne of Doldowlod Halt.

Oswestry, Ellesmere & Whitchurch, north part, at Ellesmere in August 1861 by Sir John Hanmer and John Stanton; south part, on site of later Oswestry Works on 4th September, 1861, by Miss Kinchant of Park Hall and Miss Lloyd, daughter of the Mayor.

Llanfyllin Railway (O&N), on 20th September, 1861, by Mrs Dugdale at Llyn, Llanfyllin.

Aberystwyth & Welsh Coast, in April 1862 by Mrs Foulkes of Aberdovey, near the Corbett Arms Hotel at Towyn.

Tanat Valley Railway, on 12th September, 1899 by the Countess Powis in a field behind the school at Porthywaen.

Welshpool & Llanfair Railway, on 30th May, 1901 at Welshpool by Viscount Clive of Powys Castle.

Appendix Two

Mail Trains

Mail was carried by rail to Borth from 1st January, 1864 and Aberystwyth a week later. From 1883 a sorting carriage was used (borrowed from the LNWR) and from 1888 the Cambrian provided their own sorting carriages. The vans passed on to the LNWR at Whitchurch, but from 1910 the evening mail from Aberystwyth split at Welshpool; the Whitchurch portion contained a CR van from Brecon and a through Aberystwyth–Manchester LNW van; the Shrewsbury portion, a CR brake van, sorting carriage and tri-compo., with LNW vans for Tamworth and Birmingham; it also picked up at Newtown a van loaded at the mail-order depot adjacent to the platform which ran through to London. Services were reduced in World War I ; sorting on the Aberystwyth mail ceased in 1917 and bags were passed over unsorted at Whitchurch. Sorting was restored in 1919 and finally abolished in 1939; a new carriage had been provided by the GWR in 1933. The sorting carriage, which ran in the morning on the 3.35 am from Shrewsbury, had connected there with the Cardiff–Crewe TPO and the York TPO. Mail for Portmadoc and Pwllheli was routed via Bangor and did not make use of the CR mail train.

Mail continued to be carried on the 6.10 pm from Aberystwyth in a variety of types of van, but its loading was steadily reduced as the Post Office turned more and more to road transport, until by 1977 the 'mail' consisted of one van behind a three-coach dmu.

RSOs (Railway Sub-offices) were maintained at a number of stations, including Moat Lane and Three Cocks; a daily time signal was telegraphed to them, mainly to foil fraudulent betting, at a time when not everyone had a radio in the house.

The Pwllheli portion of the up 'Cambrian Coast Express' arriving at Dovey Junction on 3rd June, 1963, with 'Manor' 4−6−0 No. 7819 *Hinton Manor* in charge.   *J. Edgington*

Dean 0−6−0 No. 2352 leaves Afon Wen with a train for Pwllheli, including two through carriages from Paddington, in August 1930.   *Author*

Appendix Three
The Cambrian Coast Express

The train which carried the above name on and off for 40 years began as the 9.50 am from Paddington on summer weekends, but was not named until 1927, when it ran on Fridays and Saturdays and later only on Saturdays. It ran via the Abbey Foregate Loop at Shrewsbury, non-stop between Wolverhampton and Welshpool, and reached Aberystwyth in 5 hours 35 minutes, considerably better than the post-War train. This was restored in 1951, but reversed in Shrewsbury rather than using the loop. In a typical year, 1958, departure from Paddington was at 10.10 am and arrival at Aberystwyth 4.5 pm. It ran non-stop from Shrewsbury to Welshpool, then calling only at Newtown and Moat Lane, though it would set down at Montgomery or Llanbrynmair on notice. After splitting at Machynlleth, the Pwllheli portion stopped at Dovey Junction and all stations except Talsarnau and Minffordd. Curiously, it would set down at Goginan or Abertafol Halts, but at no others. The main train stopped at Borth and would set down at Llandre.

From 1963, now a London Midland Region train, departure was at 11.10 am and there was no Coast portion. The last run in steam was in 1967, on 4th March. The time to Aberystwyth was now six hours flat; it was 3 minutes less in the summer of 1966 on Saturdays, when it took the Abbey Foregate Loop – a much larger saving would have been possible if it had not been given 15 minutes extra between Paddington and Wolverhampton. In 1967 also the London terminus for through trains to Aberystwyth and Pwllheli changed to Euston.

The title now lapsed for nearly 20 years, returning in 1986 as a morning train from Aberystwyth to Euston, returning in the afternoon, electric-hauled between Euston and Wolverhampton, and with a further engine change and removal of first class coaches and restaurant car at Shrewsbury. These coaches were worked back empty to Wolverhampton. In the summer of 1988 it ran on Fridays to Pwllheli instead of Aberystwyth, calling at Dovey Junction, Aberdovey, Tywyn, Fairbourne, Barmouth, Harlech, and all stations except the two halts. It would however set down at all halts apart from Tonfanau, Llangelynin, Tygwyn and Llandecwyn. It came back on Saturday morning, at 8.00 am, not named, as a very fast train as far as Machynlleth willing to pick up only at Penychain and Talybont amongst the halts. It was known as the 'Snowdonian' (down working) though not much was made of this title, which was also applied to the 7.40 am SO from Euston to Pwllheli, returning un-named at 3.05 pm ex-Pwllheli.

The return of the 'CCE' owed much to the activities of the Wirral Railway Circle, which had organised four 'Cambrian Coast Expresses' in 1971–3 to keep the name alive.

In its last years, it was not a splendid train. On the down run the buffet closed at Coventry and the removal at Shrewsbury of the first-class and buffet could take a very long time. Consequent late running, compounded by the reduction of available loops, meant that once its slot was missed much time was spent waiting for up trains in loops other than the scheduled ones. It was always late, but sometimes disastrously so, and missing its slot for the return empty stock working to Machynlleth after the MPD at Aberystwyth was closed, final arrival back there could be nearly midnight. Nevertheless the announcement that it would cease running on 1st May, 1991 was met with much protest; in fact it ran until 12th May.

At a press reception on 1st May a pair of Express Sprinters was shown off at Aberystwyth as the replacement for the 'CCE', though it would only run as far as Shrewsbury. In fact, when it went into service it turned out to be not a pair of Express sets, but one attached to a normal Sprinter. There is now no through train to Aberystwyth from London on any day. The replacement for the CCE, now 0700 from Aberystwyth, gives an arrival at Euston (change at New Street) in two minutes under five hours on weekdays. The Saturday 'fast' from Pwllheli takes 7¼ hours and requires a change at Birmingham International rather than New Street.

198

Appendix Four

Locomotives Stationed at Cambrian Railways Sheds, August 1947 (including their sub-sheds)

OSWESTRY
'Manor' 4–6–0: 7807/8/19
'Earl' 4–4–0: 9001/3/16/20/22/28/65
Collett 0–6–0: 3202/8
Dean 0–6–0: 2327/54/82/86; 2449/52/83; 2516/43/56
Ex-CR 0–6–0: 844/9/55/73/92/93/95/96/98
Large 0–6–0PT: 7405/10
Standard 0–4–2T: 1412/7/32/59; 5806
Ex-CR 2–4–0T: 1196/7
Ex-L&CR 2–4–0T: 1308
Ex-W&CR 0–6–0ST: 1331
Ex-ADR 0–6–0ST: 680

MACHYNLLETH
'Manor' 4–6–0: 7802/3
'Earl' 4–4–0: 9000/2/4/5/9/12/13/14/17/21/25/27
'Duke' 4–4–0: 9054/72/87/91
Collett 0–6–0: 2200/4/19/23/60/83/98; 3200/1/7
Dean 0–6–0: 2323/56; 2464; 2572
Ex-CR 0–6–0: 864; 894
Large 0–6–0PT: 7406
'45XX' 2–6–2T: 4501/11/12/13/49/55/60/71/75; 5507/17/24/41/60/70
'14XX' 0–4–2T: 1465/74
Light 0–6–0PT: 1965; 2151

BRECON
Dean 0–6–0: 2342/51; 2401/68; 2523/69
'58XX' 0–4–2T: 5801
Large 0–6–0PT: 9614

The above does not include narrow gauge engines; list from *Railway Observer* Supplement No. 7, August 1947.

Appendix Five

Cambrian Carriages which Survived after 1925

Renumbering list of ex-Cambrian carriages which survived after 1925; prior to this the majority of coaches built before 1900, although allotted GWR numbers, never carried them, and were withdrawn at once or worked for a year or two in the old livery.

CR No.	Type	GWR No.	Withdrawn	CR No.	Type	GWR No.	Withdrawn
1	6w. sal.	9215	1931	234	8w. cpo.	6273	1938
9	4w. sal.	9218	1936	235	,,	6274	1936
17	8w. 3rd	4136	1938	236	,,	6275	1936
20	8w. cpo.	6323	1954	237	,,	6276	1940
29	,,	6385	1951	238	,,	6277	1939
30	,,	6326	1951	239	,,	6278	1937
38	8w. 3rd	4128	1948	240	,,	6279	1938
60	6w. 3rd Bk.	4115	1930	242	6w. 3rd	4101	1928
69	,,	4121	1929	244	,,	4103	1936
77	8w. 3rd	4129	1933	245	,,	4104	1932
80	,,	4130	1939	246	,,	4105	1934
90	6w. 3rd	4124	1929	247	,,	4106	1933
92	8w. cpo.	6266	1936	250	,,	4109	1932
109	6w. cpo.	6243	1929	251	,,	4110	1929
110	,,	6246	1930	252	,,	4111	1931
115	8w. cpo.	6267	1939	259	6w. sal.	9375	1938
129	6w. 3rd	4050	1929	266	8w. cpo.	6280	1937
133	,,	4054	1929	267	,,	6281	1948
148	6w. cpo.	6251	1927	268	,,	6282	1948
150	,,	6253	1928	269	,,	6283	1939
158	6w. 3rd	4056	1929	270	,,	6284	1938
160	,,	4058	1927	271	,,	6285	1950
161	,,	4059	1931	272	,,	6286	1947
163	,,	4061	1926	273	,,	6287	1938
165	6w. cpo.	6261	1927	274	8w. 3rd Bk.	4139	1938
166	,,	6262	1927	275	,,	4137	1938
167	,,	6263	1927	276	,,	4142	1933
168	6w. 3rd	4062	1929	287	,,	4140	1938
171	,,	4065	1927	278	8w. cpo.	6288	1947
172	,,	4066	1931	279	,,	6289	1940
173	,,	4067	1932	280	,,	6294	1940
174	,,	4068	1932	281	,,	6295	1939
175	,,	4069	1929	282	,,	6298	1945
176	6w. Obs.	4070	1936	283	,,	6310	1944
177	6w. 3rd	4071	1929	284	,,	6319	1946
178	6w. Obs.	4072	1936	285	,,	6320	1949
180	6w. 3rd	4074	1928	286	,,	6321	1948
182	,,	4076	1928	287	,,	6322	1944
189	,,	4080	1926	288	8w. 3rd Bk.	4141	1938
193	,,	4083	1929	289	,,	4138	1951
196	,,	4086	1928	306	8w. cpo.	6327	1954
198	,,	4088	1929	307	,,	6328	1946
201	,,	4090	1931	308	,,	6324	1950
202	,,	4091	1929	309	8w. 3rd	4132	1951
208	,,	4097	1928	311	8w. cpo.	6330	1947
211	8w. sal.	141	1932	312	8w. 3rd	4133	1948
213	6w. 3rd Bk.	4099	1928	313	,,	4134	1947

214	„	4027	1927	314	8w. 3rd Bk.	4135	1954
229	8w. cpo.	6268	1931	315	„	4136	1946
230	„	6269	1938	325	8w. cpo. Bk.	6332	1946
231	„	6270	1938	333	8w. cpo.	6333	1951
232	„	6271	1939	334	„	6334	1946
233	„	6272	1938				

Welshpool & Llanfair Branch: cpo. Bks 1, 2; 6338, 6446; wdn 1931

Rheidol Branch: cpos. 1–3; 6335–7; 3rds 4–12; 4143–51; wdn 1938

Some 6w. full brakes remained in use:
CR 122 as GW 108; wdn 1931
CR 164 as GW 115; wdn 1926
CR 261 as GW 125; wdn 1932
CR 263 at GW 127; wdn 1926

Also Rheidol 4w. brakes 13–15 as GW 135–7; wdn 1938.

Notes:
No.   1 converted to 4w. fruit van 1925
No.   20 became workmen's coach 204 in 1954
No.   90 converted to 4w. 1923
No. 150 became 3rd class 343 in 1925
No.   46 (GW 6265) became 3rd 720 in 1935

The following Cambrian coaches had a second life as service vehicles:

No.   70 6w. 3rd Bk. as tool van 14931; 1935
No.   71 6w. 3rd as tool van 14746; wdn 1935
No. 130 6w. 3rd as sleeping van 80936; wdn 1931
No. 183 6w. 3rd as sleeping van 80938; wdn 1935
No. 197 6w. 3rd as ED van 14935; wdn 1936
No. 206 6w. 3rd as ED van 80939; wdn 1929
No. 210 6w. 3rd as ED van 14933; wdn 1936
No. 238 8w. cpo. as wireless and later ED van 80945; wdn 1969
No. 279 8w. cpo. as ED van 14326; wdn 1964

Appendix Six
Working Instructions

The Cambrian Railways' working instructions were complex and included details of action to be taken when certain trains were running late. For example, if the 2.25 am Mail from Whitchurch, due to arrive at Aberystwyth at 6.20 am, was running more than 10 minutes late, the 6.20 am up goods from Aberystwyth must leave 15 minutes early and pass the Mail at Bow Street. There were also specific instructions as to what trains could convey meat, timber, perishables or mail. They were so specific that stops on alternate Wednesdays for members of the Forden Guardians' Board Meetings were included. There were special dispensations for wagons carrying beer; in fact there was a general note 'Preference must be given to Ale Traffic for Portmadoc, Criccieth, and Pwllheli by all Goods Trains'.

Every Tuesday an extra brake coach had to be sent to Llanfyllin by the 3.45 pm ex Oswestry, returning at 7.30 am the next day; the reason is not given. To cater for Company workmen who lodged in the week and went home for weekends, a workmens' coach was attached to the 3.25 am from Oswestry and the 5.55 am Coast Line train ex-Machynlleth. Station masters and guards were ordered to ensure that the workmen did not travel in any other part of the train.

One instruction was somewhat ambiguous; 'Under no circumstances must the engine, when coming along the Porthywaen Branch towards Llynclys, be in the rear of the wagons, but must in all cases be in the front, except where this is impossible'. The guard of the last up working on this branch had the job of checking that all level crossing and siding gates were secured shut to prevent cattle straying. In the case of the Penstrowed Quarry branch, propelling from Moat Lane was allowed 'when No. 19 is unable to do the work'. No. 19 was a down goods from Welshpool which was allowed three hours from Newtown to Machynlleth to accommodate shunting time, but there may have been times when it was fully loaded on arrival at Penstrowed.

As happened with some other Welsh railways, certain individuals were named: for example in the 1904 working tables 'Mr Francis' had the job of arranging for a van and engine to run every evening in summer to Moat Lane to collect perishable traffic for Caersws and Pontdolgoch (in winter the train stopped at those stations).

There was a special letter in the columns to denote 'a momentary stop'; again, this must have caused some head-scratching, for it says: 'When these trains have been stopped for tablet or other purposes, and the distance run is thereby reduced to under 20 miles, these momentary stops need not be made'. In plainer terms, no train was allowed to run non-stop for more than 20 miles; but if a timetabled run of over 20 miles was interrupted for a dropped tablet (for instance) somewhere else, the planned 'momentary stop' could be ignored. This complex rule was abandoned once all trains had continuous brakes.

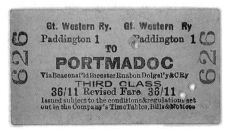

Right: this ticket was issued to the author in 1926 on alighting at Portmadoc; the halt had no ticket office and the train had no corridor. Left: this 1922 ticket included 'C Ry' on its routing direction via Bicester and Ruabon.

Appendix Seven

Aberdovey Harbour Branch

On emerging at Aberdovey from the fourth tunnel, the traveller up the Coast Line can see how tantalisingly close Ynyslas beach is across the Dovey, which for most of the day is only a matter of 300 yards wide. Had Savin been able to build his viaduct with road or footpath attached, as at Barmouth, it would have been very welcome. The Aberdovey ferry, set up as early as 1458, was notoriously subject to wind and tide; at high tides, after the Leri Cut in the 1820s had moved the river mouth from nearer Borth, the stream ran so strongly that sometimes the ferry had to go up the Clettwr river to Tre-Ddol. It was not cheap; in the 1850s a coach and pair cost 7s. 6d. (15s. on Sundays) and extra in bad weather. Users could also be caught by a rapidly rising tide; in 1880 a wooden refuge was placed near the ferry point at Penrhyn, replaced in 1933 with an iron one, which has now decayed, but no ferry has run for some time.

Aberdovey had long been a safe harbour, once across the bar; in 1850 is was said that six vessels drawing up to 9 ft could be anchored half-a-cable offshore. Although what was later called the 'sand siding' must have been used in 1863–7, its extension to a proper wharf was not put into effect until 1881; shortly after an island jetty 370 ft long was built west of the one then in use. This featured not only a rail connection across a timber bridge, but also a 'pig walk' at two levels for embarking livestock on the hoof. An Aberdovey Import & Export Company was formed in 1881, and in 1889 the Cambrian pushed through a Bill allowing it to work steamboats to Ireland and elsewhere; in fact a service was put on for a time between Aberdovey and Waterford. It lasted only a short while as the LNWR was able to undercut its rates.

The sidings were extensive and constantly changing; the topmost one was alongside the road at Bodfor Terrace. Basically, the branch came down from Aberdovey station and first threw off the 'sand siding'. Then one arm ran behind some grain and cement warehouses and turned south, crossing on the level a second arm, which crossed the bridge to the island (west) jetties. The first arm continued to the east jetties and at one period ran right round the rectangular area and with a loop across the middle. The connection to the island portion seems to have been by a turntable on both lines on the island; a traverser at each end moved wagons from one line to the other. Locomotives did not cross the bridge.

The wharves were in the news in 1918 when Marconi moored his yacht there to make wireless tests across Cardigan Bay. However from the twenties traffic fell away, and in 1923 the Great Western was asked to clear the area. The Cambrian had signed an undertaking in 1883 to clear away the island jetties 'when no longer used' – an imprecise term. The GWR did nothing, nor did British Rail; fresh discussions were started in 1959 by which time some track had been lifted. Finally in May 1964 BR stated officially that the Harbour Branch was closed; but it was another four years before full-scale lifting began. The whole jetty area including the island is now in local use; however, photographs suggest that even while working under the Cambrian, local people wandered at will; one photograph showing an Edwardian lady with parasol posing in front of a shunting 0–6–0 is especially appealing.

"The place in the Sun... where the mountains come down to the Sea"

ABERYSTWYTH

is the most convenient
HOLIDAY CENTRE
for visiting
WALES' BEAUTIFUL SCENERY

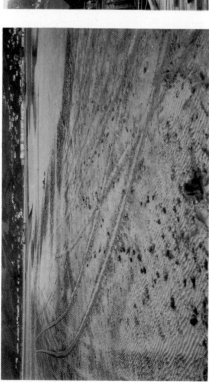

Where the *River Leri* joins the Dovey at Ynyslas: Aberdovey Harbour is at top right. In the foreground is a Cambrian chair from the 1863 beach line to Ynyslas pier brought up by a storm. *Author*

The 'island' portion of the Aberdovey wharves in 1956: in the fore-ground is the traverser for moving wagons between the two lines. It was connected to the main siding by the wooden bridge on the left. *Author*

Aberdovey station (*far left*) and harbour, from the 1901 25" Ordnance Survey of Wales. Note the main lines running behind the town and the sidings for sand collection, to the 'island' deepwater wharf, and the goods shed and storage area adjacent to Sea View Road. Penhelig

Appendix Eight

Vale of Rheidol Railway Supporters' Association: VoRRSA

VoRRSA was formed on 30th May, 1970, following a letter from the PR Department of British Rail Stoke Division that they would support such a body, and issue tickets at reduced fares. By the end of the summer nearly 600 members had been enrolled, and there followed a drive by the Association and BR, with assistance from local councils, to drum up more traffic for the line. A magazine, *Yr Lein Fach*, was issued quarterly; this covered not only events on the line, but also catered for those interested in the Cambrian generally. Letter stamps and first-day covers were issued from 1970.

Occasions in which VoRRSA took part included the 'Night Rheidol' trains in 1973, Father Christmas specials from 1977 (the first in association with the Wirral Railway Circle and Aberystwyth Round Table); also a Rheidol Express from Manchester in 1983 to coincide with a gala day. The Association also offered to pay for engine No. 9 to be repainted in the original VofR livery; in the event half was paid by Davies & Metcalfe, the theoretical builders of the locomotive, though little had survived a major Swindon rebuild. On several occasions a ten-coach-plus-van train was run, one engine being at the rear as double-heading was not allowed over the Rheidol bridge. To egg BR on to repaint the carriage stock in former GWR livery, VoRRSA paid for the first one to be done. Over the years, the Association, together with a helpful BR management, and a shed staff at Aberystwyth composed of keen and skilled fitters and drivers, achieved virtually a rebirth of what had become a rather dreary line. A former ex-LNWR camping coach was placed at the end of Platform 5 for the use of the Members; full use was also made of the line's inclusion in the 'Great Little Trains of Wales' publicity drive.

Towards the end of the 1980s the belief hardened that BR intended to divest itself of its last steam-worked railway. On 7th June, 1988 Lazard Brothers issued tender documents for the privatisation of the Vale of Rheidol. It was to be done by obtaining a new Light Railway Order, which would vest in a new BRB Company the power to transfer the order to a new owner. A notice of closure was posted on 11th June; any new owner had to guarantee to run the railway for five years.

It took some time for the dust to settle, but finally the choice was between purchase by the Brecon Mountain Railway, which already ran a short stretch of narrow gauge line between Pontsticill and Pant, in the former Breconshire, and a company titled Rheilfordd Dyffryn Rheidol, which was really a buy-out by the BR staff already running the line. After VoRRSA had taken a vote of members, it was decided to support the latter applicant. British Rail however chose the BMR bid, and the matter was closed with a decision to hand over at the end of the 1988 season. Upon taking over, the BMR informed VoRRSA that they did not require a supporters' association or any assistance with publicity, or in fact anything else. After waiting for a whole season to see whether there would be any change in the situation, in early 1991 VoRRSA wound itself up and transferred its capital and members to the Welshpool & Llanfair Railway supporters. Most of the skilled staff from the railway had resigned; there were no longer any 'Events'. It seemed a sad end to an unprecedented co-operation between enthusiasts, railway management and local authorities; but at least VoRRSA helped to keep the line open during a period heavy with closures elsewhere.

Appendix Nine

The Cambrian Coast Line Action Group

In the period of rapid line closures protests were vociferous and mainly ineffectual. The protest set in motion on 11th January, 1971 by the posting of the Withdrawal Notice for the Coast Line, intended to take effect the following 4th October, was not only the best-orchestrated of any, but was also successful. This success was largely due to the activities of John Rogers, who set up the first Action Group meeting at Dolgellau on 12th June, and was tireless in pushing against the closing door until the threat was lifted three years later; even then there were further fights to come.

The first Public Meetings were on 22nd/23rd June, 1971 at Harlech; during these John Morris, QC, MP, put the case of public hardship; a letter with 150,000 signatories was sent to the Welsh Office in August. A few days later the Transport Users' Consultative Committee declared in favour of keeping the line open. It was a false dawn; next year it was found that Crosville had been asked to draw up a programme of bus workings to replace the line. At a further meeting at Harlech the CCLAG with Council support managed to prove that the suggested bus schedules were quite unworkable.

The campaign went on and gathered strength; on 18th November, 1972 a special train was run from Pwllheli to London to enable a delegation to hand in a petition at 10 Downing Street. There were 750 supporters on the train, and many had a cold wait in the darkness as the train, scheduled to leave Pwllheli at 4.50 am, did not depart until an hour later, picking up frozen members all the way down the line. To add to the suffering, there was an engine failure and frozen points at Wolverhampton, and the class '24' had been unable to supply train-heating. A rally on the Embankment was joined by NUR and ASLEF.

Press and leaflet pressure was kept up, and on 21st July, 1974 Fred Mulley, Transport Minister, announced that the line would remain open because buses were unable to provide satisfactory substitute transport. A minor skirmish followed in 1975 when proposals to close the goods depots at Barmouth and Pwllheli were fought down. In that year a joint action group was formed comprising CCLAG, Transport 2000, Welsh Railways Action Group, North Wales Railway Circle, and Cambrian Railways Society. Many special trains were run, including one in 1978 hauled by the first class '37' to reach Pwllheli.

Then in 1980 all the forces had to be mobilised again. The discovery that Barmouth Viaduct needed extensive repairs urgently, leading to the immediate end of loco-motive working over it, caused fears that BR would use this excuse to close the line. The CCLAG focussed on the claim that repairs would cost £2½m. and succeeded in discrediting this. Pressure from CCLAG and others was effective; the cost was reduced to £1½m. and it was decided to go ahead, with the necessary temporary closing to end in May. A 'Welcome Back' jamboree was organised for 22nd May to be followed by promotions all summer, mainly by Gwynedd County Council; for a week £1 gave unlimited travel between Pwllheli, Aberystwyth and Shrewsbury.

In 1982 BR asked the Group to run summer Sunday £1 excursions from Pwllheli to Towyn and to Aberystwyth for £1.50; in four years the CCLAG with Gwynedd CC ran 42 of these trains. By this time the Group had 33 corporate associates, such as councils and other preservation bodies, and was extending its efforts to protect the Central Wales line.

It was generally accepted that but for John Rogers and the CCLAG the Coast Line would have gone by now; with four out of its five outlets to the rest of BR cut it seemed doomed. But 20 years on from the Group's foundation the trains are still running. And 10th October, 1992 marked the 125th anniversary of the first train into Pwllheli.

Index